HOLIDAY ISLAND

The footbridge at Siasconset, with Ocean View House in the background.

HOLIDAY ISLAND

The Pageant of Nantucket's Hostelries and Summer Life
From Its Beginnings to the Mid-twentieth Century

CLAY LANCASTER

NANTUCKET HISTORICAL ASSOCIATION

Nantucket Historical Association
P.O. Box 1016
Nantucket, Massachusetts 02554

Library of Congress Catalog Card Number: 93-84087

ISBN 0-9607340-9-0

Manufactured in the United States of America

This book is affectionately dedicated

to those admirable hostesses who upheld

the Nantucket tradition of gracious hospitality

and whom it was the author's privilege to have known

MARIE W. F. TUTEIN of the Woodbox

ELIZABETH B. WORTH of the Point Breeze

LENORE Y. VEO of the Nantucket House

ELEANOR J. ROYAL of the Royal Manor

JOSEPHINE A. DEVINE of the Overlook

BEVERLY S. LINDLEY of the Four Chimneys

PREFACE

A FORTHRIGHT history of early Nantucket has not been written because one of the most important aspects of life here has been overlooked or only superficially touched upon in the histories proper, and no comprehensive study of it has been made elsewhere. It will be seen, straight off, that since early times the island has been considered "another place," different from a home base—a locality to be visited. Let us begin with the name. Nantucket translates roughly as "Land Far Out to Sea," which indicates that its original inhabitants thought of it as remote. The Norsemen may have come to Nantucket a thousand years ago (we cannot be sure), but, if so, they made only a brief sojourn. Although Bartholomew Gosnold was in the area in 1602, the earliest record of white people seeing Nantucket was two years later when Captain George Weymouth sighted the "whitish sandy cliffe" of Sankaty Head. The British monarch created the Council for the Affairs of New England in 1621, and twenty-four

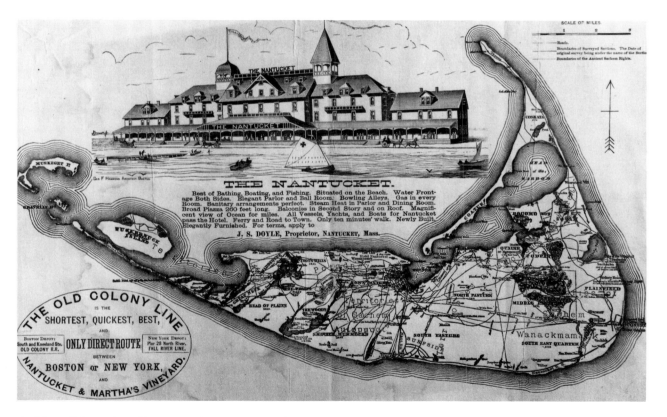

1 Map of Nantucket. The Rev. F. C. Ewer's map of 1869, as reissued by the Old Colony Railroad and the Nantucket Hotel, mid-1880s, with advertisements replacing historical notes on the original.

years later Charles I conveyed to William, Earl of Sterling, certain "Dependencies on the Coast of Maine together with Long Island, and the adjacent Islands." This last included Nantucket. In 1641 it was acquired by Thomas Mayhew, Sr., and Thomas Mayhew, Jr., of Watertown, Massachusetts. The Mayhews visited Nantucket to Christianize the natives, but they did not reside there.

The first English people to establish substantial homes on Nantucket had settled at Salisbury and were discontented over the religious bigotry and persecution then rampant in the colony on the mainland. Several representatives, led by Tristram Coffin, applied to Thomas Mayhew, ensconced on Martha's Vineyard, and an agreement was reached whereby the Salisbury people might purchase and settle the west end of the island. Mayhew had cleared his title to it through barter with the aborigines, and it was understood that any additional land was to be had in the same manner. In the autumn of 1659, Thomas Macy, his wife and their five children, Edward Starbuck, and Isaac Coleman (an orphan, aged 12) came to Nantucket and spent the winter at Madaket. They would have found the weather considerably milder here than in upper Massachusetts. It is significant that their stay was made possible only because the natives provided them with accommodations—consisting of shelter and sustenance. As the English settlers later were to engage in whaling using native methods, so at this first encounter they were taught a good lesson in hospitality. In the spring, Starbuck went to the continent and returned during the summer with ten families. The island's first real publicity reaped modest returns.

The white man's development of Nantucket was an aggregate affair. The Salisbury group formed a proprietary of twenty persons, which included the two Mayhews, and all the land was to be divided up equally or held jointly. When they came to the realization that somebody had to build houses, they invited fourteen mechanics into the proprietary on a half-share basis. In 1661, they gave out homesites according to one's standing, and the balance of the land was reserved as sheep commons. When more of the island was acquired from the natives, and when the town was to be laid out on the Great Harbor, each section was divided into twenty-one parcels, and each man took a whole or half-lot according to his status. Thus everyone received a town site, a harbor site, a moor site, a pond site, etc.; and the psychology was firmly established on Nantucket that home was wherever one slept. Of the original "Twenty Purchasers" of Nantucket, eight never came to dwell on the island (one, at least, not for long).

The chief motif and habitat of the carefree, ephemeral, but recurring existence of vacationing was the hotel. Innkeeping by the present race of Nantucket inhabitants may be traced to the middle of the eighteenth century. The legitimate hotel first put in an appearance a hundred years later. This species of caravanserai multiplied and attained its peak of opulence with the construction of the great hotels during the 1880s and 1890s. Then the movement leveled off, and it began to show marked depreciation at the outset of the Depression in the 1930s. The largest hotel ever built on the island, the Sea Cliff Inn, was taken down in 1972, but the vital period had come to an end earlier. It might be characterized as having lasted from sometime between the Great Fire of 1846 and the Civil War to about halfway between World War I and World War II, which is about a century.

Although the focus of this saga is on hotels, the subject of vacationing expands to other fields. At various stages one or another phase becomes important, sometimes to the point of overshadowing the principal symbol. The hotel grew out of the boardinghouse, and there was a hazy line of demarcation between them. The boardinghouse was doomed to extinction first, although its direct descendant, the guest house, perseveres. For summer people, the most engaging feature to grace the island was the steam railroad, to which its brief contemporary competitor—the "bob-tailed" rail cars—and petrol-powered successors have evinced no rivalry in local affection. The placid enjoyment of the island has been periodically disturbed from the early 1870s onward by entrepreneurs seeking quick and easy monetary returns through land-sale schemes. It is not a coincidence that failure attended their efforts so long as hotels retained their hegemony, or that the field opened up on the latter's decline. Prohibition begot a generation of tearooms, some with affiliated shops; and when impulses were repressed after the stock-market crash of 1929, the acceleration of art and dramatic endeavors, already established, managed to buoy them upward.

In large measure the vicissitudes that beset Nantucket during its flowering as a holiday resort reflected the social trends of America. Nantucket never became as exclusive as Newport or as tawdry as Coney Island. It catered to that vast population of summer-leisured pleasure seekers in the middle bracket, affording them a varied choice of unspecialized recreational facilities. These ranged from sailing, fishing, swimming, and beach bumming to exploring the historic and topographic wonders of this oceanic domain; and it included unrestricted participation in balls and concerts, parades and pageants, illuminations and fireworks, cycling and rollerskating, banqueting, "squantums" and picnicking, and fairs, fetes, races, and competitions. By the turn of the century there were available imported specialized games—baseball, tennis, and golf—and metropolitan theatricals, later joined by Fort Lee and Hollywood movies. Each of these items fitted into a time sequence synonymous with its popularity on the mainland; thus Nantucket may be considered a barometer to American vacationing.

There is no better moment to observe the spontaneous nature of human beings than when they are relaxed and in communion with others similarly constituted, as at a summer resort. The straitlaced tendencies and repressions of their everyday routine are released, and they become amenable to participation in activities undreamed of at home. They frolic on the shore and in the assembly hall in a manner unfitted to the parlor. They munch delicacies and consume dishes unknown in the domestic kitchen. They spend money on fancies and favors that would not appear on the family budget sheet. They are

2 *Bathers on the beach at Siasconset at the turn of the century.*

relatively free of the cares and worries that plague the residential hearth, and they can perform unhampered by the censorious scrutiny of neighbors and relatives. Conscious of a need to shed the humdrum restrictions that orthodox society imposes, humanity departs to a playland like Nantucket to seek and to be seen, to submerge itself and yet stand apart, to do the unusual by following the trend of temporary expatriation, perhaps to achieve a new perspective of itself. For whatever reason(s), the frequenters of seasonal spas constitute an interesting phenomenon. Something of the guests is to be seen in the hosts, either because of the latter's inherent qualities, sympathetic to their calling, or because of reflecting the attitude of those they serve. It goes without saying that entertainers—those who hover between what they are and what they portray—would be attracted here. But the bulk of the people who flock to a vacation spot are drawn by a factor that counterbalances the tedium of making money: It is the magic of escapism.

The doings of all these kinds of people were recorded in the island newspapers beginning in the mid-nineteenth century, and this stockpile of information has furnished the bulk of the material for the account that follows. County and town records have filled in ownership statistics. A huge assortment of photographs and other images of Nantucket provides further information about the appearance of places, and a selection has been used as illustrations in this opus.

Editorial Note: Parenthetic references in the text are expanded in the list of sources beginning on page 233. Spellings of placenames have been uniformly updated to contemporary usage.

ACKNOWLEDGMENTS

The author wishes to recognize those Nantucket residents, no longer with us, whose memories extended back more than a few decades and who were generous in sharing their recollections and correcting early stages of the work, begun in the 1970s. Among early consultants on general matters were Mrs. Marie M. Coffin and Mrs. Elizabeth B. Worth. Those on whom I relied for advice and confirmation in specialized fields were: in art, Mrs. Mary Sarg Murphy, Mrs. Isabelle Tuttle, and Miss Elizabeth Saltonstall; in theatre, Mrs. Margaret Fawcett Barnes; and for matters relating to Siasconset, Mr. Christian D. Schell. At various times I also had the pleasure of eliciting the reminiscences of Mr. George Burgess II, Mrs. Allen Backus, Dr. and Mrs. C. Kenneth Veo, Mr. and Mrs. Leon M. Royal, and Mrs. Jo Devine. They were a breed of Nantucketer we shall not see again.

I am particularly grateful for the kindness and assistance of the Nantucket Atheneum librarians, Miss Barbara P. Andrews, now emerita, and Mrs. Janice Williams O'Mara; and the former librarian of the Nantucket Historical Association, Mrs. Louise R. Hussey.

In later phases of preparation, Mrs. Helen Winslow Chase, historian of the Nantucket Historical Association, provided information and assistance. The Hon. Robert F. Mooney, himself an island historian, and Mrs. Mary Havemeyer Beman of Mitchell's Book Corner have been faithful supporters and advisors. Mr. Thomas J. Devine, Mrs. Jane E.H. Carlee, and Mrs. Giovanna LaPaglia were helpful, as was Ms. Gayl Michael. I am grateful to Ms. Elizabeth Oldham, as copy editor, for her efforts to correct errors of transcription and other inaccuracies; I am responsible for any that may remain. Graphic Arts Consortium of Nantucket provided skillful design and production supervision.

C.L.
Salvisa, Kentucky
January 1993

CONTENTS

ILLUSTRATIONS

It has not been possible to identify all photographers or to date all photographs in private and institutional collections. NHA = Nantucket Historical Association.

HOLIDAY ISLAND

The Pageant of Nantucket's Hostelries and Summer Life
From Its Beginnings to the Mid-twentieth Century

I. Inns and Boardinghouses of Whaling Days

NANTUCKETERS are ingenerate hostelers. Living on an island and depending largely on trade for their sustenance, appurtenances, and belongings, they are accustomed to dealing with people from afar and engaging in their accommodation. From the standpoint of time sequence, innkeeping is their third industry. When the English colonists first came to this sandy glacier deposit thirty miles south of Cape Cod, the only means of livelihood that seemed practical was raising sheep for wool. Then whaling was discovered and became a thriving industry. This and the marketing of oil to foreign ports attracted a continuous stream of migratory adventurers and steady retainers needing lodging. When whaling diminished through the introduction of cheaper substitutes used for lighting, Nantucket lost—along with its market—two-thirds of its population. The remaining minority found itself with the facilities, the experience, and the inclination to play host to seasonal visitors. Capitalizing on the charm of the town, typifying a vital and romantic era, and the healthful and recreational amenities of the entire island, Nantucketers set out to fulfill a destiny with which circumstances and circumjacencies had endowed them. Spending a busy summer providing recreation and repasts for those escaping from the trials and complexities of life on that neighboring land called America permits the islanders themselves a period of relative quietude throughout the remaining three-fourths of the year. This seems to suit their temperament. They have thrived on it for generations.

If innkeeping did not begin with the first settlers on Nantucket, at least the foremost of the first settlers started a career in America as an innkeeper. The prime mover of the original purchasers, Tristram Coffin, conducted ordinaries at several places in and around Salisbury, Massachusetts, before removing to the island. Perhaps it is significant that, given the first choice for a home site on Nantucket in 1661, Tristram Coffin selected a lot on the old harbor, Capaum; and he and his son Peter had the only privately owned land at that port. That Tristram accommodated newcomers to Nantucket is conjectured.

One assumes that early visitors boarded with families on the island. At some point, probably after the introduction of deep-sea whaling during the second decade of the eighteenth century, the need of late arrivals for shelter prompted the establishment of inns. The early buildings for this use would have been the same as dwellings, which, at that time, were lean-to or saltbox houses. By the middle of the eighteenth century ordinaries were somewhat common, if not in numbers at least in the other connotation of the term. On 20 May 1761 the Proprietors voted to petition the General Court of Massachusetts to pass an act forestalling "Masters and Mistresses of Houses" from "entertaining minors at unreasonable hours of the Night in Drinking, Carousing and frolicking Contrary to the Mind of their Parents and Masters" (Starbuck, *History*, p. 109). Either the inns were nuisances through their proximity to the homes of respectable people or else the latter were disturbed by the participants homeward bound. That the "Parents or Masters" were cognizant of the lateness of the hours would indicate that the guests were not lodgers of the "Houses."

The Proprietors' vote is early evidence of the persisting tendency toward abstemiousness on the island, probably prompted by the proverbial penchant of sailors for drinking, which was not to be tolerated ashore.

Houses of refreshment were not limited to the town, which from 1673 to 1795 was called Sherborn or Sherburne, reverting to its original name, identical to that of the island and county, during the latter year. J. Hector St. John de Crèvecoeur, who identified himself as a Pennsylvania farmer, visited Nantucket shortly before the Revolution and recorded that a notable diversion of the simple-hearted inhabitants was riding horseback or, in some cases, in a chaise "to Palpus [Polpis], where there is a house of entertainment. . . . By resorting to that place they enjoy a change of air, they taste the pleasures of exercise; perhaps an exhilerating [sic] bowl, not at all improper in this climate, affords the chief indulgence known to these people, on the days of their greatest festiv-

ity" (Crèvecoeur, *Letters*, pp. 205–6). Crèvecoeur commented that Europeans would have expected music, dancing, and card playing on such an outing, but those things were not included or missed here. It was prophetic that the healthful advantages of the island's superlative quality of fresh air and exercise, which were to play such an important role later on in promoting the island to visitors, were already remarked upon shortly after the close of the colonial period. The "exhilerating bowl," however, was to be suppressed.

The early nineteenth century saw no change in the accommodations for visitors. Josiah Quincy came to Nantucket on a wood sloop (no packet being available) from New Bedford in 1801, possessed of a letter of introduction to Capt. Obed Hussey, a retired whaler, who, with his wife, received the off-islander as a boarder. Quincy commented that the captain's practice of taking paying guests was for the sake of society. His was claimed to be the best boardinghouse in town. It

3 *Nantucket Town from South Monomoy. Oil painting attributed to Thomas Birch, beginning of the nineteenth century.*

4 *North side of lower Main Street looking up Federal Street, ca. 1840. Farthest up Federal is the columned portico of the old Atheneum. The pedimented building in front of it is the Federal Street House; next (toward Main) is Mrs. Elkins's boardinghouse.*

was located on a wharf (probably Old South, it and Straight Wharf being the only two then in existence) with "the sea flowing under the whole of it," which "was accompanied by a considerable dock effluvia," not noticed by the proprietors (Crosby, *Nantucket*, p. 114). Like the Pennsylvania farmer who preceded him, Josiah Quincy visited the east end of the island. After spending a half-hour at Siasconset he was taken to Tom Nevers Head, on which "remarkable headland, at the southern point of the island, there is but one house, about a quarter of a mile from the shore." Here he was given an ample repast, which was served "with neatness and good-humour," combining "a kind talkative landlady, attentive and hearty companions" (ibid., p. 117).

With the upsurge of whaling and commerce late in the first quarter of the nineteenth century, the keeping of hostelries as a secondary industry came into greater prominence. Strangers to Nantucket were fed and bedded, like Ishmael at the

Try Pots in Herman Melville's *Moby Dick*, in establishments still residential in form and scale. These often were characterized as *genteel* boardinghouses, that prospective patrons might be advised of the decorum observed therein. The new local newspaper, the *Nantucket Inquirer*, carried numerous notices of such establishments during the 1820s and 1830s, a few during the early 1840s and, after the Great Fire of 1846, considerably fewer for a whole generation or until well into the 1870s. The Great Fire was followed by a slump, and if boardinghouses did not really prosper they fared well enough and at least were not supplanted by any other form of inn.

Most boardinghouses were conducted by women. In 1821 Mrs. Elkins respectfully informed the public that she was opening a genteel boardinghouse in "that large and pleasant House lately occupied, by the Pacific bank," where she would "accommodate several steady Gentlemen with Boarding on moderate terms" and provide "Transient Boarders . . . with separate Rooms." From 1804 to 1818 the Pacific Bank had been on the south corner of Federal and Cambridge streets, after which it moved to the new brick building at the head of lower Main Street.* In 1820 the frame house on Federal Street was sold to Obed Mitchell, who conducted a store (Mitchell & Swain's) in the old banking room. Mrs. Elkins presided over the remainder of the building.

Also in 1821 Judith Robinson offered to feed "Two or three steady boarders." No address was given. It was customary in the old town for everybody to know where, or about where, everybody else lived, and, if the latter, to ask specifically on approaching the locale, as shown by Peter Coffin's directions to Ishmael for getting to the Try Pots in *Moby Dick*. Dr. A. Baker, a Nantucket dentist, advertising his profession in 1824, simply gave his address as "at Mrs. A. Hussey's Boarding House."

In 1826 Mrs. Lydia Chadwick engaged in "Genteel Boarding" at her house on Union Street, which was "commodious, pleasantly situated, retired, and at the same time not far from the centre of business." The following year Betsey Cary gave notice that she accommodated boarders. She failed to give an address, but one assumes the house to have been that on Main Street near Union taken over by Elisha Starbuck five years later. In 1830 Judith Coffin, who had been in the trade elsewhere, relocated in the former residence of Dr. Rowland Gelston, a few doors west of the Nantucket Pacific Bank on Main Street, and she continued "to entertain transient and steady boarders on reasonable terms."

Not all of Nantucket's hostelries of the period were in town. As earlier, seasonal establishments were conducted to the eastward. At Polpis, during the summer of 1822, the Nicholas Meader house was acquired by Samuel Gibbs, who announced that "good Boarding and Refreshments may be had at all times and due attention paid to all who favor him with their company." He mentions that "Within a few rods of the house is a beautiful grove of trees which forms a cool and delightful shade and pleasant retreat in the hot hours of summer." On this rocky island where early in the nineteenth century even a single tree was a rarity, the shade offered by a grove was a phenomenon.

Nantucket's traditional summer spa is the old fishing village of Siasconset. In 1823 Rachel Paddack took the house that had belonged to Reuben Joy (northernmost on the east side of Broadway, now known as "Nauma," per Forman, *Whale Houses*, p. 188), informing "her friends and the public at large" that "she would be happy to receive and accommodate such, as may call, with such fare as the season affords," concluding by saying that no exertion would "be spared on her part to render the House agreeable." Nine years later Merab Ray had assumed the "house at Siasconset which was last occupied by Rachel Paddack deceased." The later hostess, too, professed "The strictest attention . . . to the accommodation of her customers, and she solicits a share of the public patronage."

A specialized facility appearing in Nantucket at that time was a bathing house. It was in existence in the summer of 1827, when the notice was made that only those who had become subscribers, and one guest apiece, could make use of it. No location was given, but the following summer it had "removed to its former place at the New South Wharf," and in 1829 its entrance here was "adjoining P. Macy, jr's, Lumber Store." Peleg Macy II and Isaac C. Austin were the proprietors, and the rate for the season was $2 per family. Due to the propinquity of brigs and sloops tied up for long periods, one wonders about the purity of the water, but the owners vouched for the "*necessary, invigorating* and *delightful* indulgence of Sea Bathing." In 1828, Monday, Wednesday, and Friday afternoons were reserved for ladies, and the following year they had exclusive use of the premises on Wednesdays and Saturdays from 1:00 to 6:00 p.m. Bath houses were quite innovative at this early date, as the practice of salt-water bathing did not become popular in America until mid-century.

*The bank was first chartered in 1804 as "Pacific Bank"; the charter was renewed in 1812 under "Nantucket Pacific Bank"; in 1865 it was chartered as "Pacific National Bank" under the U.S. Banking Law.—Ed.

Another establishment appropriate to the wharf section was the seafood house. In 1826 Joseph Winslow supplied "Boarding, Refreshments, &c., At the sign of the Ship & Whales, No. 1 north side of old South Wharf." Available at all hours were "OYSTERS in any style; TRIPE every Saturday Evening." The Ship & Whales also offered "Lodging for persons of respectability."

Despite the last restriction, one suspects that taverns run by men on the waterfront did not attract the socially higher types. Those farther inland probably differed little from houses run by women. Elisha Starbuck invited "Genteel Boarding" in 1824. The address is omitted for his place, which was but the stepping stone to Starbuck's more ample caravanserai that was to open eight years later. Other men conducting boardinghouses were James Barrows on Centre Street and Samuel Cary at the east corner of Main and Orange streets, both inaugurated in 1829.

With the advent of the prosperous decade of the 1830s, innkeepers shared the profits of whaling. In 1831 Nathaniel C. Cary bought the old Obed Mitchell residence, lately owned by Mark Coffin, on the east side of Federal Street between Pearl (India) and Cambridge streets, and he enlarged or replaced it by an inn called the Federal Street House. Cary had owned the boardinghouse run by his brother, Samuel, at Main and Orange streets, and Samuel came to undertake the management of the Federal Street House. The new location was described as "retired, airy and central." In the autumn it was ready to cater to "transient and steady boarders." The building was of brick construction and three-and-a-half storied, with the contemporary architectural features of a fan doorway and a pedimented gable crowning the facade.*

Women, no less than men, persevered in the profession. In the fall of 1832 Anna Smith, "wishing to live by her industry," took "the west half of the house formerly occupied by Samuel Riddell (now deceased) in Fair-street—where BOARDERS" could "be well accommodated, on reasonable terms." Samuel Riddell's property was Fish Lot #24, between Mooer's and Mott lanes, across

5 *North side of Main Street at intersection of Liberty and Centre streets. Early 1840s.*

from the present Episcopal church. A few months later Sophie Barrett stated that she could serve "a married couple, and three or four gentlemen as boarders, at her house in Liberty-street," ending, as above, "on reasonable terms." At this time Abbey Betts was preparing to launch her new hospice on Main Street at the west corner of Turner's Alley (Ray's Court) in the house lately occupied by Christina Gail. In 1834 Mrs. J. S. Lawton had a boardinghouse on Main Street "opposite Josiah Hussey's, Esq." As Josiah Hussey owned no property on Main Street and lived elsewhere, this must refer to a rented store on the lower square.

Not all public houses of the period provided bed as well as board. Early in 1833 Jacob Jones proclaimed his "NEW EATING HOUSE . . . opened . . . at No. 5 Whale street," which in those days skirted the harbor between Commercial and South wharves and continued to a junction with Straight Wharf. The bill of fare included: "Pies,

*Rendering of the building shown in figure 4 is assumed to be accurate, although other structures in the Fish drawing may not be. Compare Lancaster, *Two Sketches.*

Tarts, Custards, Oysters roasted and fried, stewed, or in Soup, Fish Chowder, Hot Chocolate and Coffee, Mush and Milk, Beer, Cider, &c., at all seasonable hours." Extra entertainment, as "for parties &c.," could be had by previous arrangement. Jacob Jones's advertisement disclosed the want of "ardent spirits" at the Eating House, thus having "pledged himself to the owner of the building, George Myrick, Esq."

The paragon of early Nantucket boardinghouses and the first one worthy of the designation of hotel was the Washington House. Adopting the name of the first President was prevalent among Federal-period inns, one of the closer predecessors on the mainland being the Washington Hotel at New Bedford, kept by Henry Connor. Washington House, Nantucket, was the enlarged and renovated boarding house of Betsey Cary on the south side of Main Street west of Union. Mrs. Cary, widowed, sold the property during the summer of 1831 to James Athearn, and he and the new proprietor, Elisha Starbuck, added to the accommodations of the house. The name was bestowed upon the hostelry at the George Washington birthday celebration held there on 22 February 1832, before the official opening, and apparently while the building was still undergoing alterations. The setting for the festivities was the "spacious hall," which was part of the "addition of more than half the size of the original building . . . made in the rear," and which included "numerous sleeping rooms." They were let out individually by the night and to families for extended periods.

Besides the increased capacity at the back, the Washington House sported a colossal new portico in front, perhaps Nantucket's earliest example. The tetrastyle conceit may have been inspired by the portico on Isaiah Rogers's elegant Tremont House, built during 1828–29 at the west corner of Tremont and Beacon streets in Boston, the archetype of the modern hotel in America. Starbuck's provincial example combined its application as architectural adornment with a more intimate use as a "piazza, which affords strangers a fine opportunity to study faces and dresses as the people go by." The only known graphic representation

showing any part of the Washington House limits our information to the lower part of the portico supports. In the color lithograph made from a painting by E. F. Starbuck of the fire in Main Street on the night of 10 May 1836 (fig. 6), beneath billowing clouds of smoke are the torus bases of unfluted round shafts on square plinths.

The *Nantucket Inquirer* related particulars of the blaze on the following day. "We delay the press to announce the occurrence of one of the most calamitous fires which it has ever been the fate of this community to experience," it said. "The fire commenced at about half past eleven o'clock last night, in rear of . . . the Washington House; and appeared to proceed from the outside of the kitchen chimney. In a very few minutes after its discovery, the whole of that extensive establishment was enveloped in flames, and its numerous inmates fleeing for their lives." The conflagration consumed the hotel and the adjoining home and store of Francis F. Hussey on Main Street and two stores on Union Street. Within two hours there were only "chimneys remaining above the earth's level." Some furnishings were saved from other buildings but nothing from the Washington House. Nantucket's first notable hotel had lasted only little more than four years. It was memorialized in the name given the assembly building erected on the site, Washington Hall, which was not destined to endure very long either.

Several doors west of the Washington House, yet escaping its fate in 1836, was the Gardner House. The Nantucket Atheneum owns an oil painting of lower Main Street in which appears the foreshortened facade of the Gardner House on the extreme left. It was a two-story, five-bay white clapboard house on a high brick basement, with frontal steps ascending to a wood stoop with delicate banister railings at the entrance. George F. Worth's *Reminiscences* relates that Eliza Ann Barney ran the Gardner House, and beginning in 1841 Mrs. Barney gave the address of her sanctuary for "GENTEEL BOARDING" as "69 Main st. (near the Post Office)." The Jenks map (fig. 9) lists the "Post Office under Gardner House." Mrs. Barney made a special bid for off-island trade, stating that she would "receive transient boarders as usual, and no pains will be spared to render her establishment a comfortable and agreeable resort to travellers who may visit Nantucket." No rates are given, but in 1843 "Mrs. Barney reduces prices to $1 a day $3 a week."

At the beginning of 1833 James W. Dennison installed a "NEW HOTEL" in a recently refurbished "three story building at the head of old South Wharf," in which he was prepared "to entertain such travellers and others as may favor him with their custom." He declared his rooms to be spacious, his table always "furnished with the best that the market affords," and no pains would "be wanting to provide whatever may contribute to the gratification of his guests." Also: "Distinct from his boarding establishment and by a different entrance he has fitted up rooms for the purpose of furnishing occasional refreshment to such as may favor him with a call. He will at any hour of day or night provide such *comfortables* as may be desired by his friends—in every variety of cookery, mutton chops, beef steaks,

VIEW of the FIRE in MAIN STREET, NANTUCKET, May 10, 1836.

6 *Burning of the Washington House and adjoining buildings, 10 May 1836.*

chowder, hot coffee &c. &c. will be made ready at short notice." Ten days later Dennison was offering fifty bushels of oysters for sale at his "Restorateur." In the original announcement he had complained about the great trouble to which he had been put "procuring a stand near the center of business," for which he solicited "a share of the public patronage to remunerate him for the labour and expense necessarily incurred." Two years later appeared a notice that the "three story building . . . occupied by J. W. Dennison" was "FOR SALE, OR TO LET."

Nantucket's most enduring inn site is at the end of Broad Street, on the north corner of Centre Street. A big frame residence, facing west, had been built there for, and occupied by, Paul Gardner, and in 1831 it was acquired by John A. Parker, who, it seems, diverted its use into a boardinghouse from that time onward. At least it had

assumed the title of Mansion House in the spring of 1836 and had been "fitted up in good style . . . to receive company." The proprietor then was John Thornton, whose announcement was directed toward the transient trade, as it stated: "Ladies and gentlemen visiting the island on pleasure or business, will receive every attention that may contribute to their comfort, and the best fare the market affords." Behind the building, on Broad Street, was the North Quaker Meeting House, which, at the time considered, served as a public assembly place called the Broad Street Hall. In 1839 the building was remodeled in the Gothic Revival style, a tower added, its walls stuccoed and painted to resemble stonework, and it became the Trinity Episcopal Church.

In 1836 Samuel Mitchell purchased from Lydia Swift and Lydia Gardner the old Jethro and Obed Mitchell places on North Water Street opposite

7 *Main Street looking west from Federal Street, ca. 1840. The Gardner house is at the left. Painting attributed to J. S. Hathaway.*

Ash Street. The property may have had family connections: there had been such a preponderance of residents named Mitchell along it that North Water had been called Mitchell Street at the beginning of the nineteenth century. The location was convenient to the latest of the piers, the New North Wharf, in which Samuel Mitchell simultaneously acquired several shares and a store on its south side. The inn opened on North Water Street was called Sherburne House. It was described as "pleasantly situated and commodious," when (in 1838) it was offered to "receive and accommodate both transient or steady Boarders, for a longer or shorter period." The owner and proprietor were one and the same person. In 1842 rates were posted as $1 a day, permanent boarding $3.50 a week.

Jervis Robinson conducted several Nantucket boardinghouses in succession. In 1838 he specialized in the "GRAHAM BOARD," wherein: "Persons of sedentary habits will find great benefit from a vegetable diet." Evidently Robinson had a better understanding of the revolutionary health principles of his contemporary, Sylvester Graham, than merely using unbleached flour, as baked foods were subordinated in the system. Robinson did not consider his cuisine limited to those on a health regime, as his insertion in the newspaper ended with: "Also a few Boarders will be received with or without lodging."

The following year Jervis Robinson was conducting the "SEAMEN'S BOARDING HOUSE, an establishment for the accommodation of seamen . . . under the auspices of the Seamen's Society."* The health, or at least the well being, of those under his roof was still a factor in Robinson's program, as he sought to restrain the sailor "from the fatal effects of intoxicating drinks."

Jervis Robinson bought the "dwelling house, store & out buildings" at the northeast corner of Washington and Salem streets for $2,500 in 1839, with the intention of running an inn. In the spring of 1841 he referred to the premises as the "Nantucket Hotel" and gave its location as at the "HEAD OF STEAMBOAT WHARF," stating: "THIS House has been thoroughly refitted and refur-

8 *Trinity Church, Broad Street, 1839.*

nished, expressly for the accommodation of *Permanent and Transient Genteel Boarders. The Rooms are neatly furnished and are all properly ventilated. The bedding is entirely new and of the finest quality. The Table will at all times be furnished with the best the market affords." In line with his aversion to drinking, Robinson adds: "The Bar has been removed rom the House, and every modern improvement introduced, calculated to administer to the comfort and convenience of the public."

The proper name of the inn must have been the Gosnold House, as Jervis Robinson took out a mortgage for $60 on 23 December 1843, offering the plant as security. This transaction stated that there were other mortgages on the place, amounting to $2,805.37, indicating that Robinson was in considerable debt. On Christmas Day the property was sold to George W. Wright, called the "successor as keeper of the Gosnold House," for $10 (undoubtedly plus assuming the mortgages). A little more than a year later Wright resold it to his wife's uncle and guardian, William Hadwen, and the Gosnold House was consumed in the Great Fire of 1846. (See fig. 9, item 13.)

*Worth, *Reminiscences*, contains a list of Nantucket inns before the Great Fire, among which is the "Sailor Boarding House," located on Old South Wharf, with Alexander Bunker named as proprietor. This may have been the Seamen's Boarding House at a different time.

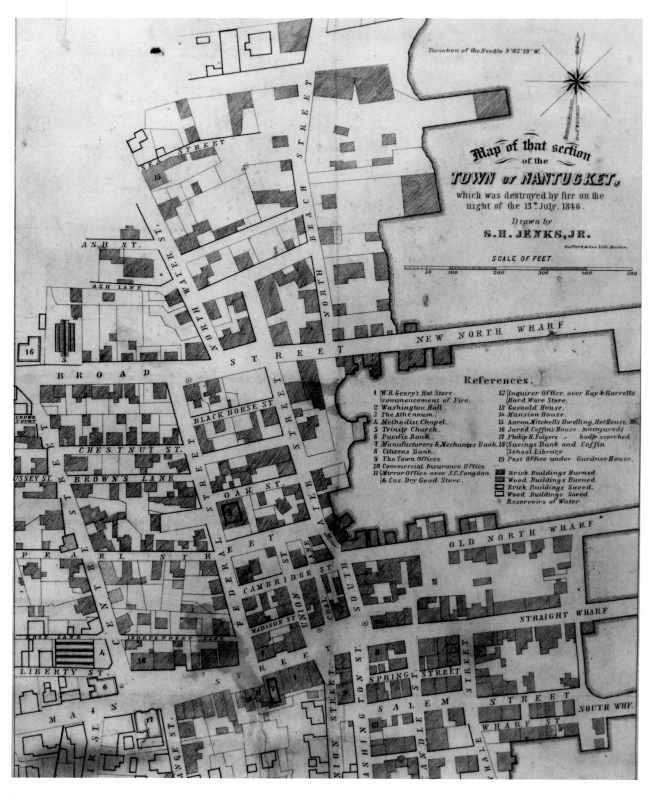

9 *Map of the section of Nantucket Town destroyed by fire on 13 July 1846.*

The name of another boardinghouse is learned from the advertisement of a teacher of the guitar, Victor Williams, who, soliciting students in 1839, gave his address as at "MRS. A. PINKHAM, corner of Centre & Pearl [India] St."

During the spring of 1841 the newspaper assumed "to say a word on behalf of a new and pleasantly located boarding house recently opened by Mrs. J. E. Macy, at the upper part of Main Street . . . [where a] few single gentlemen, or gentlemen with their ladies, can be agreeably accommodated." The house was available also to "visitors from Abroad."

After John A. Parker sold the Mansion House on Broad Street in 1829 the name was adopted by the former Federal Street House. The building still was owned by Nathaniel C. Cary, but in place of his brother the innkeeper was a woman, Mrs. Elizabeth C. Coffin. During the early 1840s the second "MANSION HOUSE" was "that large and commodious house on Federal Street, next south of the Nantucket Atheneum, where . . . [Mrs. Coffin was] prepared to accommodate permanent or transient boarders." The building was in that quarter of Nantucket decimated by the Great Fire of 1846, at which time the inn was being kept by Mrs. R. F. Parker. Within a week's time after its destruction, Mrs. Parker had set up and opened the third Mansion House in the former residence of the Hon. Barker Burnell on Orange Street.* The house was on the east side of the street, across from and a little south of the intersection of Martins Lane. It had been built by and for John B. Nicholson in 1831 and bore a resemblance to the Gardner House on Main Street. Mrs. Parker was to ply her profession here for less than nine months, after which, as we shall see, it was to be carried on elsewhere. The Nicholson house was to figure later as an inn, too.

It is an odd phenomenon that the Great Fire on the night of 13 July 1846 should have started about the same hour and close to that which originated at the Washington House ten years earlier. The later catastrophe was initiated at the rear of the William H. Geary hat store, second door east of the site of the old Washington House, whose successor, Washington Hall, burned as readily and completely as the hotel had. The 1846 fire destroyed some three hundred buildings, about twenty of which were blown up by dynamite to prevent spreading of the flames. The devastated area included both sides of Main Street eastward from Centre and Orange streets, below Main between Union Street and the harbor almost down to but not including Commercial Wharf, and north of Main Street from Centre Street (both sides above the Methodist Church to Crown Court, now Quince Street) to the waterfront up to Broad Street, then east of the Jared Coffin house (site of the first Mansion House) diagonally over to (and including) the junction of North Water and Ash Street, and up past Sea Street to about the present Harbor View Way. The burned district embraced all of the downtown business section and many industrial and commercial concerns (mostly oil warehouses and candle factories), and a substantial number of residences. The majority of those buildings were of wood, but seven or eight were of brick. Besides the Gosnold House and the second Mansion House, fire consumed the Gardner House on Main Street, Mrs. Pinkham's boardinghouse on Centre Street, the Sherburne House on North Water Street, and a large neighboring boardinghouse not mentioned before, the Spencer House on Ash Lane. Undoubtedly many other guest houses were among the casualties.

---

*The advertisement referred to had been inserted first in the July 20 issue of the *Nantucket Inquirer,* but this and intervening July and August copies are missing from the files of the Nantucket Atheneum. Mrs. Parker had been in charge of the Mansion House on Federal Street since October 1845.

II. Hostelries from the Time of the Great Fire to the Civil War

THE BUILDUP of prosperity to the time of the Great Fire had been steady for a century and a quarter from the initial launching of the whale fleet. Nantucket's other industry, innkeeping, was not only benefiting from the whaling industry, it was showing an independent course of its own. In the summer of 1845 the local *Inquirer*, taking its cue from the *Massachusetts Spy*, published a short piece, saying: "We see by the papers that Nantucket is becoming quite a fashionable place of resort in the summer, and that a larger number than usual, have resorted to the island, the present season, in quest of health or pleasure.— So far as climate is concerned, a more delightful place could not be selected. The heat and cold are both finely tempered by the ocean air. If suitable accommodations were provided, both in town and at 'Sconset, it would take a prominent station among the watering places, which collect their crowds during the summer months." The editor's lament over the shortage of hotel facilities and the advantages their increase would bring to the island is the first of many of a similar nature that were to come from that quarter.

The pre-fire opulence threw into sharper contrast the trying times that came afterward. The loss of the business district and such landmarks as the Atheneum, with its museum and book collection, and the Episcopal church, the offensive sight of the debris, and the labor connected with cleaning up were disheartening. The lesson learned by the calamity was in taking precautions against a recurrence; conspicuous in the rebuilding were the use of fireproof materials in contiguous buildings and widening the streets that flames might not again leap from one side to the other. Procuring durable substances and reapportioning the land meant additional cost, effort, and delay. It was not until the spring of 1847 that lower Main Street began to bear any resemblance to a community nucleus, and another year and a half before the gaps were filled. Shops and stores were built with more elegance than before; but the affluence was only surface, as business was not good. The market for sperm oil had diminished considerably—having been reduced fifty percent by the introduction of camphine and another thirty percent by other illuminants—and was finally given the death blow by the production of kerosene and natural gas for lighting. With the exhaustion of the chief industry, many inhabitants left the island. Glowing accounts of prizes gained in the valleys of California, sprinkled through successive issues of the *Nantucket Inquirer* and the *Mirror,* tempted the bold and enterprising to "go West" with the Gold Rush, some to remain and prosper, some to meet with disaster. Ships of the whale fleet sailed for the last time around the Horn carrying members of former crews, the vessels themselves to be abandoned in San Francisco Bay, where they foundered.

Meanwhile, immediately after the holocaust, self-preservation took precedent over other matters, and merchants hastened to find quarters for setting up and continuing business as near to their old stands as possible. Householders—especially at the north ends of Orange and Fair streets, Main and Liberty near the Pacific Bank, and on

10 *View of lower Main Street from the corner of Orange Street.*

or just off Centre Street from Main up to and beyond Broad, who formerly had let rooms to lodgers and boarders—now rented them to tradesmen and professional men for conducting their affairs. Most of the businessmen and mechanics had to replace stock and equipment. George H. Riddell, who had a dry-goods store on Main at the east corner of Orange, within a week's time was occupying "the South Front Room and cellar in the house of Rebecca Swain," on Orange near Main; hatter John Whittemore, originally on Main east of Federal Street, a month later, "having furnished himself with a new sett of Tools and Blocks," solicited customers "at the David Hussey house, Crown Court" (Quince Street); and E. and J. Kelly, formerly opposite Riddell's, in a little over five weeks had "A Good Assortment of silver ware, just rec'd at . . . No. 1 Fair St., which will be sold as low as can be purchased elsewhere, and marked in a superior style, free of expense." It has been mentioned that Mrs.

Parker was conducting the Mansion House in the Nicholson-Burnell residence at 30 Orange Street, beginning within a week after the fire. In December a Mrs. Thompson announced that she would "accommodate five or six gentlemen with board and lodging" at 43 Orange Street, which was across the street from Mrs. Parker's, on the north corner of Martins Lane, and this house was to persist in providing lodgings for a long time.

Early in 1847 the *Inquirer* insisted that what Nantucket needed was "A FIRST-RATE HOTEL . . . so much so, that we do not see how we can get along without one." It was pointed out that "if anything is to be done towards providing adequate accommodations for the visitors of this place during the coming season, it is high time that decisive steps were being taken in this matter." The third Mansion House, "the only hotel in the place," was "entirely unable to answer the demands . . . made upon it, even in the dullest supposable season." It was suggested that the

Steamboat Company should be the agent to promote and procure a suitable hostelry in Nantucket, and inasmuch as there was "not time for a house to be built . . . to meet the demands of the present year, . . . one [already in existence] must be bought and fitted up." The obvious candidate was the "mansion of Jared Coffin, Esq., on Broad street," which was offered "for sale at less than one half its cost."

That the editor should have called upon the Steamboat Company to assume responsibility for supplying Nantucket with a hotel indicates the measure of importance that it had attained. Attempts at establishing steamboat service to the island had begun a little over a decade after the successful navigation of the Hudson River by Robert Fulton's *Clermont* in 1807. The first steamer to the island was called the *Eagle*, which shuttled between Nantucket and New Bedford for about three months in 1818. The *Connecticut* made a few trips in 1824 and 1828, during which latter year it was succeeded by the *Hamilton*. Then

11 *The Ocean House, Broad at Centre Street, ca. 1871.*

12 *The Atlantic House, Siasconset, late 1880s.*

the *Marco Bozzaris* assumed the role of island steamer in 1829, with a 75¢ round-trip fare. It was altered or rebuilt and continued to run until 1832. Meanwhile, in 1830, the *Chancellor Livingston* made history by bringing an excursion party of 300 persons from Boston; but the boat was too large to pass the bar, and the passengers were landed by the *Marco Bozzaris.* It was after Nantucket merchants sponsored the building of the *Telegraph,* in 1832, that the Nantucket Steamboat Company was formed. The *Telegraph* was given the alternative name of *Nebraska,* which was lettered on her paddle boxes, while retaining the original monogram on her stern. In 1842 a second boat was built for the Nantucket Steamboat Company, the *Massachusetts,* which plied to New Bedford, while the *Nebraska* went to Woods Hole. The volume of travel increased fifteen percent. Passage was $2.00, exclusive of meals. However, it was not on passenger fares that the company was put on a paying basis but on towing and sal-

vaging ships that had come to grief (Turner, *Island Steamers,* pp. 1–31). The early steamships had tied up at South Wharf, whereas those at mid-century landed at New North or Steamboat Wharf.

The former Paul Gardner residence, later the first Mansion House, at Broad and Centre streets, had been purchased by Jared Coffin for $3,000 in 1839. Six years later it was replaced by a three-story brick building on high granite foundations and covered by a hip roof of slate. Unlike its predecessor, the new building faced south, looking down Centre Street to Main. Its architectural features, such as portico, balustraded parapet above the cornice, and crowning cupola, reflected those of the "Three Bricks" on Main Street opposite Pleasant, built for the Starbuck brothers during 1836–38. The center bay of Jared Coffin's house was wider (including the portico and triple windows on axis above), and of course it was a story taller. Tradition has it that Jared Coffin built in this location because his wife disliked the isolation of their earlier home, Moor's End, south of the intersection of Mill Street on Pleasant; but after moving into the new, centrally located mansion, it was found that she did not care for Nantucket, and her husband took her to Boston. The house was vacant at the time of the Great Fire, and its masonry exterior proved invulnerable to the flames, which came up to but did not seriously harm the house.

The Steamboat Company had considered building a hotel at the corner of Main and Orange streets, but with the land costing $1,800, construction $10,000, and because all builders on the island were busily engaged replacing fire losses, there would be a long wait before it could be accomplished. Jared Coffin had spent $15,000 erecting his mansion and offered it for immediate occupancy at $7,000. Its site was more convenient to New North (Steamboat) Wharf than that on Main Street. The Nantucket Steamboat Company purchased and furnished it and called it the Ocean House. The initial function was a reception for the stockholders and their friends on the evening of 14 May 1847. About 400 persons attended. The newspaper criticized the company for not having added "the only thing which the house seems to need, to render it about all that could be desired,—a large wing in the rear, with a spacious dining room &c., below, and a goodly number of convenient lodging rooms in the second story." The suggestion memorialized Elisha Starbuck's improvements to the Washington House fifteen years earlier. The first proprietors of the Ocean House were Mr. and Mrs. R. F. Parker. When initially announced that the Mansion House mistress was to preside alone, slander was leveled against her for allegedly favoring permanent boarders over transients, which was pointed out as contrary to the main purpose of a hotel. She had been vindicated by the stockholders and the press, and the full marital team dispelled lingering traces of apprehension.

During the following spring the Ocean House was "greatly enlarged, and otherwise improved, with good accommodations for SEA BATHERS," and it was claimed to be "in comfort and convenience inferior to no Public House in New Eng-

13 *View up Centre Street from the corner of Main Street. The Sherburne Block is the second building on the right.*

land." The enlargement was the west wing, which tied in with the existing architecture admirably and silenced the newspaper criticism at the time of the opening.

In 1848 Nantucket Island had a second fine hostelry, this one specially built for the purpose. It was the Atlantic House, on the north side of Main Street, west of New Chapel Street, in Siasconset. The frame building was two-and-a-half storied, covered by clapboards, with pilasters at the corners, a pedimented gable containing a Palladian window in front, its lower story surrounded by a square-piered open gallery, and a banister railing cresting a flat deck above. A transverse center hallway separated four rooms on each side of the two main floors. A low kitchen ell ran back from the northeast corner. The middle part of the garret had hatch skylights (toward the end of the century replaced by dormers), and once a roof walk straddled the ridge. Henry S. Crocker was the first landlord of the Atlantic House, assuming command on 13 June

14 *The Mitchell House on Union Street, replaced by the New England Telephone facility.*

with a dinner open to the public. His first announcement commented on the delightful situation, "overlooking the level Atlantic." It was for another to declare: "As a place of summer resort, no spot in the United States offers greater attractions than Siasconset. The fine, cool, bracing air, and the excellent water and sea-bathing, are admirably adapted to refresh and invigorate both mind and body. . . . Persons leaving the cities to escape from the cholera, cannot possibly find a safer retreat than Siasconset." The accessibility of Siasconset from Nantucket was made possible by stagecoach or omnibus, which accommodated the boat schedule and was run by Messrs. George S. Clark and H. A. Kingsley. (During 1849 the coach was run by Joseph Hamblin.) One-way fare was 50¢. Steamer *Massachu-*

setts made four trips a week between the island and New Bedford during the summer months.

To provide cool refreshment both for visitor and resident throughout the warm weather, there came into being during the summer after the Great Fire that institution known in Nantucket as the "saloon," elsewhere meaning something different, here signifying an ice-cream parlor. The first to appear was that of Charles L'Hommedieu, in the Riddell and Athearn block on the east side of Centre Street, opened in the spring of 1847. Later it took the name of the building itself and became known as Sherburne Saloon. The following summer L'Hommedieu also instituted an ice-cream stand in Siasconset, located "on Jefferson Avenue, opposite Mr. Smith's Hotel." In Nantucket, also in 1848, Thompson's Saloon was opened on the second floor of Union Block, over Justin Lawrence's store and E.T. Wilson's Furniture Warehouse, on Main Street opposite Orange. J.A. Ray's Nauticon Saloon came into being during 1849 in the Aaron Mitchell building on the south side of Main Street across from Federal Street. In 1851 L. A. Hooper "fitted up an Ice Cream Saloon in the rear of his well known confectionery on Centre Street." It lasted until well after the Civil War. Many years later a patron recalled the glass jars filled with candy on shelves covering the side walls of the front room, and the "arch at the back . . . with its heavy portiers looped . . . [in] richness and sumptuous elegance." In the saloon proper were served "Ice Cream, Custards, Cake, Pies, &c."

In 1850 Mr. and Mrs. R. F. Parker severed connections with the Ocean House and assumed management of the Mitchell House, the "mansion of the late Christopher Mitchell, No. 1 Union Street (the first house from Main)," which stood across from the old Town Building, now the administration offices of the Nantucket Historical Association.

The Parkers were succeeded at the Ocean House by Jervis Robinson, who, since the burning of the Gosnold House, had conducted a boardinghouse for gentlemen at "No. 7, Winter Street." Robinson was an unusual person: not only had he implemented the Graham system and expurgated alcoholism from earlier ventures, at Winter Street he sponsored the appearance of Mme. C. Amy, the "PROPHETIC PHRENOLOGIST and CLAIRVOYANT," who, for 50¢, prognosticated for the citizens of Nantucket during the spring of 1848. After Robinson assumed proprietorship of the Ocean House it seems more than coincidence that the establishment was favored by the periodic presence of "THE MYSTERIOUS LADY, MADAME BUCKLEY," who "reveals Past, Present and Future," through gazing into the "SELENITE STONE." Mme. Buckley visited the island during the fall of 1850, spring of 1852, and spring of 1857. In the fall of 1857 the Ocean

15 *The* Island Home.

16 *South side of lower Main Street during the 1870s.*

House was acquired by Eben Allen, and Robinson did not long remain. The lady of the selenite stone came no more.

In April of 1852 a building that had served as an inn in Siasconset was up for sale. It belonged to Samuel Bunker and was called the Bunker Hill House. The inn contained eight rooms and a dining hall sufficiently large to seat fifty persons. The grounds of six acres, which were south of Main Street and west of present Morey Lane, included a barn that could hold twenty tons of hay and a cistern with a capacity of seventy-five barrels of water. The Bunker Hill House was purchased for $1,050 on 10 October by Stephen B. Gibbs, who used it as a billiard saloon. Later it was moved south of the gully and became part of the Oliver F. Hussey summer cottage (Underhill, *Houses*).

Gibbs was in time to see the "venerable and veritable Sea Serpent," which supposedly appeared at various locations along the east coast of the United States during the spring of 1853, beginning with Texas in the Gulf of Mexico and ending off the outermost shore of Nantucket. In

May the Atlantic House was "opened for the reception of such ladies and gentlemen as wish to be early on the look out for him," as the monster "has been seen more frequently from Sankaty Head than from any other point on the sea shore." Interested parties were advised to secure rooms immediately. It was suggested that even if no "Serpint" put in an appearance the adventurer still would have the advantage of being at "one of the most delightful places for a summer residence in the known world."

At the beginning of June 1853, with all fantasies laid aside, the *Inquirer* further belabored the advantages of the Atlantic House and Siasconset. This was the resort of those "Travellers in pursuit of health or pleasure," as the air came "in all its purity from off the ocean," and the diversions of the house included "BOWLING, BATHING, FISHING AND FOWLING." Every steamboat was met by carriages "to convey passengers directly to the ATLANTIC HOUSE." The piece ended with the note that invitations to visit the resort had been extended to the President of the United States and Governor of Massachusetts. No mention is made as to whether Messrs. Fillmore or Boutwell graciously declined or ignored the favors offered. Three years later the chief of the commonwealth, Henry J. Gardner, and his family were guests at the Atlantic House.

Back in town, the Ocean House was not doing so well, and in the spring of 1853 it was offered for sale. The Nantucket Steamboat Company had come to the realization that ships created trouble enough without inviting more by delving into the hotel business. While hoping to unload the Ocean House, the concern turned its attention to solving the transportation difficulties. Over the preceding two years there had been talk of extending the Cape Cod branch of the railroad to Hyannis, which would make that port the feasible embarkation point to the islands, in place of New Bedford or Woods Hole. The Hyannis train became a reality in the fall of 1854; and, as luck would have it, at the same time the steamer *Massachusetts*, in taking in tow the ship *Splendid*, plowed into a ledge of rock under full steam. While she was laid up, having her hull rebuilt, the *Nebraska* took over the Hyannis-Nantucket route. Forsaking the Nantucket–New Bedford connection prompted the Martha's Vineyard Steamboat Company (organized in 1851) to reincorporate in 1854 as the New Bedford, Vineyard & Nantucket Steamboat Company, and it chartered the *George Low* to serve Nantucket until its steamer-on-order, the *Eagle's Wing*, was completed. The first voyage from New Bedford was made on 23 October. Boats of New Bedford, Vineyard & Nantucket berthed at Commercial Wharf. The two companies remained rivals until they were consolidated in 1855 as the Nantucket & Cape Cod Steamboat Company, for whom the *Island Home* was constructed during that year. The *Island Home* was said to be the finest boat of her size launched from New York up to that time. Her machinery was made by the Morgan Iron Works and her hull by the New Haven Steamboat Company. In the fall of 1855 the *Massachusetts* and the Ocean House (again) were offered for sale.

Access to the island was established from other than the three Massachusetts ports in the spring of 1856, when the Nantucket Propeller Company began operating the *Jersey Blue* between New York and Nantucket.

Two notable improvements were made to Main Street during the early to mid 1850s. The first was planting the elms. Up to this time the Town of Nantucket had no ornamental trees—at best a few that had grown inadvertently. Planting the elms has been attributed to the brothers Henry and Charles G. Coffin, both of whom owned fine brick houses on Main near Walnut Lane. At mid-century Henry made the Grand Tour of Portugal, England, and France, during which he kept notes on horticulture and brought back cuttings; and twenty years later he imported and set out around the north end of Miacomet Pond 40,000 Scotch pines and 10,000 larches from the British Isles (Gardner, *Coffin Saga*, pp. 196–240). The town as a whole took pride in the trees on its principal thoroughfare, keeping protective fences around the young saplings, and the newspapers voiced the general sentiments of indignation against ill usage by boys in their arboreal sports and by men as hitching posts.

The second improvement was lighting by piped gas, which was first used in Nantucket when a few lights were lit on the evening of 21 November 1854. The following night "a large portion of the stores and reading rooms and many of the dwellings in town were illuminated. . . . The gas burnt beautifully and answered the expectations of those who had installed it." The lighting of Main Street itself was vicarious, coming from stores downtown staying open late in the evening and from illuminated residences in the next few blocks westward. Although posts were standing for street lights in the spring of 1860, town officials still were haggling over budgeting for public illumination. Lighting the streets by gas was to prevail for only a score of years, before being replaced by electricity.

The big event on Nantucket during the summer of 1856 was the performance of Spalding & Rogers' New Railroad Circus. The circus had been an American institution since before the Revolution. It was discovered early in the nineteenth century that greater receipts could be had by taking it from place to place, and traveling shows came into existence. Some went by road and some by water. In 1851 Gilbert R. Spalding and his partner Charles J. Rogers launched their 200-foot-long *Floating Palace* on the Mississippi, housing an arena that could seat 2,400 persons. Later it was accompanied by a companion craft called the *James Raymond*, containing a concert room or theatre. The two together provided a varied, amusing, and somewhat educational show. Included was a museum boasting 100,000 curiosities. It featured a zoological exhibition of "every wild Animal existing in Europe, Asia, Africa and America. Including a full-grown ELEPHANT, and magnificent GIRAFFE: innumerable specimens of Birds, from the gigantic Ostrich to upward of one hundred specimens of the fairy Humming Bird." Also there was a statue gallery with lifesize figures of "Christ preaching in the Temple," Washington and Lafayette, the family of Napoleon, and stuffed facsimiles of Barnum's famous Siamese twins, according to the *Natchez* (Mississippi) *Free Trader* of 7 December 1855. A steam calliope was installed on the *Floating Palace* in 1858.

17 *Advertisement for the Spalding & Rogers' New Railroad Circus, 1856.*

Meanwhile, the traveling circus had taken to the dry land, its performances given by humans and horses. Spalding & Rogers' was one of the first circuses to be transported by rail, a practice that became popular after the Civil War. The advertising stated that it was not one of the "Old Fogy Wagon Shows, traveling all night over rough roads" to keep up with its schedule, composed of "WORN OUT RING HORSES" and "TIRED PERFORMERS," but a lively entertainment of "Fast Men! Fast Women! FAST CHILDREN; and FAST HORSES To keep up with the times." The cast included "ALL THE WINNERS of all the Prizes at the Great CIRCUS TOURNAMENT. . . At Washington, . . . including . . . JAMES ROBINSON, of S. C., who won the prize as the *'Best Single Bareback Rider.'* The Levater Lee Troupe! [parents, two sons, and two daughters] OF LONDON AND PARIS, Decided to be the *'Best Pantomimists, Posturers,'* &c. PLUS HORNER, of Ky., the *'Best Talking Clown.'* LE JEUNE BURTE of Paris, The *'Best Hurdle Racer.'* EDWARD KENDALL! AND Kendall's Brass Band! of New England, who won the First Prize as the *'Best Bugler and Brass Band,'* and who will make a Grand Promenade Musicale! Every morning, through the principal streets, mounted on *Eighteen Beautiful Horses!* Trained expressly for that purpose. JIM BURT, of Maryland, as the *'Best Trick Clown.'* R. WHITE, of New York, as the *'Best Horse Trainer and Maitre de Cirque.'* JOE HAZLITT, of Mass., as the *'Best Man-Monkey,'* with possibly one rival, and Aristook & Big Thunder of N.Y., as the *'Best Trick Horses.'* Besides the above winners of all the "FIRST PRIZES" were other "well known Performers," whose names were listed. The ensemble normally was transported by nine railroad cars, which could be taken off the tracks to the tent site, but for the Nantucket sojourn, precedent was broken by coming to the island aboard the *Island Home.* It must have made some of the participants nostalgic for the *Floating Palace,* which was destined to be moored at New Orleans and become a Confederate hospital ship six or seven years later.

Shows on Nantucket were at 1:30 and 7:30 p.m. on Saturday, 7 June. Admission was 25¢ (for pit) and 50¢ (for box seats), and despite "unfavorable weather had good houses, and every one was highly pleased with the performances." The troupe sailed back to America on Sunday to perform at New Bedford the following evening.

By comparison with the show in the big top, Nantucket's first county fair in the fall must have seemed rather tame. Its promoters made the point that Nantucket was no longer considered "only a barren sand heap: but now contained "many fine and profitable farms," whose tenants found "a ready market . . . here at their very door." It was time to follow the precedent set elsewhere and hold an exhibition. The newly formed Agricultural Society scheduled it for 28 October, and both professional farmers and amateur gardeners were invited to participate. The display of vegetables was arranged in the upper hall of the Atheneum and was on view all day. Accompanying exercises in the afternoon took place in the Methodist church. They consisted of several "Original Hymns," or poems, the first by the Rev. George H. Hepworth beginning:

> From Nature's ample storehouse,
> From Plenty's open hand,
> We cull in fullest measure
> The harvests of our land.

The principal speech was by Edward L. Flint, Secretary of the State Board of Agriculture. The precedent was established of concluding the fair with a ball.

The second annual fair lasted two days, 13 and 14 October 1857, and got more down to earth. Besides the exhibition in the hall, land was reserved behind the Atheneum, and plowing and spading matches were held. There was a stock show, and attention was paid to the arts and skills. On the second day a dinner was given at the Ocean House, and the ball was in the evening, music furnished by the Boston Quadrille Band. An attempt was made to attract visitors

from the mainland to the show, fare on the *Island Home* being reduced to half price.

The event reached full stride in 1859. The Nantucket Agricultural Society acquired ten acres of ground in South Pasture, below the first milestone on the Siasconset Road. They were "handsomely fenced, and suitable buildings, stands &c. . . . erected." Exhibits were shown in enclosures, and a "half mile race course . . . [was] laid out." For the first time an entrance fee was charged. The Annual Cattle Show and Fair was held on 12 and 13 October. One notes that the event had been moving forward, from the end of October to early in the month. This appears to be an attempt toward making the fair available to summer visitors. By the early 1880s the fair was being held during the first week in September, and it was to move into August, to follow the Main Street Fete, which became a biennial event beginning in 1921.

Music took an upturn in Nantucket during 1857. The Nantucket Brass Band was organized and engaged in a musical soiree at the beginning of March. It netted over $300, which helped defray initial expenses. Over the summer the band performed street drills under the direction of Dr. C. F. Robinson. In August, Mr. Arthurson, whose "singing was excellent," accompanied by Miss Jenny Twichell at the piano, gave concerts both in Nantucket and Siasconset. The spirited entertainment of the season was the versatile Peak family of "VOCALISTS, HARPERS AND LANCASHIRE BELL RINGERS," who performed on the evenings of 4 and 5 September in the Atheneum hall. Admission was 25¢, children half price. Nobody, lacking hearing defects, either inside the hall or within a radius of several blocks, would have dozed during the performance.

There were additions to Nantucket's roster of refreshment stands between 1855 and 1860. The Cottage Saloon of J. F. Murry opened during the early summer of 1855 at the old store of John S. Melvin on Main Street. It proffered "Meals served at all hours. Oysters, Meats, Pastry, Soda Water, &c., constantly on hand." Ladies were provided with a separate entrance "at the west door." Cottage Saloon lasted until the beginning of 1858. As

18 *Betsey Cary's tavern (extreme left), Broadway, Siasconset.*

indicated here, the Nantucket saloon of the later 1850s on was likely to include seafood in addition to its various sweets. In June of 1860 Mrs. Lydia C. Cottle announced the opening of her "Ice Cream Rooms and EATING SALOON" on Liberty Street. "Creams, Cakes, Pies &c. Fresh oysters in the shells, served every day." The following month Mrs. Fish's "OYSTER AND ICE CREAM SALOON" was "prepared to furnish Oysters, Chowders, Cake, Pies and Ice Cream" at its headquarters on Orange Street.

In September of 1857, Eben W. Allen, builder of Allen's Block (now 43–45 Main Street) and lately in the dry-goods business at the west corner of Main and Orange streets, purchased the Ocean House for $5,500. The building came furnished, contained forty-four rooms with accommodations for one-hundred persons, and had a stable attached. Allen reopened within a fortnight, and then or over the winter had gaslights installed in the parlors, dining room, halls, and principal chambers. Jervis Robinson remained proprietor.

At the close of the 1859 season Allen had the Ocean House "thoroughly rejuvenated" and added "a neat balustrade . . . in front of the main building" (a balcony of wood, later replaced by one of iron). Basement rooms (formerly unimproved) were fitted up as a "Billiard Saloon" and gentlemen's smoking room, the latter having an outside entrance on the east side of the building. The manager was L.A. Hooper. After the summer season the Ocean House offered weekly dances for winter residents. The first was the Thanksgiving Hop, with a door fee of 50¢ for a gentleman and two ladies. Succeeding dances were only 25¢.

The commodiousness and luxury of the Ocean House may be thrown into sharp relief through comparison with a small and rustic hostelry of the same period. In 1860 a writer for *Harper's* visited Nantucket to add his impressions of the island to a series on New England. His trip included a jaunt to Siasconset, "the Newport of the Nantuckoise." He made a distinction between the two parts of the village: the old community on the bank, which, he said, resembled "a group of hen-houses," and the "new suburb . . . which totally eclipses the fishing hamlet in size and appearance," consisting of "a number of pretty private cottages and a neat hotel." The inn (Atlantic House) and summer cottages were closed, as it was off-season, and the visitor proceeded to the inhabited section, where he found a small shack that answered for a tavern. Entering it he found that the "public reception room" was a "cuddy, measuring about eight by ten [feet, which] seemed to serve also as a general storehouse of groceries, provisions, and fancy goods." Among them were: "Dried codfish, bottled beer, sugar-candy, fishing lines and hooks, eggs, whiskey, ginger-cakes, opodeldoc [a saponacious liniment containing camphor and other oils], pork, cigars, cheese, Ridgeway's Ready Relief, tobacco, ship biscuits, pain killer, jack-knives, lucifer-matches, and jewelry." The place was as tidy as its restricted size and ample contents would allow.

The proprietress introduced herself as Mistress Elizabeth Cary. She was known locally as "Mother Cary" and was the same Betsey Cary who preceded Elisha Starbuck at his enlarged Washington House in town a third of a century earlier. She was described as a "little old woman with a motherly vinegar aspect," who was civil enough, once she ascertained that she had a cash customer. At his request she procured a boat for him to engage in blue fishing, and provided bottles of porter, lunch, and fishing tackle for the outing. Accompanying the story in *Harper's* is an engraving of "Mother Cary," clothed in a "glistening black silk gown" and wearing a white turban, collar and apron, seated among her stores and offering a bottle. Her establishment in Siasconset was at the southwest corner of Broadway and Mitchell (New) streets, the house now enlarged and called "Shanunga." Betsey Cary must have fared well enough, as she owned a residence on School Street in Nantucket Town at the time of her decease in 1862.

Mother Cary's tavern and general store were symbols of the decline that had afflicted Nantucket since the disasters of the Great Fire and

failure of the whaling industry. The author of the *Harper's* article was not referring to her part of the village when he called Siasconset the Newport of the island. It was ironic that he made the reference at all, inasmuch as the Rhode Island town was prospering in comparison to Nantucket. During the early period of oceanside vacationing, it was only natural that an island which frowned upon drinking, gambling, and suggestive beach attire would take a back seat to another that did not. In mid-September of 1857 the *Nantucket Inquirer* carried an editorial prompted by reports coming from the mainland, saying: "Things are . . . much worse than we wish they were, but not quite so devastating as might be supposed from some of the epistles." Business admittedly was dull, but Nantucket was "neither dead nor sick unto death." It must be remembered, too, that the close of the summer season was the time for reflection on and defense of the island's plight, sympathetic to entering the post-season doldrums that lasted three-fourths of the year.

When warm weather brought a substantial return of vacationers, the dreary requiem became a nimble jig. The summer of 1858 was one of the best since the Great Fire. In the middle of July the newspaper reported "a gala week for Nantucket, a large number of people in pursuit of comfort and pleasure, arriving here, causing our streets to present a lively appearance. Every boarding house was filled to its utmost capacity, and a large number [of visitors] were cared for by connections and friends, and many private dwellings were profitably opened to the strangers. The weather was delightful and all appeared highly pleased with their trip to this 'side of the sea.' On Thursday evening a ball was given at Pantheon Hall, which was largely attended, and kept up with unabated vigor until 4½ o'clock Friday morning. Smith's Quadrille Band furnished the music, and it is needless to say that it capably sustained its enviable reputation." Then, as now, there was nothing like the combination of consecutive sunny days and abundance of paying guests to quicken the spirits of Nantucketers.

It was an opportune moment for what may have been the first locally produced summer the-

19 *Betsey Cary in her tavern at Siasconset, 1860.*

atrical on the island. The popular three-act comedy, entitled *The Serious Family,* was given at the Atlantic House on the evening of 18 August by the Dramatic Club. The group had presented it at the Atheneum on 11 and 12 January, and decided one day in advance to repeat it at Siasconset. A few minor parts were taken by other than members of the original cast. It was said about the reprise that "for an amateur club, the thing was well done, and offered a pleasant attraction to a large company of ladies and gentlemen, many of whom went from town to witness it." The play was followed by a social hop, which lasted until almost dawn. Proceeds of the presentations in town had gone to help the community's destitute, and that at the Atlantic House was "a complimentary benefit to its worthy hostess, Mrs. Parker." Mrs. Parker must have been alone and in strained circumstances, as the notice of her closing the house for the season in September mentioned that those wishing to "benefit" her "will confer a favor by so doing."

Acting on impulse and using a national achievement as an excuse for a celebration to wind up a successful season, Nantucketers seized on the completion of the Atlantic cable in August and the exchange of congratulatory messages between Queen Victoria and President Buchanan to stage a demonstration on 1 September. "Stores were closed and business generally suspended. At sunrise the bells were rung, but on account of sickness were not rung during the day. Main street was liberally dressed with flags, many of them bearing appropriate inscriptions . . . 'Ocean Telegraph—the conquests of Peace greater than of War. — Aug. 5th, '58,' England and America were represented cozily joined together. The names of Cyrus W. Field, and of the commanders of the Niagara and Agamemnon," who were responsible for laying the cable, were in evidence. The evening was enlivened by "displays of fireworks from the hill near the residence of Sheriff Gardner. The Nantucket Brass Band occupied a position in the vicinity. . . . The streets, hill sides, and houses in the neighborhood were thronged with people." The event mainly was organized by Charles Cook and the pyrotechnics were supervised by William Summerhays. The Atlantic cable was hardly a matter for rejoicing, insofar as Nantucket was concerned, as it bypassed the island; and it ceased working shortly after it was laid, negating celebrations anywhere.

Enthusiasm over the cable event contrasted sharply with reaction to the proposal in 1860 for memorializing the bicentennial of the settling of Nantucket. The subject was broached at the beginning of March, and at the town meeting held six weeks later the committee outlined plans for a reunion and demonstration and asked for the sum of $3,000 to cover expenses. They were voted down. The account of the meeting in the *Inquirer* ended with the forlorn recommendation to "let us do what we can." What came of the idea was a rather commonplace event bolstered by a grandiose title, "GRAND CENTENNIAL PICNIC & CLAM BAKE," which was held at the fairgrounds on Saturday afternoon, 18 August. Admission was a nickel for pedestrians and a dime for equestrians and those in carriages. Proceeds profited the Brass Band. Refreshments were served continuously. The band played its "choicest music," and the clambake proper began at five o'clock. The event was neither appropriately commemorative nor successful. A week later the leader of the band, Zados Thompson, "dissolved his connections," following a drive to sponsor a band concert for "one night a week upon the square, resulting in a collection of seven dollars."

Nantucket Island, no less than any other segment of the United States, was coming more and more under the ominous clouds of secession and national cataclysm rolling up from the South. There seems to have been no special consciousness of the blow to be dealt the hostelry industry during the approaching conflict as there had been to whaling during the Revolution and War of 1812, and as there was to be to tourism during World Wars I and II. The anxiety was almost intangible and not quite realistic. At the beginning of 1861 the rumor spread that Siasconset was "about to adopt secession resolutions" and was on the verge of hoisting the Mexican flag in place of the Stars and Stripes (Mexico had abolished slavery in 1829). Uneasiness increased with the installation of Jefferson Davis as President of the Confederate States on 18 February, but a measure of steadiness returned with the inauguration of Abraham Lincoln as sixteenth President of the United States on 4 March. A little over a month later Fort Sumter, in Charleston harbor, surrendered to the rebels, and two days after that Virginia severed connections with the Union. Richmond became the capital of the Confederacy. On 29 April a mass meeting was held at the Atheneum Hall to adopt measures for defending the island from possible invasion and supporting the Union cause. The Hon. William R. Easton took the chair, and Andre Whiting was chosen secretary. A committee of twenty was named to devise the desired ends. Foremost was the organization of a home guard, composed of sixty young men, within the next three weeks. It should be mentioned, too, that the Nantucket Brass Band, which officially had disorganized four months before, recently had reassembled and was on hand to lend martial airs to current events.

With the fall of Fort Sumter, President Lincoln issued mobilization orders, and Gov. John A. Andrew of Massachusetts called for two regiments, of which Nantucket was to supply its share. Besides the volunteers for the home guard and army proper (and later draft), Nantucket's part in the war was mostly vicarious, taken out primarily in talk and assembling supplies for the troops by women and school children. In the summer of 1861 the Coast Guard, under Commodore R.B. Forbes, came to the island on short notice. Their gunboats had been left at Barnstable harbor, and they arrived on the *Island Home* early in the afternoon of 8 July. Welcome was extended by Captain Summerhays of the Nantucket Guards, marshal of the day, and Philip H. Folger, after which the Citizens Committee, Home Guards, and Brass Band led the march through town to the fairgrounds, where a tent had been erected in which a hearty meal was offered. The coast guards then went through howitzer and rifle drills. They camped on the grounds overnight. The next day they were given a clambake (consuming forty bushels), and in the evening they were treated to a military ball at Pantheon Hall in Union Block. Next morning they were escorted back to the *Island Home* and returned to America. The populace of Nantucket must have felt they had done their duty and solidified their relations with a worthwhile ally when, a few days later, the Southern privateer *Jeff Davis* appeared off South Shoal and "committed depredations" and "made several captures," not specified in the account, as the particulars were known already to Nantucketers. Upon its departure the schooner was pursued by several Northern vessels.

Following this single incident during the first summer of the war, Nantucket remained remote from the theatre of operations and observed the conflict somewhat dispassionately. During the early part of the winter of 1862 the *Inquirer* declared that the "war has been prosecuted for the benefit of army and navy contractors, the manufacturers of shoddy [goods], and negroes." The one important consideration, it declared, was the restoration of the Union. Its advice was: "If the President is wise, he will kick from him all such counsellors as Summer, and Chandler, and Lovejoy, and Thad Stevens, and plant himself, firmly and squarely on the conservative platform. If he will do this, and stand by the constitution as it is, he will greatly strengthen himself at the North, and in sixty days there will be a Union party in every southern state. Six months of labor in the right direction will restore the Union, just as six words in the right direction would have saved it twenty months ago."

News of developments on the continent was taken in stride on the island: the Emancipation Proclamation at the beginning of 1863, the decisive battle at Gettysburg in July, Sherman's march to the sea and devastation of Atlanta, and the Confederate invasion of Maryland in 1864. The fall of Charleston, cradle of the rebellion, and of the Confederate capital, Richmond, in the spring of 1865, were followed in rapid succession by the surrender of Lee, the assassination of Lincoln, and the capture of Davis. The war was over. The islanders sealed the end of a trying era by laying to rest the bones of their fallen heroes in the Soldiers' Lot of Prospect Hill Cemetery and erecting on upper Main Street the Soldiers' and Sailors' Monument, which was dedicated on Memorial Day in 1875. The base of the obelisk is inscribed with the names of the 73 Nantucket men among the 339 who served in the conflict and lost their lives.

III. Reconstruction:
Establishing the New Island Industry

FROM 1861 to 1865 there had been considerable activity on the hostility front between the Atlantic Ocean and the Mississippi River on the mainland, but there had been little on the hostelry front between the Atlantic House and Ocean House on the island. Hotels and lodging places on Nantucket ceased advertising, and that the minds of the islanders were directed toward America is indicated by the fact that the only notices in the *Inquirer* after 1861 and until the spring of 1864 were for the Parker House in New Bedford, the White House in Hyannis Village, and Frank's Hotel in New York City.

On 11 May 1864 the proprietor of the Ocean House at Nantucket announced that it again was "open for the reception of company." Eben Allen had, "During the past winter . . . erected a Bathing House on the Cliff Shore, where persons can enjoy sea-bathing." It will be recalled that in 1848 the Ocean House had provided "good accommodations for SEA BATHING," which probably were in or near the town and took less into account the socializing aspect of beach lounging. After the Civil War, people wore specially designed costumes for this purpose, those of the ladies including "Bloomer pants . . . of red flannel" with the hair "protected by a cap of oil silk, a course clip hat . . . with red carpet binding." The latest Ocean House facility was ready in July, being "open on pleasant days between the hours of 10 and 1 o'clock in the forenoon, and from 4 to 7 afternoons. Tickets for sale at the Ocean House, a package of ten tickets, $1.00. Single tickets, 15 cents." That Allen was successful in his new role as innkeeper is confirmed by the

citation given him in the newspaper during the fall: "We have rarely found a more pleasant home at a hotel than at the Ocean House. Everything is scrupulously neat, and the table abundantly supplied with well prepared food. The landlord and his wife are models of their craft in their attentions to their guests."

Other hostelers were emerging from the cocoons spun around them during the war. In the same edition of the *Inquirer* with the notice of the reopening of the Ocean House appeared one for a local boardinghouse. The editor included a gratuitous recommendation of it on the same page, couched in language similar to that of the compliment to the Ocean House proprietors: "We call attention to the advertisement of Mr. Cromwell Barnard in another column, and can assure the travelling public that they will find his house commodious and a model of neatness, all his family kind, intelligent and devoted to the comfort of their guests." The paid announcement gave the location on Union Street "three doors from Main Street." The building originally was a duplex dwelling in which adjacent hallways have been thrown together and supported in the middle by a round post, with the south stairway removed; currently it is a bed-and-breakfast inn at 7 Union Street.

The street that was to become the leading guest-house row in Nantucket for the next quarter of a century is that at the summit of Quanaty Bank above Union Street. Orange Street maintained the foremost line of whaling captains' houses during the entire 1800s, and it is fitting

20 *No. 7 Union Street (the Barnard House in 1864).*

that it also should have tended toward Nantucket's second industry. The first lodging house to advertise after the moratorium of several years ended in the spring of 1864 was "the large established house, 40 Orange Street" (in subsequent issues the address was corrected to 43), which "will continue to take steady and transient boarders." One notes use of the term "will continue," this

being the former establishment of Mrs. Thompson, on the north corner of Martins Lane, following the Great Fire. It was owned at this time by the Myrick family, and in 1868 Leonora B. (Mrs. George F. Whippey) and Charlotte Myrick sold the house to a cousin, Adeline Fanning, who used it for the same purpose. Seeking to sell it in the spring of 1873, Adeline Fanning characterized it as: "the largest house on the island . . . containing twenty rooms . . . [it] has three porches, cellar, coal and wood houses and other conveniences, and is well calculated for a hotel." The property was not sold at that time, and when Miss Fanning died four years later she left it to Leonora and Charlotte (then Mrs. Marchant) and two other cousins, Lydia B. Myrick and Ann E. Gorham. The kinswomen kept it for another two years.

The house on Orange Street that was to rank foremost as a caravanserai during the balance of the century was across the street, at that time designated 48. It had served, briefly, as the third Mansion House under the management of Mrs. R.F. Parker before she went to the Ocean House. The proprietor at the time of its reopening as a boardinghouse in the spring of 1865 was John Winn, who proudly gave an historic sketch of the twenty-five-year-old building. The "house was built, owned, and occupied by that whole souled man and mechanic, Mr. John B. Nicholson, at an expense of between $8,000 and $9,000, and subsequently owned and occupied by Barker Burnell, through whose benevolence it received some tasteful additions; and more recently by Capt. Zenas Adams." He omits its nine months' occupancy by Mrs. Parker. John Winn extols the setting: "Said house is located upon one of our pleasantest and most elevated thoroughfares, affording an extensive view of our harbor and adjacent waters, and from the cupola of which can be seen the shores of our island at any point of compass, or at sea as far as the eye can extend." After soliciting "The patronage of a portion of the traveling public" as well as "permanent residents of our island," the piece is concluded with the notation that the "house may be known by the traveller as the 'ADAMS HOUSE.'" Winn purchased the property from Zenas L. Adams in the fall of 1864, and the concluding remark sounds as though Captain Adams had earned a good reputation through taking in guests following his acquisition six years earlier. It was a two-story, five-bay clapboard house on a high brick basement, with a small portico at the entrance. The "tasteful additions" given it by Barker Burnell may have included the two-story, one-room extension flush with the facade at the south end, though the mansard roof crowning it would have been later. The Winn regime lasted eight years.

In the fall of 1865 Irene Fisher, who, "having fitted up her house, No. 45 Orange Street, nearly opposite Adams House," offered to "take boarders at the following rates: Meals, 50 cents; lodgings, 25 cents." The season corresponding with the Agricultural Society's fair, Irene Fisher stated that during this event she would "be at the grounds and will furnish meals at the above rate." Her house stood on the south corner of Martins Lane and had been purchased by its current owner in January of 1864.

Orange Street soon acquired a place devoted exclusively to eating. In May of 1866 Sara B. Ross opened a "REFRESHMENT AND Ice Cream Saloon in the rooms formerly occupied as a Daguerreotype Saloon, over the Store of Mr. George Clark, where she . . . [would be keeping] constantly on hand, Ice Cream, Cakes, Pies, Meats, Chowders, &c." A year later a second "Ice Cream Saloon" appeared on Orange Street, run by Mrs. Andrew Winslow, "at the house . . . next door north of Reuben G. Folger's Furniture Ware Rooms." The furniture store no longer exists; Mrs. Winslow's saloon was in what today is 22 Orange Street. It carried the usual fare for such places, "Ice Cream, Cakes, Pies &c.," and would cater for parties "on giving due notice at the Saloon." On 1 May 1868 an "ICE CREAM and REFRESHMENT SALOON" was available to the public "a few doors below the Post Office, Main Street." The "Ice Cream Rooms [were] up one flight." The location seems to be that of the Nauticon Saloon of J.A. Ray nine years earlier. Later in the summer of 1868 Mrs. George C. Ray "re-opened" her ice-cream saloon, no address given.

In the spring of 1865 George W. Macy made a social hall out of the rooms over his store in the Union Block on Main Street, second door from Centre Street. Macy ran into trouble with the Institution for Savings, on the second floor of the corner building, which on 27 June filed an official dispute over sharing its stairway with clients of a public hall. The matter must have resolved itself within the fortnight, when the opening of the new entertainment place was announced in the newspaper. It was called Wendell's Hall, "Wendell" being Macy's middle name, derived from his paternal grandmother, Sarah, daughter of John Wendell of Boston. The contemporary report states: "Everything about the establishment indicates taste and refinement. The ladies' drawing room is fitted most conveniently, and the large room in the third story is well adapted for supper parties. The latter contains a fine billiard table; and the *tout ensemble* shows that the proprietor means for his patrons to find there every means for rational enjoyment." The same piece comments on the need for such a place and says that undoubtedly "this enterprise will prove a complete success."

The Atlantic House at Siasconset had been debilitated by the war, and when it resumed operations afterward it was under the proprietorship of Reuben Chadwick, who announced frankly that it was "NOT A HOTEL." His notice in the press sought "to inform the public that he does not keep a Hotel, his means not admitting of his furnishing the house in a style worthy of being called by that name." For the time being he was limited to the status of an inn, in which regard he professed to "furnish as good meals as can be got elsewhere on this island." In a modest way he also could "Furnish lodging rooms, at short notice, if early application is made."

With the hotel, inn, and boardinghouse ventures on the way to becoming the primary sustaining institutions of the island's economy, a rival snare for the summer visitor was laid during the early postwar period. It was in line with sheltering vacationists, only on a more ample basis and without the constant waiting on them required in hostelries. The new enterprise was the renting of cottages to families for the season. The first advertisement was placed in the *Inquirer* ten weeks after the surrender at Appomattox Court House. It read: "TO LET, FOR the Season, a well furnished cottage house. Apply to WILLIAM H. WESTON." It was joined a week later by another using the same caption but being more explicit about the advantages offered. "TO LET, For the

Season a furnished cottage house. The house stands near the Cliff, and commands a fine view of the Sound and entrance to the harbor. The bathing houses are also nearby. The situation is a desirable one. For particulars apply to this office." Pleasant vistas and convenience to bathing led to the development of the North Cliff. The new undertaking was to build up momentum for a decade, then burst out onto a number of tangents, which will be largely the subject of the following chapter.

The *Barnstable Patriot* announced at the beginning of 1865 that there had been a meeting "in Nantucket, proposed and guided by gentlemen from abroad, to take measures to make that place a 'first class watering place.' As to '*making*' it a '*first rate*' watering place, that was done long ago by the Great Architect. . . . All that a Committee can do is to *advertise* it and let the world know what an invigorating and healthful air pervades it. . . . The sick will hurry to it as they did of old to the healing waters of Babylon." The last word undoubtedly was meant to read "Bethesda." The article is equally faulty in suggesting that only those who are ill would be attracted to the island. The idea was passé. From this time on the euphoric quality of Nantucket was to be addressed to the able-bodied rather than the invalid, in line with the connotation of enjoyment added to the former restricted meaning of the word "recreation." That by summer some inkling of the trend was recognized on the island is suggested by the following paragraph from the newly combined *Inquirer and Mirror,* which is headed "Summer Resort" and takes a down-to-earth view of the matter.

"As for a place for summer resort, Nantucket has strong attractions. It will probably not become the resort of fashion, but a fashionable resort. It has an Ocean House, and a first-class house it is too, but then it is not likely to be patronized like the Newport Ocean House, where visitors congregate not for recreation so much as display. Nantucket has no drives where millionaires may exhibit their showy equipages, and drivers in top hats and white gloves, but it has drives where the balmy air is scented with the fragrance

21 *View from Unitarian Church tower, looking south along Orange Street. The Myrick-Fanning boardinghouse is the dark building with two chimneys (beyond the white house with roof walk) on the right. That of Irene Fisher is next beyond. The Adams House is across the street, partly hidden by the tree.*

of ferns and other wild herbs, and freshened by ocean winds. These visitors who seek rest and recreation, real recreation, seldom go away from our island with disappointment." The author cites a couple of the recently found diversions for vacationists: "We have fishing 'of the tallest kind.' What sport more exciting than shark fishing! Next to that comes blue fishing. . . . It was formerly a just cause of complaint, that we had no

bathing house; now Mr. Allen of the Ocean House has supplied that want. Come then, all who wish rest, recreation and communion with nature by the sea, and make Nantucket your place of sojourn for weeks or days."

The local repulsion to Newport snobbery was given expression in a number of journal transcripts closely following. One, in the fall of 1867, states: "We should dislike to see our good old

22 *Methodist Episcopal Church, 1823 (portico 1840), Centre at Liberty Street.*

town, mother of so much stability of character, degenerate into a position so unbecoming to her fair fame and record." It goes on to say: "Sensible people are growing weary of so much tawdry exhibition of vain, unsatisfying manners. Bogus gentility has ruled long enough in America; it is high time that we pay more regard to the essential virtues. . . . During the summer campaign just closed, Nantucket has been unusually favored by a company of intelligent and quiet guests, who, with due respect to our early enterprise and honorable career in the past, can yet join us in the hope that we may one day retrieve our lost fortune." The final sentence may be interpreted as meaning that Nantucket looked to summer tourism for whatever prosperity it was to enjoy in the future. In this connection it should be mentioned that an earlier piece, published at the height of the season, had admonished local people to be reasonable in what they charged visitors for their provisions and services, or, as it was worded, to "be careful not to kill the goose that lays the golden eggs," as people "go where the most can be got for the money."

One thing that did much to promote the island in those days was the visual entertainment people derived from the stereoscope, with its three-dimensional pictures achieved through double slides taken from slightly different positions. The foremost producer on Nantucket was Josiah Freeman. In the fall of 1867 he offered "A LARGE lot of Stereoscopic views of the streets, and other interesting features of Nantucket." The series included a number of views taken from the Unitarian Church tower. Visitors bought sets for themselves and friends to while away cold winter evenings gazing at images of the summer vacation setting.

A characteristically Nantucket outing that was revived at this time was the "squantum." The term is doubtless of Indian origin and means a cruise with a party for destination. The month of August, 1867, was said to be "prolific of squantums. Hardly a day has passed, but one or more of these pleasant gatherings has taken place at some favorable spot on the shores of the island,—Madaket, Quidnet, Koskata [sic], Shemmo [sic], Pocomo, or Squam. On Wednesday last [21 August] . . . there were three large squantums . . . ; the one at Shemmo numbering about thirty persons, enjoying a chowder at noon, and a genuine old-fashioned Indian clambake in the afternoon. These gatherings are great novelties to strangers who participate in them, and are becoming more and more popular every year." One, a year later, "came off at the farm of Capt. James C. Eldridge, at Polpis," in which a group of twenty five participated. Mrs. Eldridge served chowder at twelve o'clock, and the clambake was at four-thirty, after which the participants sailed back to town. In 1870 Benjamin C. Eldridge advertised that he would furnish "chowders and clambakes for parties wishing to have an old-fashioned squantum." A later notice gives Benjamin's address as "farm at Polpis," which address, with the same family name, would seem to establish a connection between him and Captain James.

Old-style events were pretty much the order of the day. In August of 1865 a reunion of Nantucket high-school graduates was held for the first time. An association was formed with Joseph S.

Barney elected president. The main events of the reunion were an oration delivered by the Rev. Ferdinand C. Ewer in the Methodist Church on Centre Street, a collation served to 700 alumni and alumnae, and a ball given in a mammoth tent at Main and Milk streets. A second reunion was held in 1866 and a third in 1869, each with a similar program. But by the last occasion the school-reunion fever had run its course.

The good summer of the decade was that of 1868, just ten years after an earlier season of any special consequence. It was claimed that the number of visitors to the island was the largest to date. However, the season got off to a late start. The gayest of events occurred on the evening of 30 July, when the Neptune Club gathered in front of the Pacific National Bank "and regaled the inhabitants with the spirited club songs, duets, etc." Then to the rhythm of fife and drum they "marched to the Ocean House where, filing into line, they gave three round full cheers for the Proprietor Mr. E.W. Allen, who politely acknowledged the salute by a cordial invitation to 'come in.' In a few moments the spacious front parlor was filled with a delightful company—a delegation from the Adams House, together with the guests of the hotel, and a few invited friends." More vocal performances followed, of which the best received was Mr. Spinney's "Babylon Is Falling" and "Rocked in the Cradle of the Deep," sung after the manner of "ye olden time," and his "Cornet Solo" with piano accompaniment, the sound of the cornet being produced by the singer's voice. An "impromptu dance in Atlantic Hall, under the management of Messrs. Alley and Gibbs, closed the festivities."

Atlantic Hall stood on the south side of Main Street east of the Charles G. Coffin house and opposite the Henry Coffin house. The building had been built as a Friends meeting house in 1829, and in 1853 it became the Nantucket Straw Works, where hats were made. The factory later was called the Atlantic Straw Works, and when in 1867 the stock was transferred to 4 Fair Street for distribution, the old building was transformed into a social hall, adopting the later name of the hat manufactory. Many delightful gatherings

23 *Atlantic Hall, Main Street, ca. 1880.*

were held here over the next fourteen years. The last manager of the straw works, A.T. Mowry, and the building itself were to figure rather prominently in several aspects of the summer entertainment program in years to come.

On the evening of 28 August 1868 a Grand Concert and Ball was held in Atlantic Hall. It was anticipated as being *"the* occasion of the season," and the event justified the prognostication. Music was furnished by the North Bridgewater Band under the direction of W.E. Thomas. The hit of the concert was a trumpet solo, "Haste Thee, Winter." The ball began with the Grand March and developed into a Circle. The dancing was described as "a miniature universe of laces, silks, muslins, organdies, and tarlatons." Waists were

high, skirts were full, and trains were flung over the arms of the dancers. The ladies in "elegant attire" hailed from "New Bedford, Boston, New York, Brooklyn, and the Pacific State." Management of the hall was in the capable hands of E.H. Alley, who was to be the owner of several hotel pavilions on North Water Street.

In the summer of 1868 the *Inquirer and Mirror* ran an editorial on "BATHING," saying: "This healthful pastime is steadily becoming more and more popular among us. There are excellent conveniences for bathers at the Cliff shore . . . But a sea-bath there involves either a long walk or the . . . expense of conveyance." It pointed out that "a few bathers have recently betaken themselves to the 'Clean Shore,' as a place more accessible."

24 *Nantucket Atheneum, Pearl at Federal Street.*

Reference is made to the cove between Steamboat Wharf and Brant Point. But bathers were inconvenienced here by lack of facilities for changing clothes, and the newspaper recommended that if "some enterprising person would put up a row of bathing houses . . . it would be a decided accommodation to visitors and others, and would very much more than pay interest on the money expended."

The suggestion was taken by Charles E. Hayden, who designed and saw to the construction of the Clean Shore Bathing Rooms, which were opened on 1 July of the following year. There were twenty-one units, and the announcement read: "For convenience of arrangement, and ease of access to the water, the rooms cannot be surpassed, and every inducement will be offered to make them a place of popular resort. The beach is one of the cleanest to be found on the island." A reader's enthusiastic letter about the Hayden establishment, reprinted on the same page, describes a "long bridge leading to the outer bathing house, itself containing ten comfortable apartments." Hayden's Clean Shore bathing plant was to be enlarged and survived into the 1920s, when it passed into other hands (see chapter seven).

In 1869 Nantucket patronized an entertainment that was an indigenous American type of vaudeville begun in the 1840s. This was the black-face minstrel show. The company was that of Sam Sharpley, and it performed at the Atheneum on the evenings of 11 and 13 September. By then the summer people were gone, but island citizens were promised not only "a rich musical treat, but fun enough to last them through the coming dull winter."

The notable diversion of this period locally conceived was the Atheneum Fair of 1870. It opened on Tuesday, 9 August, at 10 a.m., and the admission charge was 25¢. To either side of the upper hall were long tables on which were sold all sorts of needlework, and at the north end were two tables displaying "Fancy Articles," with a "Flower Booth" between them. Among the offerings of the latter were native white pond lilies,

such as were to be sold on Main Street a half-century later. At the south end was the "Post Office," where "four young ladies did their best to suit all tastes in the way of epistolary favors." The reviewer commented that the specimen he commissioned was of a rather personal nature. Downstairs, in the West Room (present reading room), one young woman "dealt out oracles from the Fate Tree"; another was "Rebecca at the Well," baiting fish hooks with prizes for 10¢ per nibble, and a third portrayed the "Old Lady in the Shoe," this one "enthroned at the *heel* of her mansion, with dolls of all hues and styles swarming upon the sides of it. Unlike her prototype in the nursery tale, she knew what to do with them; for the unnatural little parent was *selling off* her numerous offspring to any chance customer who offered a sufficient price for one or more of them."

A part of the West Room was screened off for an exhibition of "queer conceits." Some were quite amusing. A selection of titles and the objects themselves are: "Cause of the Revolution—B. Otea," a package of tacks in a tea caddy (tea tax); "The Pioneers (attributed to) Mintz," two ears of corn surmounted by a wedge of mince pie; "Monuments of Greece—W. Hale," two tall sperm candles; "Toilers of the Sea—B.I. Valve," clam shells; "A Poultry Yard," three chicken feet; and "The Four Seasons," containers of salt, pepper, vinegar, and mustard. The East Room (now the stacks) displayed the museum collection, mostly old portraits. The original library room, across the north end of the building, simulated the Boston Common in miniature, with basin and fountain, and here refreshments were served. Some "valuable articles were raffled off or disposed of by guessing-matches." The Atheneum Fair was such a success that it was extended to Friday. Porter's Bridgewater Band furnished music during the evening sessions and played for "the supplementary Grand Ball at Atlantic Hall" on Friday night.

The homey humor manifested in the exhibition of "queer conceits" at the Atheneum Fair resurfaced in August of 1871 at a theatrical called "Spirit of (18)'76," given at Wendell's Hall in Union Block. Described as a "satirical bur-

25 *Mrs. Eliza Barney's house (1872), Main Street.*

lesque," the situation was that of a Rip Van Winkle character, Tom Carberg, who returns to his native place after an absence of a decade. In this case the return is looking ahead five years, and poor Tom is not relieved by the decease of Dame Van Winkle but plagued by a bevy of matrimonially inclined and eager suffragettes, in whose hands reside the new tax levies. Others failing, the "Infernal Revenue Assessor" (the Widow Badger) finally fixes on Tom a new "bachelor tax." The hall was "crowded to its full capacity" for the performance.

The year 1871 is to be remembered as that during which the first substantial residences were built in Nantucket Town in a quarter of a century, or since replacements were made after the Great Fire. The block on Main Street to the west of the Pacific National Bank was a favored loca-

tion. The first completed was that of Mrs. Alice Swain, which stood next beyond the Frederick W. Mitchell brick house (69) and was a two-story frame building with its gable, elaborated in the Eastlake manner, toward the street. The second was that of Capt. David Thain, of Philadelphia, on the east side of the Mitchell house, and for which the William Barney house was demolished as well as two-fifths of the Masonic Lodge Hall (1805). The *Inquirer and Mirror* reported on 22 April that the Swain house was "newly finished" and "the basement built for the large and elegant mansion of Capt. David Thain." The Thain house was two-storied and symmetrical, having bay windows flanking the doorway, a bracketed cornice, and a hip roof crowned by a cupola. Both the Swain and Thain houses were razed during the early 1960s (see *Historic Nantucket*, April 1964,

26 *The Ocean House. Engraving in advertisement, 1872.*

p. 5). Also in 1871 the well-known artist Eastman Johnson was in the process of making Nantucket his summer home, and he had purchased part of the Jethro Coffin and Dorman estates on North Shore Hill where he was having a studio erected. A year later Mrs. Nathaniel (Eliza) Barney bought a house and lot from Alice Swain and had the building replaced by the finest Nantucket residence of the period. It is currently 73 Main Street, east of the Henry Coffin brick house. The H-shaped form, with Eastlake details, is two-storied and covered by a hip roof on bracketed eaves and topped by a railing and cupola. It was restored during the 1960s.

During the decade of the nation's centennial Nantucket made considerable strides in caring for its guests. The beginnings were humble, as the island was just coming out of a long-standing economic slump, but the development set the stage for the hotel period of greatest affluence.

In the summer of 1871 William G. Folger announced: "A few transient boarders can find good accommodations and pleasant rooms, at reasonable prices, at No. 51 Fair Street." Henry Walling's Nantucket map of 1858 shows Folger living in the middle house between Farmer and Twin streets, now 47 Fair Street.

In the fall of that year Eben W. Allen disposed of the barn and carriage house at the rear of the Ocean House by auction, to be removed from the land. The structures were purchased by Messrs. Fisher and Bodfish. Clearing the back of the lot was preparatory to disposing of the hotel itself. At the beginning of 1872 the advertisement offering the Ocean House for sale claimed for it fifty rooms, stated that the windows in the main house were of plate glass, and that the dining room could seat 150 persons. Allen was to keep it another summer, and the hostelry was sold in mid-November for $15,000 to Allen L. Howe and William A. Elmer of Boston. The transfer included all of the "beds, bedding, linens, crockery, furniture, silverware, kitchen utensils, and all the movable property now in and belonging to the 'Ocean House.'" Under its new owners the hotel opened on 10 June with George W. Macy as proprietor

and R.H. Cook as clerk; daily rates for room and board were $3.00 for transients and $2.50 for permanent guests. A correspondent for the Fall River *Herald* called the Ocean House "the best hotel of its kind that I was ever in." He praised its food, its tidiness and its staff: "Here you can get bread, whose principal constituent is not Saleratus [baking soda]; here you invariably find everything clean and neat; here you may eat nicely cooked blue-fish to your heart's content . . . everybody, from Mr. Macy, a very pleasant and agreeable man, down to the porters, seem to deem it a favor to make you comfortable." The tradition of hospitality established by the Steamboat Company and furthered by Eben Allen was being continued by the Boston owners.

A play given at Atheneum Hall in March of 1872 was an off-season affair, but it had for theme the taking of paying guests by a Nantucket household. This, the second presentation given by the Sherburne Dramatic Club, was called *Down by the Sea*. The setting was the home of John Gale, fisherman, and his family, including two sons named March (long lost at the beginning of the play) and September Gale. The summer boarders were a wealthy gentleman, Mr. Raymond, and his loving and dutiful daughter, Kate. Two other characters were Jean Grapeau and Captain Dandelion. The review stated that the presentation "opened with five successive *Gales* . . . under full headwind, and kept up the interest until the close." It was performed under a proscenium arch, lettered with the Shakespeare quotation: "All the World's a Stage," supported on pillars, "the tasteful work of Mr. Alexander I. Macy," fast becoming Nantucket's foremost decorator. The evening's entertainment began with musical numbers conducted by G.D. Crane (one of the musicians was Charles H. Robinson, about whom we shall hear more directly) and closed with a short farce, entitled *Tit for Tat*, which had everybody laughing as they left the hall on both evenings of the performance.

Capt. Edward McCleave, who had bought a strip of land on Main Street in 1859, in May of 1872 fitted a little frame building on it. Situated between the barber shop at the west end of Gran-

27 *Children and sand barrow on the beach at Siasconset.*

ite Block (opposite Federal Street) and Charles Lowell's store, here at the beginning of July Bailey B. Cornish II launched an ice-cream saloon.

Another was set afloat about this time at Siasconset by Mrs. Alfred Folger II. It occupied "a new building just erected by Mr. Folger, in the very center of the village."

Not far away was a more general type of inn. It was on the east side of Broadway, near the end of Main Street, and was called the Franklin House. Guests of the inn were "furnished with unexceptional meals at reasonable rates . . . [by] Mr. and Mrs. V.O. Holmes. . . . The 'Franklin House' takes its name from Franklin Folger who formerly owned this estate [and] . . .was an apostle of genealogy." The little building was known as "High Tide" before its destruction and replacement about 1900 (Hussey, *Evolution of Siasconset*, p. 21).

The Atlantic House, meanwhile, had been holding its own. Since last considered, in the mid 1860s, Eliza Chadwick had taken over the management after the decease of her husband. In 1873 a small detached building had been erected for a billiard room, and the following year the stable accommodations were improved. In 1876 Mr. and Mrs. Valentine O. Holmes had left the Franklin House and were running the Atlantic for Mrs. Chadwick. Two years later it was leased to W. Sargent of Boston. In 1880 Mrs. Chadwick managed the Atlantic House jointly with Levi S. Coffin.

The New York *Tribune* pointed out the lack of seashore amenities at Siasconset in 1872, especially lamenting the plight of children visiting the hamlet: "Poor little things! There is no amusement for them . . . but paddling in the sand." It commented that they "run fairly wild." The criticism makes one ask what kids like better to do on a vacation? Although there was as yet no bath house, surf bathing had been given encouragement through the construction of a "plank walk leading down to the water from the bluff," and "a buoy with rope attached" contributed to the safety of bathers. Henry Clay Folger was credited with being instrumental in providing these improvements.

A major step in Siasconset's upward climb toward attaining the status of a notable summer spa was the acquisition of a new hotel, which in another decade was to eclipse the Atlantic House. In the winter of 1872 Charles H. Robinson (the musician) and Dr. Franklin A. Ellis purchased land on Sunset Heights, below the junction of Main Street and Gully Road, or Grand Avenue. Robinson was a builder and put up the new hotel, which, overlooking the water, was named the Ocean View House. Both permanent and transient boarders were accommodated with "all the comforts of home at as low rates as can be found . . . either in the village . . . or in town." A restaurant was "connected with the house, and meals

28 *Summer boys on blackfish.*

. . . [were] served at any and all hours. . . . Those in search of sea-breezes, salubrious air, surf-bathing, good fishing and other delights of a first-class watering place, should not fail to visit this pleasant retreat, where they may be assured of a hearty welcome and attentive care from P. THURSTON, Proprietor." Peleg Thurston had "kept a table on board the Island Home" during the preceding summer.

The original Ocean View House looked like summer cottages of the period, such as were being built at Oak Bluffs on Martha's Vineyard. The walls were of flush vertical boards without stripping, the gables elaborated with Gothic bargeboards on overhanging eaves, and pinnacles at the apexes. Fenestration had hood molds, and over the pointed window in the second story of the center gable was inscribed "OCEAN VIEW HOUSE," in a curved line hurdling the opening.

The front room was "a fruit and confectionery store, leaving a room about thirty feet in length for . . . [the] restaurant." The building also contained a parlor below, and "seven lodging rooms in the upper story." At the entrance to the grounds, "from the main road at Siasconset village" was erected a "very handsome gateway."

In the restaurant a social dance was given on the afternoon of July Fourth, 1873. Music was furnished by the Nantucket Brass Band. As there was a Grand Promenade and Ball scheduled for Atlantic Hall in the evening, Independence Day participants could canter down to Siasconset by sunlight and back in town by starlight.

The aftermath of the first season of the Ocean View House was unpleasant. Early in September the *Inquirer and Mirror* announced that Proprietor Thurston had "stepped out" after "having 'stuck'

29   *The Ocean View House, Siasconset. The original building of 1872–73 is to the left. The 1876–77 pavilion is to the right.*

30 *Looking eastward from the summit of Gay Street. The Atlantic Silk Works, later the Waverly House, is at the right.*

his confiding friends to a considerable amount, and left them to whistle for their just dues." Thurston answered the charges through the New Bedford *Mercury*, stating that "the hotel enterprise at Sunset Heights proved a losing venture," but that he would "return to Nantucket and settle his bills as soon as possible." Whether he did or not is not known.

When the seaside hotel again welcomed the public on 19 June 1875 the parlor and dining rooms had been enlarged, "the latter capable of accommodating fifty persons," and a croquet ground added. The proprietor was Walter S. Chase. The season was successful, and a second pavilion was built in front during the following winter. It was shingled and in the bracketed style, with gables on all four sides, making it virtually three-storied. Its east porch continued

southward as a pergola to the front door of the older building, and it connected with extensions across the north end of both structures. The former parlor was combined with the dining room, which now could seat eighty persons, and the later parlor was on the first floor of the new building. Sleeping facilities were increased by twenty chambers.

A number of bath houses were built during the summer of 1875. In 1876 Chase had a partner in running the house in the person of Millard F. Freeborn. They believed in advertising and made arrangements with the Hon. William R. Easton to have the roof of his big building on Steamboat Wharf painted black, on which Alexander I. Macy added white letters reading: "Go to the Ocean View, Siasconset." The advice was in plain view of all passengers debarking from the boats.

31 *The Bay View House, Orange Street.*

In August Messrs. Chase & Freeborn bought one-third interest in the enterprise. The following summer they imported a handsome three-seated wagon, with the name of their inn blazoned on either side, to convey guests to Sunset Heights. The combination of roof-top invitation and available transportation was irresistible.

To pick up the thread of our story back in town: a number of hostelries were inaugurated in 1873. One was at the west end of Gay Street, in the building that had been the Atlantic Silk Works from 1836 to 1844. For its new role, almost thirty years later, the plant was "thoroughly renovated and fitted up in first rate style for the accommodation of the travelling public. The landlord, Mr. W. A. Searell, has taken time by the forelock, and opened his hotel on Monday last," which was 26 May. William Searell called his place the Waverly House. The frame Greek Revival building on the south corner of

Westminster Street is two-and-a-half storied plus a high brick basement. A piazza was built on it in 1875, since removed.

Two women made known their intentions of starting boardinghouses in the spring of 1873. One was Jane James, who "opened her house on James' Court, Liberty Street, opposite Winter, . . . prepared to accommodate boarders, or persons wishing only lodgings." The announcement recurred into the summer of 1875. The second landlady, Avis M. Enas, offered "BOARDING . . . within 3 minutes' walk of the steamboat landing, and three doors from Main Street." The house was that in which Cromwell Barnard had run an inn nine years earlier, currently 7 Union Street. In 1878 Mrs. Enas had the yard on the north side of the house graded for a croquet ground, occupying the space back to the present bank on a line with the garage. Her notices continued to run through the summer of 1885.

Several guest houses were on Orange Street. A "Genteel Private Boarding House" was conducted by 'B. COLESWORTHY, 53 Orange St.," which must have been at the corner of Plumb Lane.

A hostelry that was to endure about a decade and a half was that of Freeman E. Adams, at the north corner of Gorham's Court, then 74 and now 38 Orange Street. The building is a fine Greek Revival residence built in the late 1830s and known as the homestead of Frederick Gardner, who had bought and lost it several times before Adams acquired it in 1856. In June of 1873, after having made "extensive additions to his house during the past winter, . . . [he opened] it . . . for the reception of steady and transient boarders." The addition was a two-story ell at the rear, adjacent to Gorham's Court, since removed. The public was promised: "The table will always be supplied with the best the market affords, and no pains will be spared to insure the comforts of its patrons." In April of 1874 Freeman E. Adams's announcement was headed by the new name given the inn, the "BAY VIEW HOUSE." It had been suggested by the "high and central location, [which] commands a pleasant view of the island, the harbor and the ocean." The vista undoubtedly attracted the landscape painter, W. Harry Hilliard, who was a guest there the following summer and invited the newspaper editor in to see his work. During succeeding years Adams turned over the management of the Bay View House to John W. Macy, owner of the neighboring Sherburne House, in 1876; E.D. Hatch, in 1877; and F. M. Gorman, of North Orange, and F. C. Newton, of Manchester (both students at Andrew College with hotel experience in the White Mountains and at Oak Bluffs), in 1878.

Farther north on Orange Street the old Adams House set out on a new career in the spring of 1873, when John Winn sold it to John W. Macy for $6,000. Macy chose the same name for his caravanserai as had been used by Samuel Mitchell for his on North Water Street before the Great Fire, the Sherburne House. Like Mitchell and Winn, John W. Macy was his own proprietor. He did little or nothing toward improving the premises, except that in 1875 he had an awning put up in front. The following year he managed the Bay View in addition to the Sherburne House and evidently overextended himself, as in the fall he was forced to auction off his holdings. The outcome was that "Joseph B. Macy purchased the

32 *Rear of the Bay View House, with guests on upper level of porch.*

33 *Sherburne House, formerly Adams House, Orange Street.*

Sherburne House for $3000; the cottage or Bates House, on Orange Street for $1000; the Peleg Macy House on Union Street for $500; and the store-house on Whale Street for $200." Rumor had it that Macy bid in the property for John Winn, who allegedly wished to continue running the Sherburne House as a hotel. As Winn's deed to John W. Macy in 1873 held a mortgage, he was technically still the owner, and the transfer of papers on 12 October 1876 was from Winn to Joseph B. Macy. The property was still in Winn's hands when it went to the next purchaser nine years later. For the winter and spring of 1876–77 the Sherburne House was let for a boys boarding school, with an enrollment capacity of twenty five. Students were prepared "for College, for Business, and for Schools of Technology." Board and tuition for the term were $325. George H. Cary of Pittsfield was proprietor.

When reopened as a hotel in the spring of 1877 the Sherburne House was leased for the season to the "Messrs. Mowry Brothers," who were to use it "simply for lodging purposes, in connection with the Bay View House," except that they had engaged "a violinist, pianist and cornet player to provide their music . . . [for] weekly hops in the dining-hall." The Mowry brothers then were involved with the Springfield House and the Nantucket cottages and real estate in general, of which more anon. In 1878 the Sherburne was spruced up in that it was given a new coat of paint by William H. Coffin. Captain Comfort Whiting undertook its management. During the following year the proprietors were Mr. and Mrs. Thomas H. Soule II; and the "estimable housekeeper" was Mrs. E.T. Adams, who christened the season on the evening of 18 June by inviting a "select company" to "look over the various departments," after which "a collation of creams and cakes were served in the dining hall," which was profuse with "cut flowers." The room then was "cleared and prepared for a social dance, music for which was furnished by Messrs. W.B. Stevens and K. Reynolds." It lasted until midnight.

During the 1870s Orange Street was confronted with a rival for guest accommodations in North Water Street. The southern half had been burnt out by the Great Fire of 1846 and rebuilt within the next few years, but most of the lodging houses were to be among the older buildings at the upper end. The first was at the corner of

Chester Street. It was one of the largest residential buildings in town and had been partitioned into two good-sized dwellings in 1836. Elijah H. Alley acquired it during the winter of 1863 and spring of 1864. The building had a high brick basement story, Federal-style pilastered doorways, and clapboard walls, and Alley added a full third story within a well-conceived mansard roof. After taking in boarders for a decade, Alley decided to transfer the load to other shoulders. In the spring of 1874 he advertised: "HOTEL FOR SALE or TO LET! That entire building situated at the corner of North Water and Chester streets, which has

34 *Elijah H. Alley's hotel, later the Springfield House, North Water at Chester Street.*

recently been put in thorough repair by the subscriber, and is in every way calculated for a first-class hotel, is now offered for sale or to let. Said house is three stories high, has twenty-five lodging rooms, and a dining room in the basement large enough to seat eighty persons." The kitchen also was at ground level, and there was a good well of water. Every room was equipped with gaslights the longer side of the building facing east. "An excellent view of the harbor and sound . . . [could] be had from any of the windows," and it was "located but a short distance from the steamboat landing or either of the bathing houses." The proximity of North Water Street to bathing facilities was a major factor in promoting its patronage during the next decade. It would seem that Alley continued to conduct the hotel himself during the summer of 1874.

Toward the end of August his effort to find another proprietor bore fruit. We read "that Mr. A.S. Mowry, of the Springfield House . . . has leased for a term of years, the extensive hotel which has recently been fitted up by Mr. E.H. Alley. . . . Mr. Mowry . . . will no doubt fill both houses another season." The Springfield House was in the two-story building that is now 21 North Water Street. It had been purchased for $800 in May of 1872 by Almon T. Mowry, whose brother, Albert S., thereafter conducted it as the hostelry named after what they considered their home town in Massachusetts, although Albert was born in Fitchburg and Almon in Millbury. At the end of 1876 the Mowrys engaged C.H. Robinson (builder-owner of the Ocean View House) to "make an addition . . . to the north side." The Springfield House stayed open all winter, and in March of 1876 it played host to "Prof. Maria Mitchell of Vassar College," Nantucket's native and renowned astronomer. Not all guests were as desirable as Miss Mitchell. In midsummer there was issued: "A Warning. The attention of proprietors of Sea-Side Hotels is called toward W.L. DICKERMAN, of Foxboro, Mass., as they are likely to be swindled out of their board if he serves them as he has A.S. MOWRY, Prop'r. SPRINGFIELD HOUSE, Nantucket, Mass."

Probably the name Springfield House was applied to the Alley building as well as to that on the east side of North Water Street at the time Mowry assumed proprietorship. In the same column with the announcement of Maria Mitchell's visit is the observation that Mowry was "preparing for a crowd this coming season," and that "two new billiard tables have been added to the many attractions." The original building being of limited size and without a basement story, the tables must have been put in the Alley pavilion. A newspaper comment in the summer of 1878 says: "The name of the Springfield House has been placed in the concrete walk in front of it in white marble mosaic—the first work of the kind ever done here." Nineteenth-century photographs show the letters, about nine or ten inches high, in the pavement at the base of the steps to the east door of the corner building. Certainly the Alley building was considered the main part of the Springfield House at that time. Rates were $2.00 to $2.50 per day, and $9.00 to $15.00 per week.

A Springfield House dinner menu in the collection of the Nantucket Historical Association Research Center, dated 26 August 1878, is handwritten on a printed form listing the courses, available dishes being: "Fish Chowder, Macaroni, Baked Bluefish, Beef, Lamb, Beefsteak Pie, Succotash, Corn, Potatoes, Beets, Stewed Tomatoes, Apple Pie, Berry Pie, and Plum Pudding." Printed at the bottom of the card are the beverages: "Bass's Pale Ale, Lager Beer, and Wines." Oddly enough, the Springfield House made a point in its advertising of stating that it kept "NO BAR."

In August of 1878 Elijah H. Alley bought Nancy K. Fisher's house, now 27 North Water Street, for $415. Alley had acquired the adjoining corner lot in 1856, shortly after demolition of the Nantucket Cordage Company's ropewalk, which extended the entire block along the south side of Easton Street; and inasmuch as his own home was across the street, diagonally opposite his hotel building, Alley had substantial holdings on three corners of this intersection. The new acquisition, a two-story, five-bay clapboard house, was enlarged at the top during May of the following year, in the form of a third floor within "a French

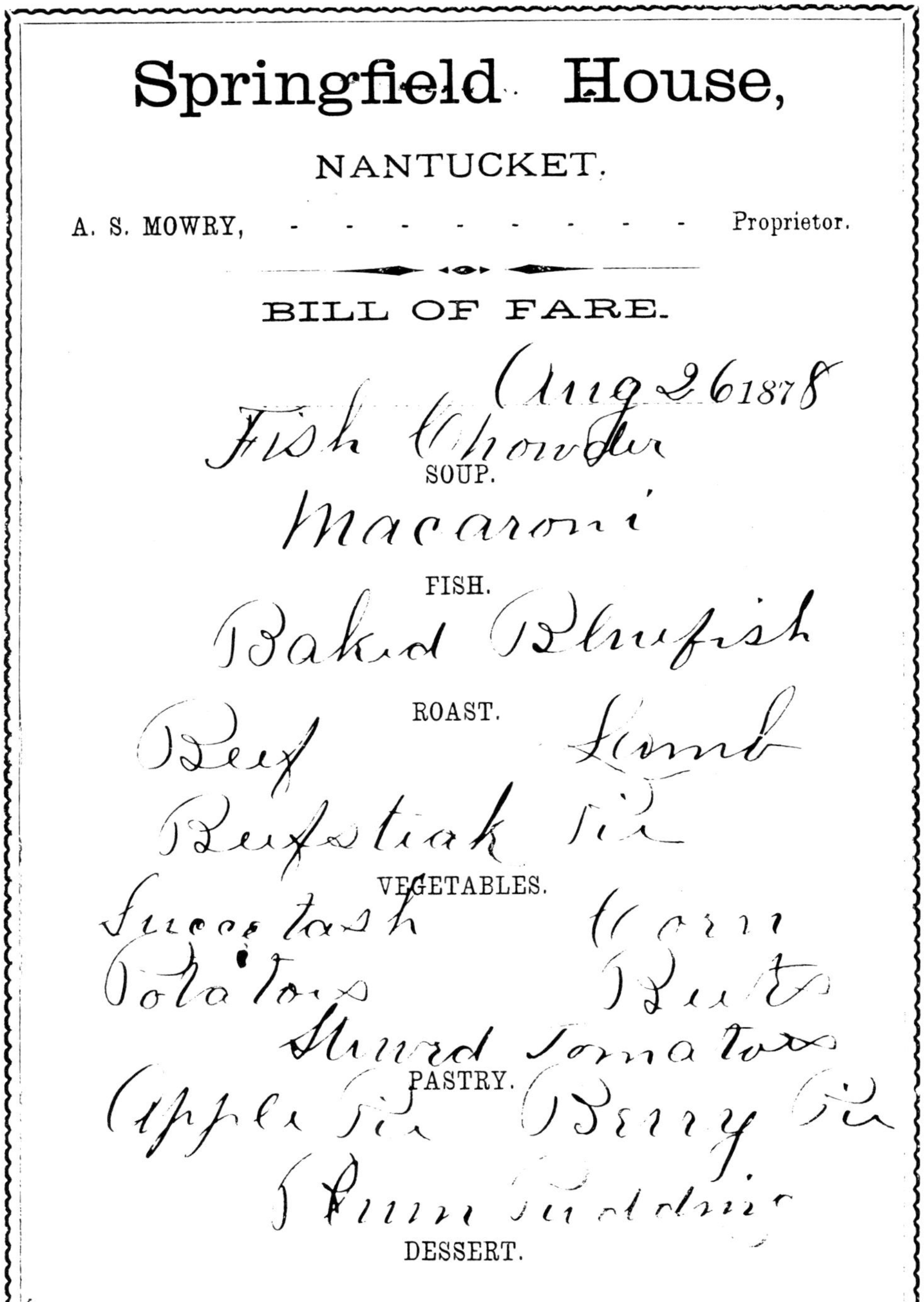

Springfield House,

NANTUCKET.

A. S. MOWRY, - - - - - - - - Proprietor.

BILL OF FARE.

Aug 26 1878

Fish Chowder

SOUP.

Macaroni

FISH.

Baked Bluefish

ROAST.

Beef   Lamb

Beefsteak Pie

VEGETABLES.

Succotash   Corn

Potatoes   Beets

Stewed Tomatoes

PASTRY.

Apple Pie   Berry Pie

Plum Pudding

DESSERT.

Bass's Pale Ale, Lager Beer, and Wines.

35 *Dinner menu, Springfield House, 26 August 1878.*

roof 36 x 46 feet, and it [the building] contains twenty-five rooms. If affords an excellent view of the harbor and sound, and will be fitted with all modern conveniences, to be used during the summer, in connection with the Springfield House, opposite, for lodging purposes. The work is being done by Mr. James H. Gibbs." Also, a "spacious piazza" was put up across the front. When opened for the season of 1879 the building was known as the "ANNEX HOUSE." The Springfield complex was the mecca for devotees of "BATHING, BOATING AND FISHING."

Despite enlargement of the inns on Orange and North Water streets during the 1870s, Nantucket's leading hotel remained the Ocean House. When Ulysses S. Grant, the first incumbent President of the United States to set foot on Nantucket, arrived on 27 August 1874, he was entertained there. The Presidential party, including Mrs. Grant and General Belknap (Secretary of War) and his wife, arrived on the *River Queen*

(used by Grant during the Civil War, now back on the island route) at ten o'clock in the morning. They were greeted by a firearms salute and met by conveyances to conduct them on a tour of the town. The chief executive was taken in Frederick C. Sanford's carriage. They drove from Steamboat Wharf down South Water to Main Street, west through the business district to Orange, south to York, through to Pleasant, back to Main, east to Centre, north to Chester, east to North Water, south to Broad, thence to the Ocean House. The entourage was welcomed by cheers along the entire junket, and many stores and residences were bedecked with flags. The Ocean House was elaborately decorated with red, white, and blue streamers dropping from the eaves to the lower balcony, and on the portico "were arches of flags and flowers with the portrait of our guest in front." President Grant and Mrs. Macy led the procession to the dining hall, followed by Councillor Macy and Mrs. Grant and

36 *The Springfield House, main pavilion on right (note name in sidewalk) and the Annex House on the left.*

some fifty other guests. The collation consisted of "cold meats, turkey, chicken, roast beef, lamb, ham and tongue; salads, lobster and chicken. Dessert, cakes, Charlotte Russe, lemon and wine jellies, ice cream, pears, peaches, bananas, apples and grapes." The head of state charged Postmaster-General Jewell with expresssing his appreciation to the populace gathered outside, himself making no such appearance. The party resumed places in the carriages to return to Steamboat Wharf. A rein got caught under the harness, and this and the throng of people alarmed the Sanford horses, which bolted forward but soon were got under control. Nevertheless, the First Lady alighted and walked to the boat, while the President calmly kept his seat until the equipage reached the wharf. At noon the *River Queen* set out for Hyannis amidst a din of warm farewells from the islanders. Grant occupied the old state suite during the voyage.

The year after the President's brief visit, Charles H. Robinson was engaged in making improvements to the Ocean House. Among them were: "New water pipes . . . [and water] closets arranged for the convenience of guests," and a "cover over the balcony in front."

On 1 May 1878 the Ocean House was sold at auction to F.C. Sanford for $5000. In 1879 the high brick wall on the west side was removed and replaced by a "more graceful fence."A seventy-room addition was made in 1882, and kitchen and sanitary facilities came four years later. J.S. Doyle was proprietor.

Beginning in 1875 the *Inquirer and Mirror* listed the names of "HOTEL ARRIVALS" during July and August for the six major inns on the island: the Ocean House, Sherburne House, Bay View House, and Springfield House in town, and the Atlantic House and Ocean View House at Siasconset.

Lesser establishments of the mid- to late-1870s in Nantucket, given by the names of their proprietors and contemporary addresses, the types of accommodations, and date (in parentheses), include:

Philip Joseph's Providence House, 137 Union Street (boardinghouse, 1873–74).

Cordelia M. Coffin, Lily Street (furnished rooms, 1873). She lived next north of the Reuben R. Bunker house, then occupied by Lucretia M. Brown.

George A. Chadwick, 8 Vestal Street (boardinghouse, 1874–81).

William J. Chase, Chester Street (furnished rooms, 1874). This is the house on the north corner of Centre Street and is pictured in the C.H. Shute series of stereographs in the NHA collection.

George W. Galvan, Main Street (boardinghouse, 1875). The house is that on the east corner of Grave Street (Quaker Road).

T.G. Nickerson, "No. 2 North Water Street, corner of Chester Street and opposite the [original] Springfield House" (boardinghouse, 1875). This would be the building south of the Alley hotel.

Mrs. Susan C. Veeder, 155 Orange Street (boardinghouse, 1875). Susan was Mrs. Charles A. Veeder, whose husband's land was in the vicinity of Warren Street.

L. Dexter's, Main Street, "Four Doors Below Post-Office" (boardinghouse and restaurant, 1875). Take-out orders were averred to be "sweet and fresh."

Reuben P. Folger, no address, had a piazza built to accommodate summer boarders (1876). Six years later Mrs. R.P. Folger's boardinghouse was "No. 7 Fair Street."

W.H. Myrick, North Water Street opposite Sea Street (boardinghouse, 1876).

Capt. Charles Luce, 114 Orange Street (boardinghouse, 1877–78). The house actually faced Cottage Court, and the property ran to York Street.

37 *Swain's Inn, Centre at Lily Street.*

J.B. Swain, 94 Centre Street (boarding-house, 1878 on). This is now 78 Centre, north corner of Lily Street. The house was run by Samuel Davis in 1878 and leased for five years by James B. Coffin beginning in 1879; its name then changed (temporarily) to the Brattleboro House.

Several refreshment stands had come into existence during this period. One of them had quite a showy soda fountain. In the summer of 1873 the C.H. Jaggar store installed an A.D. Puffer Carbonated Spring Soda Apparatus. The body of the counter was of Italian marble, on a base of Sienna marble, and it had a "complete set of silver-plated tubes and connections for drawing the syrups . . . and coolers of the most approved style."

William B. Stevens's Union Ice Cream Saloon was five doors above the post office on Main Street (1874).

The address of Mrs. Winslow's ice cream saloon was given as 38 Orange Street (1877–79). We have noted the opening of this establishment in 1867.

Mrs. Allen H. Gifford's ice cream saloon was at 37 North Water Street (1879).

Outside of Nantucket Town, in the summer of 1875, Julius Ives converted the Myrick farm in South Pasture (its entrance opposite Lovers Lane) into Myrick's Grove by planting additional pine trees and making it into a picnic ground, with tables, benches, and a water cooler, adjoining which was a "level lot" for a baseball field. A box was kept near the cooler for depositing pennies, "the price of admission for each man, woman, or child being one cent."

In Siasconset a boardinghouse called the Sea View may have been under construction in 1873 when a writeup appeared in the newspaper in August about "the first successful attempt at driving a tubular well on the island," and notices about its being open to the public were inserted in 1875.

Robert B. Coffin had a "Summer Boarding" place "near the bank" in 1878.

In 1879 mention is made of the "Parker House," first as a sign gracing a "'Sconset villa," and later as being "closed Sunday." To what it catered is not specified.

Another circle of activity was around the Great Harbor, to the south and east of the old seaport. In the spring of 1874 William C. Gifford advertised that he had "taken the 'De Wolf Farm' on the south shore of the harbor, "where he was "prepared to receive permanent or transient boarders." His hostelry was called the Sea-Side House.

The out-of-town inn that came into existence during this period and was to grow and flourish for a full century was the Wauwinet House at the Head of the Harbor, below the narrow neck of land called the Haulover. Its location had the advantage of proximity to both harbor and ocean. The original building was quite small, perhaps 30-feet square, a story-and-a-half form with a few chambers lighted by dormer windows over the entertaining room occupying the first story, which had end walls that swung on hinges and could be opened up to the breezes. A porch across the front looked out over the water and offered a distant vista of the town. A narrow pier extended out into the water. Materials for the building were delivered to the site at the beginning of February, a week later the frame was standing, and by the first of March, 1876, the structure was "recently completed." Its name was that of the sachem Wauwinet, chief of the native tribe that had lived in the area before the white man came. Charles A. Kenny and Asa W. N. Small were the proprietors.

The opening event was invitational, an excursion made jointly by the Masons, Odd Fellows, and Daughters of Rebekah, which is the women's chapter of the I.O.O.F., the two divisions having shared headquarters in Sherburne Hall on Centre Street. A gathering of 163 met at Steamboat Wharf around seven o'clock on the morning of 14 June and found places in nine yachts for the sail up the harbor. Fog had moved in, but the trip was enjoyable. The guests landed and inspected the premises, after which the noon meal was served, consisting of "clam chowder, boiled lobster and all sorts of pastry." Music by Prof. L.H. Johnson accompanied the repast and continued for the quadrilles, polkas, and waltzes that followed. Then came the group singing, while those less interested in vocalizing engaged in a game of croquet on the grounds. Preparations for the homeward voyage began at about five o'clock, with speeches of thanks and three rousing cheers for the hosts, and the boats were back at their moorings by dark. Regular passenger service to

38 *Gathering at the original Wauwinet House.*

the Wauwinet House was undertaken by Captain Codd's little steamer *Island Belle*. Further clambakes and dances were scheduled by way of incentive to patronage.

During the following spring a second inn was erected at the Head of the Harbor for Sylvanus B. Howes on land he purchased. Originally to have been called Wonoma, after the daughter of the sachem Wauwinet, when opened on 26 May the name had been fixed as the Sea Foam House. The title was painted on a "handsome sign" by Alexander I. Macy.

Like the Wauwinet House, the Sea Foam staged parties, some of them in the evening, requiring special arrangements for transportation. Unlike the Wauwinet House, it did not prosper, and Howes sold it to William T. Swain for $341.82 in October of the same year.

The year 1879 closed the decade and issued in a new kind of July Fourth celebration, which,

although not followed consecutively with others of its kind (due to distraction over the railroad, beginning in 1881), nevertheless set a tradition. Heretofore, Independence Day festivals had been scattered: Sunday school picnics at the fairgrounds, clambakes for grownups on the south shore of the harbor, and perhaps a firemen's torchlight parade in the evening, as on the previous Fourth. In 1879 the celebration was centralized and of all-day duration, beginning with the deafening tolling of church bells at 4:30 a.m., punctuated by the firing of a five-pounder gun. At daybreak a disreputable looking group of about one hundred "Antiques and Horribles" assembled on the Lower Square and were formed into line by S. P. Marden, chief marshal of the occasion, assisted by M. Rothenberg. The latter, in Oriental costume and on horseback, led the parade, which went down Union Street, came back Orange, marched west on Main to Fair, south on Fair to Lyon, through to Pleasant, back to Main, through Gardner and North Liberty to Pearl (India), east to Centre, north to Chester, east to North Water, south to Broad, and across Federal to Main. The motley crew all along the way were greeted with "half-awake smiles and shouts by the early disturbed residents, who were provoked to mirth by many most comical costumes."

At 9:30 there was a rowing regatta of "pair-oared working boats." The five entries started from Steamboat Wharf and rowed to and around a stake boat off Coatue Point (a mile away) and back. The race was won by John J. Gardner and Charles E. Veeder, the latter the spouse of the proprietress of the boardinghouse on Orange Street. A yacht race followed. There were twelve

entries, and they made the junket to Coatue and back twice. The prize for the four-mile event went to Captain C.E. Smalley's *Lillian*, best known as a conveyance to festivities at Wauwinet. There was also a tub race for juniors at 1:30. Only two teams got in the running. They paddled over the required course, and the winners were young Avery Gardner and George Folger. The other pair came home swimming—pushing their tub.

The evening was enlivened by another march, the "FIREMAN'S PARADE," which traversed Main Street as far as the Civil War Monument and then back to Steamboat Wharf, where "an excellent view was offered of the FIREWORKS." The pyrotechnics were set off from the plank walk of

39 *The* Island Belle.

40 *The Sea Foam House, at the Head of the Harbor.*

Hayden's Baths. The last of the rockets were launched in quick succession, as a light rain had begun to fall, the denouement of the misty weather that had been dampening the partici- pants all day. Those not too limp from wet and marching repaired to the "FIREMAN'S BALL," which began on 10:30 in Chace Hall on Federal Street, corner of Main.

IV. Land Booms
and the South-shore Railroad

THE STORY of Nantucket hotels during the last quarter of the nineteenth century is intimately tied up with land speculation and "cottage-city" schemes, an offshoot of the movement that was rampant along the Atlantic coast of the United States over much of the triple "New" section— New England, New York, and New Jersey. The old leisure-class practice of spending holidays at mineral springs in the mountains slowly shifted to summering at the seashore. Selling lots for cottage sites was the last and least amenable stage in providing visitor accommodations. It had begun in the personal relationship between host and guest in the boardinghouse, had become less intimate in the inn or hotel but still maintained constant, daily contact, and was reduced to a preliminary and perhaps final meeting between owner and client in the summer-cottage transaction. The sale of a building lot entailed only a brief encounter between speculator's agent and buyer at the time of the sale, often in the form of a public auction. As we have seen, the boardinghouse reigned supreme on Nantucket up to the time of the Great Fire; the hotel had begun in rudimentary form and it came to the fore in the second half of the decade of the 1840s; the renting of cottages began at the close of the Civil War, or during the mid-1860s. Not only were services diminished, but the scale was larger in each successive stage mentioned: the furnishing of bed and board by the landlord of the private establishment was magnified to transactions encompassing hundreds of acres by the entrepreneur. The social climate of Nantucket in the nineteenth century was such that the final form of the move-

ment was more successful in dividing up land than in bringing multitudes of seasonal visitors to the island.

The later land divisions here considered resemble the early proprietary parceling of shares in only one or two respects. The initial staking of homesites in 1661, of sixty square rods per full-share holder, made possible the settling of the island. The homesites combined into an irregular, gerrymander shape from Capaum Harbor down to the head of the east cove of Hummock Pond. Subsequent divisions were regular and in compact areas around the lower arc of the Great Harbor, inside Nantucket Town. The principal ones were the Wesco Acre Lots (1678), roughly between Liberty and Broad streets west of Federal; the Fish Lots (1717), from Main Street down to Mulberry between Quanaty Bank and Pine Street; West Monomoy (1726), below the Fish Lots down to Milestone Road and between Pleasant Street and Consue Meadows; the Warehouse and Beach shares (1723), east of South Water and Union streets; Bocochico (1744), interlaying Wesco Acres and the Warehouse shares; and the Brant Point Meadow shares (1733), east of North Water Street and Cliff Road. Others were removed from the town expansion, such as South Monomoy (1726), around the south end of the harbor, and Quidnet and Siasconset at the east end of the island. From about the middle of the eighteenth century onward, after whaling had succeeded sheep grazing, much of the common land was divided for individual use, some of it becoming farms. Private ownership afforded vulnerability to subdivision schemes a century and

41 *Footbridge at Siasconset, showing first of Charles H. Robinson's cottages on Sunset Heights.*

more later. The proprietary layouts were mainly for the use of members' dwellings, the exceptions being the Warehouse and Beach shares and lots fronting on downtown streets, which were for commercial use (often residential as well), whereas the later speculations were for seasonal occcupancy by nonresidents of the island, and therefore by people not primarily concerned with its well-being. However, a good percentage of the late-nineteenth-century promoters of land division were natives, or at least were or had been residents.

It will be recalled that the first of the new generation of substantial houses built in Nantucket since those of the whaling era date from 1871; and in that year Eastman Johnson purchased land on North Shore Hill, where he had a studio erected for his own summer use. The following year this locale became the seedbed of the new industry, with two factions in competition. The first was an individual, Charles C. Mooers, who between 1865 and 1871 had purchased several pieces of ground, and in the fall of 1872 he offered "Sea Shore Lots at 'THE CLIFF'," having a "delightful situation . . . and . . . near to the beach, and to well conducted BATHING ROOMS." Lots of "convenient size" were priced from $150 to $200. In March of 1872 a group composed of Charles G. and Henry Coffin, Charles H. Robinson, and Matthew Barney purchased thirty-five acres between North Street (Cliff Road) and the shore, and they advertised, simultaneously with Mooers, "CLIFF LOTS" at "The Highest Part of the Cliff." Lots were "50 by 75 Feet," and there were "nearly two hundred in all." They featured "a beach and SEA SHORE PRIVILEGE OF ABOUT 2000 FEET," and a thirty-mile view over the Sound.

One of the backers of the Cliff Lots development, Charles H. Robinson, in partnership with Dr. Franklin A. Ellis, bought property on Sunset Heights, Siasconset, where they built and opened the Ocean View House in 1873 and offered the balance of the land as building lots. They were made accessible by "a broad avenue, called Ocean Avenue laid out along the edge of the bank, three-quarters of a mile in length." As on the Cliff, lots were 50-by-75 feet in size. In midsummer "a number of finely executed plans, in elevation, of cottages, drawn by C.H. Robinson & Son" were displayed in the window of Macy's Express Office on Main Street. It was recommended that "any one wishing a cottage at 'Sconset Heights' will do well to examine these plans." The style of Robinson's cottages is exemplified in the original pavilion of the Ocean View House.

In the fall of 1873 Robinson was given the commission for building the Lifesaving Station at Surfside, now the youth hostel, and of which a facsimile was erected in 1970 as the Lifesaving Museum at Shawkemo. Early that summer (1873) Surfside had been the setting for a meeting to snare investors in a gigantic development extending three miles along the south shore between Miacomet and Madequecham ponds. Among interested parties in attendance were Charles G. and Henry Coffin, George Wendell Macy, and Alfred Swain of Nantucket; "Blackwell and Utley, the well known real-estate men of New York, Mr. Ives of Geneva, Messrs. Cottress and Marshall and

Mr. Charles F. Coffin of Boston, and Mr. Bendle of the Meridian Manufacturing Company." The Surfside stock was to be divided into a hundred shares at $1,000 per share. (Robinson may have had an interest in it, as those in attendance repaired for dining to the Ocean View House.) Not for the better part of a decade did lots of the Surfside Land Company begin to move, and then due to the interim provision of mechanized transportation to the site. Layouts containing around 500 lots were to change design here over the following quarter of a century. Basically all of them were a fizzle.

Equally ambitious and equally abortive, without hope of redress, was a similar undertaking by the Nantucket Sea Shore Enterprise, headed by S. D. Tourtellotte of Worcester. A thousand-acre tract at Madaket, stretching from Smith's Point to Long Pond, with an ocean front of two-and-a-half miles, was bought and divided into about 1800 lots. In the spring of 1873 there were to have been built "a hotel and a few cottages . . . for occupancy next summer." Illustrating the whole scheme was "a very beautiful map . . . neatly executed on oiled silk." Its attractions included a few leftover spaces in the English garden-city manner, such as the triangular Trinity Park, circular Central and Observatory parks, and the oblong space accommodating the namesake of Hither Creek Park. Anybody familiar with the island knew the western cusp to be made up of shifting dunes and swamps, and a lot there to be as secure as a sand castle in the wash of a rising surf. Few lots were sold, no houses were built, and for many years no further attempt was made to exploit the area west of Hither Creek. Today, about half the site of the Sea Shore Enterprise layout is under water.

In 1872 Hervey B. Leete of New Haven acquired some twenty acres at Tetawkemmo (Quaise), not on but in sight of the harbor, and in 1875 he and Dwight Wooding tried to market about 500 building lots, 25-by-125 feet in size, of which only a few were sold. The land eventually went for taxes, and of course no cottages materialized.

42 *"PLAN OF GREAT NECK and SMITH'S POINT," by Cherrington & Marble and A. J. Marble, Worcester, 1873.*

The area east of Hither Creek (including part of the Tourtellotte fiasco) was the scene of several pretentious divisions during the mid-1870s. One endeavor was Nauticon, promoted by Winchester and Joseph A. Veazie of Boston. The larger part of Great Neck was parceled into 467 house lots, 50-by-100 feet in size. A few were disposed of but no improvements were made. The Veazies also were involved in prospective booms in neighboring Smooth Hummocks, between Nauticon and Surfside. In 1874 the Veazies staked off one part (Share #16) into 108 lots, another (Share #8) into 473 lots, and a third into 380 lots. The following year they conveyed part of those lands to Francis Hinckley, who offered 488 lots. Others active in that section at about the same time were Trueman B. Towne, who in 1875 had 162 lots for sale, and a group whose holdings extended to the west (beyond Hummock Pond) and to the north. Members of the group whom we have encountered before were Charles G. and Henry Coffin and the latter's son (Charles F. Coffin), and Benjamin Robinson and son (Charles H. Robinson); associated were George Easton, Alfred Swain, George W. Macy, A.M. Myrick, and Nathaniel Barney. They held almost 950 acres, of which more than half was in Smooth Hummocks; over 200 acres were in Head of Plains, and another 130 acres in Trott's Hills, on the Sound and west of the Cliff. Lots were considerably larger than in preceding projects; the last, for instance, divided into 27 parcels.

The division of Trott's Hills (though without appreciable fruition) in 1874 and former progress at the Cliff signaled further activity in this region in 1875. The laying out of Sherburne Bluffs, immediately west of the latter and sponsored by the same men, was designed by J. Davis Robinson, architect. Consisting of thirty lots, it extended to the water, with Averet Avenue separating the beach from the development proper. Two sets of bathing rooms were to be built for purchasers' use.

In 1876 a much larger undertaking was to the southwest. It was known as Wannacomet Bluffs. Lewis A. Taylor and John H. Hersey of Springfield had it cut up into 240 lots. It was to no avail, and the water company was to occupy the area a few years later.

The development of Beachside, along the north shore of Brant Point, was begun by Henry Coleman, Elijah H. Alley, Franklin A. Ellis, and Frederick S. Raynard. On 27 November 1872 they paid $500 to George Easton for a tract fronting 3,146 feet on the water and running back from 400 to 600. Bay Avenue was proposed along the beach with Hulbert and Walsh streets parallel to it (the latter from Henry Street westward), and there were nine short streets running crosswise. Beginning 1 November 1880, Charles C. Mooers replaced Ellis and Raynard, and the three owners became active in disposing of lots. The first was the 200-foot square between Charles and Dix streets on the waterfront. It was purchased by Edwin J. Hulbert for $200, and he built the first house in Beachside.

In 1881 Charles H. Robinson and Alfred Swain launched a small subdivision called Clifton Springs at the end of Lincoln Avenue on the Cliff.

During the fall of 1882 "most of the [water] frontage west of the residences upon the Cliff" had been acquired by "Mrs. Elizabeth W. Johnson, wife of Eastman Johnson, a partitioning having been set off to her from the common and undivided lands, by vote of the proprietors," and the land was "on the market for building purposes." It extended to Capaum Pond. Eastman Johnson himself bought the "land bordering upon and enclosing the Reed pond at the Cliff," but his intentions were for his own pleasure, rather than commercial, as he planned to clean out and stock the pond with fish.

In 1884 Isabella A. Orr was operating in this general vicinity, having had T. William Harris of Boston make a survey of her land on Lincoln Avenue near North Beach Street, adjoining holdings of Joseph S. Barney, John Winn, and Ansel Hamblen. In 1886 Henry Robinson and Henry A. Willard laid out 27 lots along Willard Street on Brant Point.

An active campaign was being waged simultaneously on the outskirts of Siasconset, taking on a somewhat different character from that occurring elsewhere. Almon T. Mowry, brother of the proprietor of the Springfield House and himself

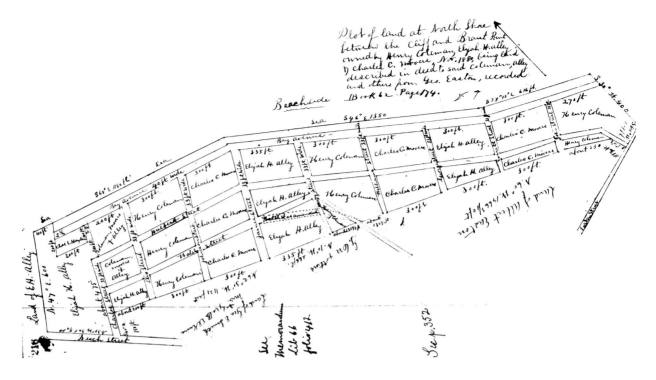

43 *Plan of Beachside on the north shore of Brant Point, as laid out in 1880.*

involved in it and in the Sherburne House (1877), was operating as a realtor disposing of small pieces of land divided into a few lots, such as that of W. Williams, W. M. F. Round, and G. A. Sawyer. Elsewhere in the hamlet the practice abounded of building cottages to rent furnished during succeeding seasons. In 1881 A. Judd Northrup had written a book called *'Sconset Summer Life: A Summer on Nantucket Island* (published in Syracuse, New York), which describes the phenomenon in its somewhat embryonic stage, but established nevertheless. A second edition of the book was to come out in 1901. In the spring of 1883 the newspaper announced: "The baker's dozen of cottages which Mr. Charles M. Robinson is now building for H. K. White, Esq., of Detroit, in the village of 'Sconset, are rapidly approaching completion, and furniture for them is on the way here. Every one of them is already rented for the season of 1883." At the beginning of July a Siasconset cottage advertised for rent contained "eight rooms and a store room, just completed and fully furnished for housekeeping. For particulars, address E. F. UNDERHILL, Siasconset, or inquire of Capt. William Baxter, or Levi S. Coffin." Edward F. Underhill was to make a thriving business of renting cottages: in 1887 we find him asking $90 to $190 per season. He added to his initial stock and in 1890 had three dozen cottages available. Toward the end of the century he was issuing charmingly illustrated notices of "FURNISHED SEASIDE COTTAGES," and inviting requests for circulars "about 'SCONSET . . . containing a brief history of the place, with maps, views and ground plans of the houses." Underhill coined and popularized the sobriquet "patchwork village," using it in the title of some of his published writings, most of which came out under the imprint of Underhill, E. T. & Co., New York. They include: *A Picture Book of ye Patchworke Village, 'Sconset by ye Sea* (1885), *The Credible Chronicles of the Patchwork Village* (1886), *'Sconset by the Sea* (ca. 1893), and *'Sconset in a Nutshell* (n.d.). Underhill wrote several articles as well: "'Sconset

Then and Now—A Retrospective Glance at the Patchwork Village" (*Inquirer and Mirror*, 20 August 1888) and "The 'Sconset Railroad" (*Boston Herald*, and *Nantucket Journal*, 6 August 1891); and the series, "The Old Houses on 'Sconset Bank" (*'Sconset Pump*, summer of 1888, and *Nantucket Journal*, August–September 1889).

Edward T. Underhill had started off in the orthodox manner of selling land, in 1882 laying out 50 lots between Ocean Avenue and Atlantic Avenue (Morey Lane), before drawing in his reins, keeping and building on them himself for summer rentals. The principal land-boom exponents at Siasconset were the Flaggs. In 1883 William J. Flagg offered 13 lots between Sankaty Road and the bank, and two years later he and Eliza L. Flagg had the more ample tract, Sankaty Heights, containing 87 lots along the ocean. In 1884 Isaac M. Thomas, Harriet H. Gray, and Ellen M. Round had available 31 lots in the south end. In 1885 Charles H. Robinson laid out more land on Sunset Heights; and two years later Emily P. Rice and Robert B. Coffin were disposing of 39 lots on Atlantic Avenue. A house lot that sold for $225 at Siasconset in 1883 brought $325 in 1885, and an offer of $450 was made before the close of the summer season.

Elsewhere than at the two year-round communities, the major theatre of new developments during the early 1880s was around the Great Harbor. In 1882 Mrs. Z. D. Underhill, of New York, "bought of Mr. Joseph Vincent his lots at Shimmo amounting to eighty acres for $2,000." The land extended from the DeWolf farm (Gifford's Sea-Side House of 1874) to Abram's Point. It is not clear whether Mrs. Underhill meant to build only her own cottage there or portion off lots. There is no question about the intentions of Mrs. Ellen M. Round, who, the same year, had 55 lots staked out at Wauwinet. They were arranged in two alignments, to either side of a straight road, leaving a space for the hotel in their midst. In 1883 the Coatue Land Company developed the area just south of Mrs. Round's, making it into 83 lots; and at the same time the company laid out a plan for 39 blocks, containing 275 lots, at the far end of Coatue, from the second point

westward. When that land was sold to William F. Kidder in 1890, members of the Coatue Land Company at the time were Josiah Freeman, Almon T. Mowry, and William S. Chadwick. In 1884–85 Matthew Barney and Andrew M. Myrick had land parceled out at Squam and Pocomo, the latter, at least, laid out on a grid plan.

In 1884 Ellen M. Round bought a strip of land between Sesachacha Pond and the ocean, with a pond frontage of 470 feet. It was divided into 40 lots, most of them on the water. Sales of harbor and Sesachacha Pond lots were inconsequential.

Real-estate flurries of the last half of the 1880s were mostly expansions of those areas that had been proven viable, including Lincoln Heights (1886) at the Cliff, Aurora Heights (1886) at Siasconset, and Dionis City (1887) west of Capaum Pond.* A group from Boston and Brooklyn, New York, laid out a 17-acre tract called Monomoy Heights in 1889. This region at the south arc of the harbor was the former South Monomoy, divided into the usual 27 portions by the proprietors in 1726, along with West Monomoy (lower Orange Street), but whereas the latter had been assimilated into the town, the more remote South Monomoy had not. More than a hundred and sixty years later it was staked into 347 lots; and although they did not sell all at once, Monomoy Heights, with a view of the town and harbor equal to that of the North Cliff, was destined to rival it as a cottage colony. Attempts continued at Surfside. Throughout the autumn of 1889 agent Almon T. Mowry ran weekly notices offering lots gratis on guarantee of a contract to build a cottage "in VERY LIBERAL TERMS." Even that failed to start the ball rolling, and in 1891 a good deal of the Surfside property was sold to, or taken over by William H. Gwynn of Cohoes, New York. There were other, smaller projects germinating on the south shore, such as Mary, Georgiana, Fanny, and Ida Elkins's 27-lot layout to the east of Surfside.

During the last decade of the century, attempts at marketing lots occurred mostly at both ends of Siasconset, particularly at Low Beach; at Wauwinet, Maxcy's Pond, Pine Lands (part of which became the fairgrounds), Quidnet

*Henry Barnard Worth, "Nantucket Lands and Land Owners," Bulletin of the Nantucket Historical Association, Vol. 2, No. 4 (1904), p. 116.

FURNISHED SEASIDE·COTTAGES,

AT SIASCONSET, NANTUCKET.

AN ANCIENT 'SCONSET COTTAGE.

Fifty miles out in the ocean, one can have all the benefits and none of the discomforts of a sea voyage.

Life is undisturbed by the clank of machinery, the creak of ship's timbers or the roll of the vessel.

No fear of drifting on land in darkness or in fog, or being driven on a lee shore in gales.

Cool and quiet by night and by day 'SCONSET is a haven of rest for brain workers and tired out business men, and is a natural sanitarium for those suffering from nervous exhaustion, hay fever or malaria. It is a paradise for children.

Laziness drifts into sleep and sleep awakens into laziness; so gradual is the change, it is hard to tell where one ends and the other begins.

The most restful climate for invalids and convalescents.

Influenced by the tonic properties of the ocean air extinct appetites are born again and manifest aggressive activity. It is not unusual for an invalid to gain 25 to 40 pounds during a season.

◆ ◆ ◆ ◆

UNDERHILL.

'SCONSET BEACH DORIES.

AN ANCIENT 'SCONSET COTTAGE.

NANTUCKET is the island of long lives. More than half of its people live to from 70 to 100 years. The average duration of life is 64 years, nearly double that in any other part of the world. 'SCONSET is its most wholesome spot.

Life is passed basking in the sun, on the grass, or on the beach, resting in hammocks or under awnings, riding or sauntering over moors redolent with a perfume of wild flowers, fishing, or playing the current outdoor games, viewing the gorgeous sunsets or the ocean in sunshine or in storm, laving in surf of a uniform temperature of 70 degrees in July and August, while the average highest of the air is from 68 to 70.

Picturesque cottages with six to nine rooms fully furnished are to let there at from $90 to $175 for the season.

If you want to know anything more about 'SCONSET write for a circular, containing a brief history of the place with maps, views and ground plans of the houses.

◆ ◆ ◆ ◆

108 Fulton Street, New York.

44 *Edward F. Underhill's advertisement for "Furnished Seaside Cottages," 1898.*

(Sesachacha Pond), Beachside (Brant Point), and still at Surfside. Most of those ventures were more "boom" in their aspirations and advertising than in actuality. It seems that the more inflated they were the flatter they collapsed. The magnitude of improvement needed, both in building and landscaping, was largely responsible for their failure. Another factor was accessibility, which played an important role in what successes there were near to Nantucket Town and Siasconset and, to a lesser degree and temporarily, in proximity to the hotels at Wauwinet and Surfside, which were provided with regular service by yacht or train. With regard to hostelries in relation to cottage suburbs, we already have seen that the Ocean View House was the counterpart to Robinson's lot sales on Sunset Heights. Also, it may be observed that two of the island's greatest hotels, the Nantucket and the Sea Cliff Inn (built during the mid-1880s, to be discussed in the following chapter), were lively ornaments of Brant Point and North Street (Cliff Road), each surrounded by its satellites of lesser boardinghouses and summer cottages.

Quite aside from the prosaic process of reaching vacation quarters, transportation was and is a matter of vital concern to islanders. The story of steamboat connections with the mainland, since before the Civil War to almost the close of the nineteenth century, is largely that of the *Island Home* (1855), which has been mentioned. The estrangement from New Bedford occasioned by the loss of the *Eagle's Wing* in 1861 was reconciled a year later with the building of the *Monohansett,* into which the engine of the *Eagle's Wing* was installed. The *Monohansett* soon was chartered to the government and served to carry dispatches to the war fleet operating off Cape Hatteras and Wilmington, North Carolina, during the Civil War. The boat was returned to Massachusetts in 1866 but not put on the island run. The *River Queen* was built in 1864 and used by General Grant during the period of belligerence, afterwards serving Martha's Vineyard until acquired in 1873 by the Nantucket and Cape Cod Steamboat Company. The next year the *River Queen* brought General Grant, then President, to the island; and it and the *Island Home* operated in the first two-boats-a-day season. The *River Queen* was sold in 1881, and for many years it was operated on the Potomac River.

In 1886 the Nantucket and Vineyard lines consolidated, forming the New Bedford, Martha's Vineyard & Nantucket Steamboat Company, which acquired the ship *Martha's Vineyard* for excursion purposes; and in the same year the ship *Nantucket* was built especially for service to its namesake. The boat was 190 feet long and of 629 gross tons, a worthy mate and successor to the *Island Home* after her decease in 1895. The last craft acquired for the Nantucket Sound fleet during the nineteenth century was the *Gay Head*, built in 1891. It was the largest boat to date, 203 feet long and weighing 701 tons. She was propelled by revolving buckets, a system that took up less space than paddlewheels and was entirely enclosed by the boat's superstructure (Turner, *Island Steamers*, pp. 64–73).

More intimately connected with summer events on Nantucket, begotten by and for land ventures, the progenitor of several hotels, and for a third of a century the life line between Town and Siasconset, was the dry-land complement to the steamboats—the Nantucket railroad. Rail service to Siasconset had been proposed and a survey made during the mid-1840s by Judge Edward M. Gardner, but nothing came of it. Establishing a railroad on the island was broached again in 1875, the proposed destination being Surfside. It is significant that at the time there were no civilized amenities at Surfside, and the only aspirations for a summer colony were laid out on paper. The first real evidence that a railroad might materialize was on 12 August 1879 when four civil engineers from the continent accompanied Philip H. Folger to Nantucket and began making plans for a course. They started at the Springfield

House, corner of North Water and Chester streets, measured westward out Chester and West Centre (West Chester) streets to the edge of town. They continued past Maxcy's Pond to Trott's Hills, turned left and followed Long Pond to the south shore. Here they swung eastward; proposed crossing the crook of Hummock Pond about 300 feet from the beach, passed Miacomet Pond, Nobadeer, Madequecham, and Toupchue ponds; then they veered inland to Philip's Run and concluded along Milestone Road into Siasconset. Arthur H. Gardner, publisher and editor of the recently begun *Nantucket Journal*, commented that the forthcoming project was to be financed by "capitalists from abroad," which meant Boston and New York, and that "the girting of our island with an 'iron belt' [may] have the effect of dotting the plains with . . . cottage cities." Here, in a phrase, was the initial motivation behind the railroad. Its circuitous route from Nantucket to Siasconset was meant to serve the Cliff, Trott's Hills, Great Neck, Head of Plains, Smooth Hummocks, Surfside, and Sunset Heights, all of which were potential developments at that time. When Folger returned during the fall he was accompanied by Joseph Veazie, one of the promoters of Nauticon; and, although there were nine or ten backers of the railroad, Folger and Veazie alone applied for and received a right of way for the line from the Proprietors of the Common and Undivided Lands of the Island of Nantucket. The map of the proposed road drawn in the late fall mostly followed the route earlier described, with the exception that it was to begin at Steamboat Wharf and go out North Beach Street, omitting the Springfield House; and it was to continue from Toupchue along the shore past Tom Nevers Head and Low Beach to the base of Sunset Heights, instead of entering Siasconset via the carriage road.

Work on grading was begun in the spring of 1880. The exit from town now was via Washington Street toward the south rather than out the north end, and the western circuit was abandoned in favor of a straight drop to Surfside. The reason for the change was economic: landowners on North Beach Street asked exorbitant prices for a track strip, the price of railroad iron had

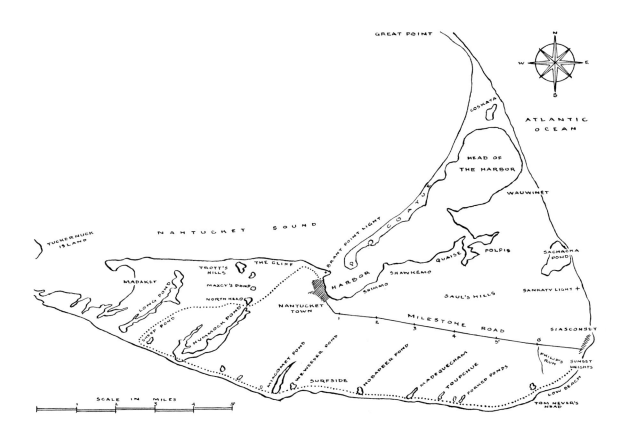

Labels on map: GREAT POINT · N · ATLANTIC OCEAN · COSKATA · HEAD OF THE HARBOR · WAUWINET · NANTUCKET SOUND · BRANT POINT LIGHT · COATUE · QUAISE · POLPIS · SACHACHA POND · TUCKERNUCK ISLAND · TROTT'S HILLS · THE CLIFF · HARBOR · SHAWKEMO · SANKATY LIGHT · MADAKET · MAXCY'S POND · SHIMMO · SAUL'S HILLS · LONG POND · NORTH HEAD · NANTUCKET TOWN · MILESTONE ROAD · SIASCONSET · DEEP POND · HUMMOCK POND · MIACOMET POND · WEWEEDER POND · NOBADEER POND · MADEQUECHAM · TOUPCHUE · FORKED PONDS · PHILIP'S RUN · SUNSET HEIGHTS · SURFSIDE · LOW BEACH · TOM NEVER'S HEAD · SCALE IN MILES

45 *Map of Nantucket Island, showing first proposed route of the railroad from Nantucket Town to Siasconset, 1879.*

gone up, entrepreneurs (at least those connected with the railroad venture) had decided to concentrate on Surfside, and perhaps investment in the company had not come up to expectations. A second Veazie, Winchester, came to the island as engineer to survey for the new route, and a contract for the work was given to Loren Downs of Boston. About half of the laborers came from America; the balance, and the teams of horses needed, were local. Grading got under way at the beginning of May. The primary problem, and the one that took longest to resolve, was building a causeway over Goose Pond. Beyond Orange Street the roadbed required a good deal of sandfill over the Clay Pits, and a cut had to be made through Michael Foley's property. From there grade was accomplished fairly easily by men with shovels

over the flat commons to the beach about 500 yards east of the lifesaving station at Surfside. The work continued along the shore eastward, and by the end of June it had reached Forked Ponds, about halfway to Siasconset, where it suddenly came to a halt. Work stoppage was attributed to trouble in the home office at Boston; nevertheless, the same directors were reelected in October, but it was too late in the year for the endeavor to be resumed.

In April of 1881 circulars were issued announcing proposals, affirming stability, and inviting investment in bonds of the Nantucket Railroad Company. The following month it swung into action by purchasing rails and rolling stock; and Downs brought workmen to the island and began repairing and raising the level of the roadbed. The arrival of the rails at the end of May and the use of two small flatcars on the lengthening track facilitated the work considerably. The system was a narrow gauge of 36 inches. Perhaps the two most exciting moments in Nantucket's history were in early July: the first when the engine, tender, and two cars were unloaded from the barge *Roslyn Sherman* on the first day of the month, and the second when they went into service, on July Fourth. The locomotive, a product of the Baldwin Works of Philadelphia, had been used for several months on the Danville, Olney and Ohio River Railroad in Illinois. It was shipped to Nantucket via New York, where it was equipped with a patented spark arrester to prevent its setting fire to the pine groves; and on the flanks of the tender its name was inscribed in gold letters: "DIONIS." The choice had been that of Charles F. Coffin, general manager of the company, and it was in memory of Dionis Coffin, wife of the patriarch Tristram. The two passenger carriages were of the open summer style, each containing fifteen transverse benches, entered from the sides, capable of seating seventy-five to ninety persons. The cars had been employed on the Long Island Railroad and were redecorated after coming to the island.

Initially, the tracks began just north of Main Street, where the station was only a part of a store, and Surfside was the end of the line. There the railroad company had a substantial depot built. It was to function as a refreshment and general recreation center, as the sea and beach were the only other attractions the area offered. The barnlike structure was about 100 feet long and stood back 50 feet from the narrow platform bordering the tracks. It had vertical-board walls pierced by sash windows and corbel-arched doorways, with chevron stripes painted on the double doors. A veranda extended the length of the front facing the tracks, a ticket booth projecting into the shelter at the center. A kitchen was built as an ell at the back by Charles H. Robinson, and presumably he was responsible for the entire depot. The building was not finished for the opening exercises, which occurred on the Glorious Fourth, but it figured prematurely in that memorable event.

On Monday, 4 July 1881, the locomotive and tender were hauled to the provisional starting point. The boiler and tank were filled with water and the fire was kindled. The engine was trimmed with flags. Early in the afternoon it took on a privileged party consisting of General Manager Coffin, Civil Engineer Veazie, Contractor Downs and Mrs. Downs, Superintendent Philip H. Folger, Treasurer John M. Norton, and Town Crier Billy Clark, the last having been most enthusiastic in hailing the landing of each article of equipment and stock by blowing his horn from the top of the Unitarian Church tower. Amidst shouts from the spectators, *Dionis* started off and ran out as far as Hooper's station, where she stopped,

46 *The Surfside Depot.*

47 Dionis *and carriages at Surfside.*

then backed to town. She then coupled with the cars and was ready for the first run of three miles to Surfside.

The passengers were invited guests and included a representative of the *Inquirer and Mirror,* probably R. B. Hussey, who described the excursion to the sea: "Shortly after 2 P.M., the train moved away from the station corner [at] Main and Candle streets, and slowly around the sharp curve near the foot of Coffin street (this curve has been lengthened), when engineer Stansbury 'opened on her' gradually, and away the train went over the Goose pond, the Clay Pits, by Hooper's station, through the short stretch of pines, to the open commons, where the speed was increased, and we went whirling along towards the station at Surf-side, which was to be the scene of festivities at a later hour. The eveness of the road was freely commented upon, and the officials were loud in their praise of the work of Mr. Downs, whose beaming face near by gave evidence of the

gratification he was deriving from listening to the words of praise; and he was justified for feeling . . . supremely happy. The run over to Surf-side occupied but a few moments, when the train returned to transport other guests to the scene of the festivities. The platform was crowded as it drew up at the station, and as 'all aboard' sounded from conductor Keene's lips, the cars filled rapidly, and shortly after the appointed hour, several hundred persons were being borne along on A REAL NANTUCKET RAILROAD. We listened attentively to the comments on all sides, and were greeted with 'Ain't it funny'; 'This is just lovely'; 'Here's the Goose Pond'; 'I could ride all day'; 'Well, I never expected to ride on a railroad through Weeweeder valley,' and other similar remarks. Pleasant faces greeted one on every hand, and the novelty of the occasion added greatly to the pleasure of the ride, which was enjoyed to the fullest extent by all participants. The familiar scenery along the route seemed ladened with a different and peculiar charm. Passing along the pleasant shore of the harbor, thence across the flats, the Goose Pond, the Clay Pits, out into open fields, thence entering a sweet-scented grove of pines, and beyond rushing out upon the broad, level common, with the sea in front, drew out frequent expressions of delight, as the tastes of different members of the company were called forth. As the train drew up at the station at Surf-side, one lady gave utterance to the only fault-finding heard for the day, which fully expressed the feeling of all in attendance. It was that the ride was not long enough."

The passengers alighted and inspected the premises, strolled down to the beach, and stood in groups chatting. Tables were arranged inside the station and on the veranda, and the guests were invited to partake of a "most excellent shore dinner of Quahaug chowder, baked clams and bluefish cakes, fruits, tea and coffee and iced lemonade." The meal was prepared under the direction of J. Bradlee Starbuck and served by girls of the high school graduating class.

The collation was followed by a literary and musical diversion. After the eating utensils were cleared away the audience faced an "improvised pavilion." The Rev. Daniel Round presided. The opening number was a song entitled "Soft Glides the Sea," rendered by the glee club, among whose members were Mr. and Mrs. Almon T. Mowry. The first speaker was Allen Coffin, author of the *Life of Tristram Coffin*, a book recently published by the *Inquirer and Mirror*, its contents figuring in the oration. The name of the new railroad engine being identical with that of the patriarch's consort provided a link with the current celebration. The glee club followed Allen's talk with a second song, "Hurrah for Old New England." The next speech was by the Hon. William R. Easton, and his preoccupation with the shooting of President Garfield two days earlier lent a dreary note to the meeting. It was remedied by Joseph B. Barney, agent of the Nantucket and Cape Cod Steamboat Company, who spoke imaginatively on what the old settlers of the island would think if they returned to witness the current improvements of railroad, Wannacomet water tank, and proposed jetties. The last speaker, Dr. Arthur E. Jenks, con-

centrated on the advantages of the railroad, which was, after all, the theme of the meeting. It closed by everybody standing and singing "America." There was a delay in the return trip to town as a coupling had broken and had to be repaired.

Nantucket summer life was focused mainly on Surfside during the next two months. The depot was completed and the name "SURF-SIDE" painted in bold letters on its roof. A well was dug, and steps were built down the embankment to the beach. The formal opening of the railroad station was on 21 July, with dancing in the afternoon and evening, accompanied by violin, cornet, and piano under the direction of Prof. J. H. Backus, and there were fireworks at night. Refreshments were served, and the train provided continuous service. Other events included weekly clambakes on Thursdays, which drew the older people. Monday evenings were for roller skating. The hall was illuminated by Chinese lanterns, and the young folks glided about to the strains of Cushing's orchestra. As a special event, on the evening of 1 August, C. B. Whitney, manager of the roller-skating rink in Atlantic Hall, gave an exhibition of fancy skating. On 4 August there was a ball, with music furnished by Diamond's Quadrille Band. The south shore was so alive with activities that the Arthur Gardner newspaper declared: "Surf-side seems destined to become the 'jumping-off place' for tourists to Nantucket." "Jumping-off" at Surfside precluded regrets for the tracks not now reaching Siasconset, the intended destination of the railroad.

Launching the Nantucket Railroad shared honors with, and participated in, another memorable event during the summer of 1881. This was the Clan Coffin Celebration, the Coffin family reunion, which had been talked about and planned for about as long as the railroad itself. Two books were published in conjunction with the reunion, one being Allen Coffin's *Life of Tristram Coffin*, previously mentioned, and the other Harriet B. Worron's *"Trustum" and His Grandchildren, by One of Them*, a volume padded to four times the size of the other. The gathering of the clan was scheduled for 16 to 18 August, with two meetings at Surfside on the first and third afternoons.

48 *The Coffin Family Reunion, Surfside, 16 August 1881.*

The opening day, Tuesday, began with rain threatening, and in the morning a business meeting was held in Wendell's Hall. The sky cleared as the train began hauling Coffins out to Surfside. At 1:30 P.M. the clan posed for a group picture photographed by George H. Gardner of Boston. Hill's New Bedford Brass Band arrived in time to occupy the rear row in the exposure. A shore dinner was served at 2:00 o'clock. About 300 participants found seats in the flag-and-bunting-draped depot and another 200 at tables on the veranda and elsewhere. George A. Chadwick supervised the cuisine, which provided clam chowder, baked clams, baked corn, baked fish, lobster salad, relishes and beverages, and watermelon for dessert. The literary exercises following were presided over by Allen Coffin, secretary of the association, and were much the same as those at the christening of the railroad. Tristram Coffin, of Poughkeepsie, was the principal speaker and discussed the early history of the family, particularly his forebear of the same name. Poems were read by Judge Owen T. Coffin of Poughkeepsie and Susie W. Folger of Boston, and music was furnished by the band from New Bedford.

Wednesday's meetings were of the literary variety and were held in the Methodist Episcopal Church in town. The climax of the three-day event was the Thursday session at Surfside. A banquet was scheduled for 3:00 o'clock, and diners came out by train beginning early in the afternoon. The bill of fare consisted of "a relish . . . tomato soup, baked blue-fish, Madeira sauce, broiled Sword-fish, stewed lobster and wine sauce, eight varieties of cold meats, green peas, corn, potatoes, cucumbers, tomatoes and lettuce, several varieties of cake and pastry, tea and coffee, with vanilla, strawberry, lemon and chocolate ice cream, Troy pudding, bananas, grapes, watermelons and cantaloupes for desserts." By the time the meal was consumed a storm had begun to brew, and it was decided that the ball to follow ought to be held back in town. It took place at Atlantic Hall.

Nantucket as a summer resort certainly was on the map in 1881, and in that year it became a bird's-eye lithographic vista as well (fig. 49). Made from sketches taken the previous year and reproduced by J. J. Stoner of Madison, Wisconsin, the view was "delineated with strict fidelity . . . [to] streets, houses, public buildings, etc." Copies of the 22-by-30-inch print sold for $2.00. Near the upper left corner of the print, tracks of the Nantucket Railroad are shown crossing Orange Street;

they disappear into the Foley gulch, emerge beyond onto the commons, and extend to a hut indicated as the "U.S. Life Saving Station" at Surfside. All of the prints examined, except that at the Library of Congress (presumably early copyright), show a train—engine and two (closed) cars—on the stretch approaching the ocean. Hotels identified in town are the Ocean House, Springfield House, Sherburne House, Bay View House, and American House. A view of Siasconset set in the upper righthand corner similarly calls attention to the Atlantic House and Ocean View House. Vignettes at the bottom show perspectives of the Ocean House, Sherburne House, Springfield House and Annex, and the Ocean View House at "Sconset Beach." At the upper right angle of the vista proper, beneath the Siasconset insert, is the "Water Works Reservoir"— the Wannacomet water tank, mentioned in Easton's talk at the July

Fourth meeting at Surfside, erected in 1879 to supply the town with running water. Among other public improvements mentioned by Easton were the jetties, which would provide a deeper channel so that larger boats might enter the harbor. As they were just begun in 1881, they did not figure in the Stoner panorama.

Building the railroad had removed the great obstacle to the sale of cottage lots on the south shore by providing regular transportation to and from the site, and in 1882 the Surfside Land Company set out to make the most of the situation. A new community layout was created at that time, eliminating the previous fan-shaped intersections of the principal roads in favor of a regular grid, with all streets crossing at right angles. The road from town formed the main axis and terminated at the street nearest to the water, forming a T-shape, and both were given the name

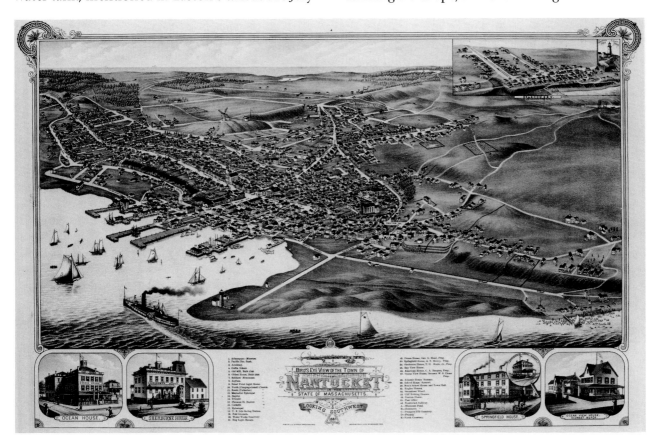

49 *"BIRD'S EYE VIEW OF THE TOWN OF NANTUCKET," 1881.*

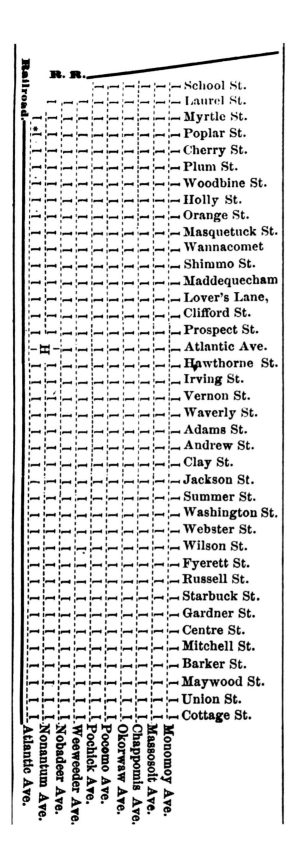

of Atlantic Avenue. Nine long streets parallel to the top bar of the T were crossed by sixteen short streets to the west of the Atlantic Avenue stem and twenty-two to the east. The railroad tracks bordered the plan on the west and south sides and cut across the corner, with the depot just below. To expedite sales, Charles F. Coffin, late general manager of the Nantucket Railroad Company (and still a director) and now treasurer of the Surfside Land Company, was given space in the station for an office. By the end of July sixty cottage lots had been sold, the number was tripled in August, and by the end of November nearly 300 units had passed into private hands.

Social life at Surfside during the summer of 1882 started with the Independence Day celebration, which also was the first anniversary of the railroad. Festivities were a reprise of the dinner and literary exercises of the year before. The meal was catered by James Patterson of the Bay View House and consisted of clam chowder, cold roast chicken or turkey, cakes, pies, strawberries and fruits, for which was charged 50¢. The main speaker was the Rev. J. A. Savage, whose subject was railroads. The program included music by the glee club and concluded with everybody singing "America." An innovation was the drill performed outside by the Cunningham Rifle Company of Brockton. Balloon ascensions planned never got off the ground, as each time the attempt was made to inflate a balloon with hot air it ignited and burned. The pyrotechnic display in the evening was successful, described as "large and brilliant." It was followed by a grand ball in the depot, with improvised orchestra and floor managers.

Due to the sounds of the surf and revelries on the beach and in the depot, many people failed to hear the conductor's call announcing the train's departure. The *Journal* championed their cause and suggested that the engine blow its whistle. It was agreed to give two short toots three minutes before pulling out. When it was put into practice for the first time on 22 July, Miss Isabella Orr had

50 *Grid plan of Surfside layout, with street names, 1882.*

just driven up and the noise frightened her horse, which turned completely around, throwing its mistress out of the buggy, and galloped away toward town until stopped at the McIntosh farm. The lady was not hurt and soon would be dabbling in Cliff lots; and the carriage was not seriously damaged. Nevertheless, there were complaints about blowing the whistle. It was pointed out that the steamboats did it methodically without startling horses and advised that persons with nervous animals ought to keep them away from mechanized conveyances.

The Surfside depot lived up to its previous year's record by being the entertainment spot of the island. On Friday evening, 28 July, Orville and Florence Coffin, children of Charles F. Coffin, gave an invitational party. On the following Monday evening a complimentary dance was held in which there were nearly a hundred participants. On Thursday, 10 August, the *Monohansett* brought an excursion party of 500 to the island, and most went to Surfside for a clambake at noon. The *Island Home* arrived a few hours later with Hill's Full Cornet Band, which marched from Steamboat Wharf to Main Street and presented a sample of its talent before boarding the train. Many townspeople followed and were rewarded by an outdoor concert at Surfside during the afternoon. A grand promenade was held in the station during the evening, followed at 9:30 by a dance, for which slight adjustments in the ranks of the musicians produced Hill's Quadrille Band. It was estimated that around 2,300 passengers were transported during the day.

Bathing rooms were added to the station complex, and their use for changing to beach attire cost ten cents. Another dime was charged for renting a bathing suit. In August Capt. Matthew Webb, the illustrious swimmer of the English Channel, was engaged for an exhibition in the surf. Hill's Band was on hand to add music to the spectacle. Beginning at 4:00 o'clock on the afternoon of the 26th, the captain cavorted in the brine and dived from the top of two ladders lashed together on the deck of a whaleboat. His daring bordered on foolhardiness, which sealed his fate the following year when he attempted to swim the rapids below Niagara Falls and was knocked unconscious against the rocks and drowned.

A few days after Captain Webb's demonstration, the Secretary of the Navy, William E. Chandler, and his wife reached Nantucket aboard the *Tallapossa*. Although not forewarned, a reception group with carriages assembled and took the visitors to the Atheneum to inspect the artifacts and curios in the museum, and to the Pacific Club to meet the elderly whalemen. They were given a train ride to Surfside, and before his departure Secretary Chandler called at the Orange Street summer residence of Henry A. Willard of Washington.

On Thursday morning of the following week, from his roost in South Tower, town crier Billy Clark sighted the steamer *Dispatch*, ornamented with the Presidential ensign. Billy blew his horn to attract attention and relayed the news below. The *Dispatch* dropped anchor at the outer bar, and F. C. Sanford sent an invitation out by sailboat to the chief executive to come ashore as his guest. Following acceptance, Chester Alan Arthur and his party were taken to Sanford's house on Federal Street for refreshments. Here Mr. Arthur stepped out on the portico to greet the crowd that had assembled. The President was driven to the Cliff to see Charles O'Conor, his former legal adversary, and artist Eastman Johnson. He was conducted back past the Civil War monument to the Agricultural Society's grounds, thence to the Pacific Club. There he was offered the use of the railroad for a jaunt to Surfside, and he and his retinue climbed aboard. It was Sanford's first ride on the Nantucket train. The *Journal* reported that "A brief stay was made at the prospective city by the sea, the President expressing himself much pleased with the locality." Except for the lifesaving and railroad stations, there was little but "locality" to comment upon. Back in Nantucket, President Arthur was shown the Atheneum and returned for final refreshments to Sanford's home. Here the Boston Metropolitan Band, which chanced to be on the island accompanying the Massasoit Encampment of the I.O.O.F., tendered a street concert. The chief executive returned to the *Dispatch* around 5:00 o'clock. Sanford had entertained both U.S. pres-

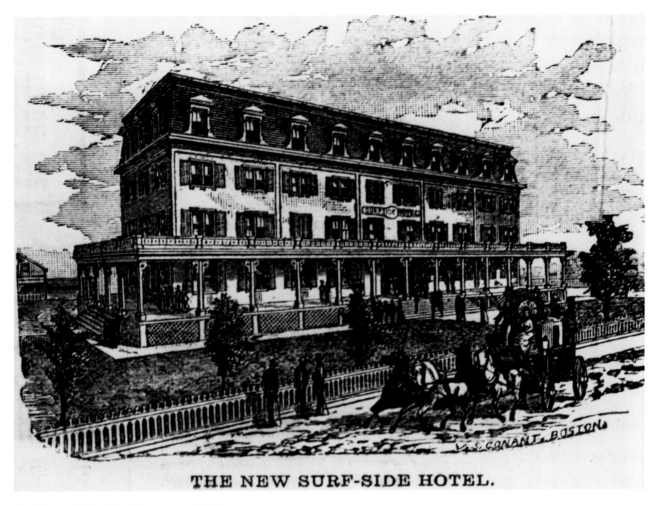

THE NEW SURF-SIDE HOTEL.

51 *The Surfside Hotel. Engraving, 1883.*

idents to have visited Nantucket up to that time.

The Surfside land sales and railroad were prelude to the Surfside Hotel. The hotel was meant to justify the building of the railroad and to augment the disposal of lots. Originally intended to have been situated near the junction of the two Atlantic avenues on the 1882 layout, instead the Surfside Hotel was sited near the east end, at Nobadeer, which involved extending the tracks about a mile farther.

Like the rolling stock of the train itself, the Surfside Hotel was a second-hand importation from America. It had been designed by Walker and Company of Providence, Rhode Island, and

the main part of it was built as the Riverside Hotel on the Providence River. If it had been built as pictured in the *Inquirer and Mirror* on 13 July 1883, it would have been a sizable edifice, more than 300 feet long, consisting of a twelve-bayed main block of four stories and two-storied superstructure and twin six-bayed wings of three stories, the top floor of each unit enclosed in a mansard roof. An arched veranda was to have encompassed the main level, with deck above, and a roof loggia adjoined the crowning pent. The superstructure and wings were not realized at Riverside.

The acquisition of the Riverside Hotel was announced on 10 September 1882. Within a month Charles F. Coffin was at Riverside seeing about taking down and transporting the building, Philip H. Folger was in New York to obtain railroad iron and flatcars to be used in lengthening the roadbed and hauling the hotel parts to the site, and the digging of the cellar had begun at Nobadeer. George Paddack of Providence, formerly of Nantucket, was engaged to disassemble the building and load the schooners for its shipment to the island. Only the twenty-six dormers were kept as units, the rest being crated and sent over as materials, which spent the better part of the winter stacked on Commercial Wharf. Around the beginning of March they were carted to the south shore and dumped in piles for sorting. Brick foundations were laid by J.S. Appleton, and construction was conducted by John S. D'Arcy of Boston. Steam heating and piping were by Walworth Manufacturing Company of Boston. Plumbing was by Codd & Deacon, roofing by H.S. Valentine, plastering by Brown & Ring, and painting by H. Paddack & Company of Nantucket. Toward the end there was considerable scurrying to get the building finished by the 25 June deadline.

The Surfside Hotel was a four-story block on an elevated basement measuring 40-by-125 feet. A bracketed piazza, 10-feet deep, was at the principal level and a mansard at the top. The ten-bayed facade was divided by tall, slender pilasters into five divisions, and fenestration was coupled, except for the dormer windows in the mansard roof. The name was on a quarterboard between the second- and third-story windows over the main entrance at the center. The basement contained a billiard room (40 x 50 feet) at the east end and storage rooms elsewhere. The dining hall on the first floor corresponded to the billiard room. The office, coat, and luggage rooms and the staircase were off the 24-foot-square entrance hall. The main parlor (25 x 40 feet) was at the west end, and between it and the entrance hall were two small supplementary parlors (each 12 x 15 feet) at the front and two supper rooms of equal size at the back, a passageway separating them. Each of the three chamber floors provided eighteen lodging rooms arranged to either side of a crosswise corridor, and toilets, linen room, and maids' closets were adjacent to the stairs in the middle. The kitchen was in a separate pavilion of two stories and basement, 30-by-40 feet, set 25 feet behind the hotel proper and connected to it by an enclosed way. A laundry was below and servants' dormitory above the "kitchen, where a Whiteley range, broilers, baker, etc., of the most approved character . . . [were] used in the culinary work." A large pantry and dish closets were on the south side. It was noted that "water will be supplied the entire house by a steam pump, and arrangements . . . completed for heating the house by steam for the comfort of such guests as may remain late in the season." Furniture was in the Eastlake manner, of ash for the guest rooms and ebony in the parlors, upholstered in plush and silk. Included with the purchase at Riverside was an elaborate wooden fence 800 feet long, which was set up on the ocean front.

Charles H. Moore, formerly of the Maverick House in East Boston, was the proprietor, and the rate was $3.00 per day.

The completion of the Surfside Hotel in 1883 provided a new setting for the Independence Day celebration and second-anniversary party of the Nantucket Railroad. It was billed as a "Grand Gala Day for Nantucket!" during which "EXTRA TRAINS WILL BE RUN!" The offerings—dinner at 12:30; literary exercises, at which Arthur H. Gardner presided and Allen Coffin gave an oration called "The American Citizen," a eulogy on Charles Sumner; songs by the glee club; a display of fireworks and a grand ball—almost duplicated those of the previous year. There was even a sales pitch for the lots, vaguely disguised as a lengthy recitation (some eighty lines) in verse, entitled "A Welcome to Surfside," by William H. Macy. Undoubtedly many people boarded the train more to inspect the imported caravanserai by the sea than to partake of the program.

Entertainments and recreational and social events, such as were held at the Surfside depot during the two previous summers, now were enacted at the hotel. Hill's New Bedford Band was there on 18 July, giving outdoor concerts in the afternoon and evening and playing for the hop

52 *The Ocean View Annex, Siasconset.*

that followed in the dining room. Another concert was on the 26th. On 3 August there was a dory race of eight entries. It was exciting because the sea was rough and some of the boats overturned. Two weeks later there was a swimming match, the contestants and spectators repairing to the hotel afterward for refreshments. Theatricals also were presented in the hotel, though not of notable quality. During the middle of August the south shore was lashed by a heavy surf, and ten days later it was hit by a storm. Many townspeople thought that the Surfside Hotel would collapse, but its time had not yet come. The hotel closed for the winter on 13 September.

In extending the tracks from the Surfside depot to the Surfside Hotel in 1883, the railroad was one mile closer to Siasconset, its original destination. In the late fall it was announced that the railway would be continued to the village the following season. Efforts toward achieving this end became visible during March of 1884. Iron rails and ash

ties came periodically to the island until the third week in June, and a force of laborers was at work under the direction of C.M. Stansbury, grading the roadbed and laying tracks along the beach. The imminent realization of the line to Siasconset prompted the building of a new hotel at the terminus. To be precise, it was a separate pavilion of one already existing, the Ocean View House, then ten years old.

Materials for the structure had been unloaded at Capt. William T. Swain's lumber wharf in October of 1883, when it was announced that the new pavilion was to be "118 feet front, 32 feet rear and three stories high . . . [and it was to] contain, exclusive of the grand parlor, which will be 32 x 22 feet, 34 rooms, 10 on the lower floor, and 12 on each of the other two." The placing of the building was to be "upon the rising ground at the southward of the Ocean View House and near the property of R. Gardner Chase." To take full advantage of the ocean vista a spacious piazza was "run along the entire front." Old photographs show the porch to have been fourteen bays long. Ten were double-storied with a railing and deck at the third level; posts continued up another story for four bays at the south end, supporting a jerkin-headed gable containing two double windows. On the east slope of the roof also were three dormers, two with triple windows and the third polygonal with four windows (two in the splayed sides) and a balcony in front. The dormers and several windows in each flank gable indicate the fourth story to have sheltered sleeping rooms, perhaps for the help. At the rear was a wing with toilet facilities on each level. The water was forced up by a steam-powered pump. Furniture for the house was ordered from Webster, Folger and Company of Boston. Levi S. Coffin was the proprietor. Like its predecessors, the third building of the Ocean View House was designed and built by and for Charles H. Robinson. Accommodations at the complex in Siasconset were superior to those of the Surfside Hotel.

The Nantucket Railroad began passenger service as far as Surfside on 25 June, at which time the tracks had been laid to within a mile of Siasconset. The completion was achieved on 1 July, and ceremonies were scheduled for July Fourth. But between waiting for the state inspector to approve the addition to the line and for a spell of bad weather to subside, the official event had to be postponed four days. Its occurrence took place on what Nantucketers called the "Glorious Eighth." Although the day began with dark skies that kept the timid at home, the clouds cleared away nicely; and the train, running at ninety-minute intervals, brought the largest crowd that had ever assembled at Siasconset. The tracks approached via Low Beach to the foot of the embankment under the Ocean View House.

After the arrival of the noon train the rites began with Master Ray Barnum (young scion of Gen. Henry A. Barnum, a regular summer resident) stepping forward to implant an American flag at the end of the tracks. Nearby stood town crier William D. Clark, who had driven the first spike at the informal laying of the first rail in 1881, now armed with gilded sledge hammer to drive the "golden spike." It was a sort of reenactment of the ceremonial completion of the transcontinental railroad at Promontory Point, Utah, fifteen years earlier, though it would have been held more appropriately where the two stretches of track met at Surfside. On the other hand, Siasconset was the coveted goal, and the formality of the event was of less consequence than the place. Billy Clark lifted his hammer, the newly organized Mechanics' Band struck up with "Yankee Doodle" and, as Billy pounded the glittering spike in the sleeper, loud cheers and applause resounded from the multitude. The Golden Spike ritual over, everybody climbed the bank to the hotel, where they were favored by another musical selection from the band. Then the collation was served inside the Ocean View House. The after-dinner recitations were staged on the veranda of the new pavilion, which participants used for a podium, and the spectators found places to either side and on the lawn in front. As on the corresponding occasion at Surfside the previous year, Arthur H. Gardner presided and Allen Coffin gave the main address. Coffin recalled Judge Gardner's proposal to construct a railroad to Siasconset forty years earlier, and he likened the lack of support then to the islanders' initial response to the current project. Its backers deserved all the more credit for persevering, Allen declared. The Hon. William R. Easton told of early railroad evolution in England and America. The cottage builder and Siasconset enthusiast Edward F. Underhill came next, and after a nonsensical introduction provided a few historical facts about the village. The last to expound was Dr. Arthur E. Jenks, who rounded out Allen Coffin's theme by pointing out the obstacles that had been overcome in building the Nantucket Railroad. Musical numbers from the band interspersed the speeches, and rousing cheers for the railroad company, the band, the landlord of the Ocean View House, and Engineer Stansbury concluded the meeting.

Six runs a day were scheduled between Nantucket and Siasconset, and one other went only as far as Surfside. Round-trip fare to the end of the line was 80¢ for an adult, half-price for children.

53 *The excursion train at the Siasconset depot. The Ocean View Annex looms above (right).*

To Surfside alone was 35¢ for grownups and 15¢ for juveniles.

With Siasconset only twenty minutes farther away than Surfside, many of the summer functions migrated to the eastward. Hill's Band performed at both shore points. A clambake at the hamlet, early in August, brought more people than had come to the golden-spike ceremony, and was surpassed later in the month by the Grand Illumination on the 21st. There had been illuminations in Siasconset before, but they were mostly for local enjoyment. The railroad made the 1884 fete an open show. An extra run was made, leaving town at 6:15 p.m., the regular 7:00 o'clock trip postponed to 7:30. Those who took the earlier train had time to look over the quaint, variously lighted cottages. Some had old-fashioned lamps or candles flickering, some sported colored lights, and some were hung with Chinese lanterns. The last train was packed with people, their arms, heads, and legs sticking out like the quills of a porcupine, their discomfort soothed by the thought that at least they had got aboard. About 3,000 persons crowded the crest of Sunset Heights for the fireworks, the main attraction of the evening. The pyrotechnics were under the direction of Prof. Benjamin M. Wedger of Boston. The first part of the display consisted of a number of surprise effects: bombs bursting, rockets shooting skyward, luminous serpents writhing in the air, revolving wheels emitting sparks, and parachutes floating slowly out to sea, their changing hues casting pale reflections on the water. Meanwhile, a torchlight brigade, composed of resident youths and headed by the Sherburne Drum Corps, marched through the crowd and paraded up and down several streets of the village, returning to the bank in time to witness the set pieces. The first was called the "Revolving Sun." It was followed by the "American Star." The third and last was the most engaging and was dedicated to the Nantucket Railroad. It was designated the "Emerald Wreath." A field of spinning colored fires formed a large circle of olive leaves with green lance jets in the center. Then there appeared the numerals "1884" in crimson lights, soon after replaced by the name "'SCONSET" in silver radiance. It was the grand finale of a spectacular show. The little *Dionis* hauled the pyrotechnophiles back into town at 12:45 a.m.

In 1885 the railroad reached its zenith regarding services offered. Its road had been laid as far as was ever intended. Tracks at the town end had been extended northward to Steamboat Wharf and a station built the year before. With the Surfside Hotel assuming the party functions of the Surfside depot, half of the latter building was taken down and transferred to Siasconset to be put up as a railroad station at the terminus. The line also was to have two complete trains. Besides the *Dionis* with her two open cars, which was to continue on its regular schedule, an excursion train was assembled for special occasions. It was headed by a bogie (0-4-4) engine made by the Mason Locomotive and Machine Works of Taunton, Massachusetts, and had been recently used on and leased from the Boston, Revere Beach and Lynn Railroad. It was christened *'Sconset*, and the name was inscribed in fraktur letters on the sides of the fuel compartment. A baggage car was fashioned out of one of the flatcars brought over to transport materials to the Nobadeer extension. It was a box-like affair with a sliding door near one end of each side and three small windows at the other. With benches placed inside it could be pressed into passenger service. A second car was strictly for passengers, and it was the first piece of rolling stock purchased new for the Nantucket Railroad. Manufactured by the J. G. Brill Company of Philadelphia, it was a closed coach with sixteen upholstered seats on each side of a center aisle, capable of carrying sixty-four persons.

The memorable event at Siasconset during the summer of 1885 was a repeat of the Grand Illumination, which was scheduled a few days later in August than before, and further postponed because of boisterous weather. It finally came off on the 28th, when atmospheric conditions were all that could be desired. Fireworks again were under the direction of Professor Wedger and were equally spectacular. Attendance was good, though not up to that of the previous occasion. The show was prolonged in that one of the most enjoyable parts of the evening was the return to town. The *Journal* described the final episode: "The fireworks lasted until 10 o'clock. With a view to the accommodation and speedy transit of its patrons, the railroad company had provided an extra train and both were in waiting to proceed to town as soon as the exhibition was over. The first train, drawn by the 'Dionis,' was composed of the two open cars, and the second was drawn by the 'Sconset,' and consisted of the new passenger coach and the baggage car. Both trains were comfortably filled and were run about half a mile apart, arriving in town shortly before 11 o'clock. It was a novel sight for Nantucket—two trains of lighted cars, half a mile apart, following along the shore line to Surf-side, thence across the 'commons' to town in the 'dead hours of the night.'" The railroad had gained an accepted place in the summer life of Nantucket; in fact, it constituted a major attraction.

V. Fin-de-Siècle Boardinghouses and Bonanza Inns

DECENTRALIZATION ATTEMPTS by ill-advised land speculators, enthusiastic railroad investors, and substantially encouraged hotel proprietors on the south shore failed to lure the real vacation nucleus of the island away from Nantucket Town. This was because the community provided a full line of entertainment and recreational facilities, all within a relatively small compass. As patronage increased, so did Nantucket accommodations. Its inner growth and development were accompanied by new outcroppings on its perimeter. Its immediate frontier was proven expansible by cottage-lot sales, particularly in the Cliff and Brant Point regions, which came into full flower during the 1880s.

Nantucket's primary attraction to vacationers from inland America by this time had become salt-water bathing. In 1876 Charles E. Hayden's Clean Shore Bathing Rooms, north of Steamboat Wharf, were enlarged to include four rooms that were "arranged expressly for warm salt water baths. A fine bath tub, set wash bowl, with hot and cold water for each, and other conveniences comprise the furniture of these apartments, which are well lighted and roomy." A forty-barrel tank was built to furnish water. In 1880 Hayden began operating a second establishment on his recently acquired property at the north end of Beachside (end of Charles Street), called the Cliff Shore Bath Houses. They provided twenty-eight rooms, which were oriented exclusively toward beach activities and did not include tubs. The opening of the Cliff Shore Bath Houses was on 5 July, and patrons were conveyed there by water, in Barzillai Burdett's sloop *Dauntless*, which left

"her moorings near the foot of old North Wharf . . . every morning (Sunday excepted) at 9, 10, 11 and 12 o'clock . . . until 1 o'clock P.M." Fare for the trip was "TEN CENTS EACH WAY."

For those of more intellectual interests, particularly in the historic past of the old whaling port, the museum in the Atheneum had been set up on a formal basis during the summer of 1879. Its collection had increased slowly until it was about on a par with what had been destroyed by the Great Fire of 1846. Items were arranged on the first floor among the bookshelves. The main exhibit was the "mammoth SPERM WHALE'S JAW, seventeen feet long, in perfect condition, with all the teeth in place." There was also a model of the "camels," that trough-shaped device for hauling large vessels over the sandbar into the Great Harbor before the jetties were built, the model shown embracing a ship in proper scale. There were, besides, "hundreds of strange things . . . collected from nearly every part of the globe." Explanations of the "wonders" were given to strangers by Joseph S. Swain, whose title elsewhere was recorded as "janitor." He was available to "Parties desirous of entrance in evenings." Entrance fee at any time was 15¢.

A new diversion was introduced to Nantucket in 1881 when the floor was relaid in Atlantic Hall, and it became a skating rink. The sales pitch that accompanied it testified: "Roller skating has become a fashionable pastime. It is particularly healthful and is indulged in extensively by the best classes in the large cities and thus throughout the states." Social proprieties were to be main-

54 *Hayden's Clean Shore Bathing Rooms. View from the North Tower.*

tained in Nantucket, as the management reserved "the right to refuse admission to objectionable parties." Skating was accompanied by live music "furnished by the Skating Rink Orchestra, under the lead of Prof. Gardner, of Brockton." Sessions were from 3:00 to 5:00 and from 8:00 to 10:00 p.m., admission was 15¢ in the afternoons and 25¢ in the evenings, package of six tickets $1.00. C. B. Whitney, the exhibition skater at Surfside, was the proprietor, and his brother, George Whitney, was in charge of the skate room. Winslow Improved Skates were used (skate checks were 10¢). The Nantucket Roller Skating Rink first operated on the evening of 18 July 1881. This being leap year, there was a special party in its honor on the evening of 19 August. A band performed from 8:00 to 8:45, and an "EXHIBITION OF FANCY SKATING" began at 9:30; otherwise there was general skating to an eight-piece orchestra led by John Holmes until 11:00 o'clock. "No gent . . . [was] allowed upon the surface during the music, unless accompanied by a lady."

At the close of the season, Fred V. Fuller hired fifty pairs of skates and kept the rink operating on Mondays and Fridays at the usual hours, the admission rate reduced to 10¢ and 20¢ (price of skate checks remained the same), and music was

furnished. On other days the hall could be engaged for parties.

Several eating or snacking places came into existence at this time. A new restaurant on Steamboat Wharf was conducted in 1879 by Charles A. Kenney. In 1880, specializing in "OYSTERS, cooked to order," it was run by Alfred Scudder. He was followed by Calvert Handy, who called it the Old Colony. Nantucketers still repeat with glee the call of the lookout man to the cook in the galley: "Big crowd getting off the steamboat; throw another bucket of water in the chowder!"

On Main Street, "A FEW DOORS FROM THE POST OFFICE," the Washington House and Restaurant was in business in 1880. Its name and description of the location would indicate that it stood on the site of Levi Starbuck's old Washington House, later Washington Hall. The 1880 replacement was run by J. B. Watkins, and boarding was "$1 per day, lodging 50 cents." Watkins provided everything from "Meals" to "Sodas, Confectionery, Cigars &c."

In the spring of 1881 the Misses Chadwick, daughters of George A. Chadwick, opened an ice cream saloon "in the store on Orange street lately occupied by Mr. F. J. Crosby," where "cake, pies

55 *The catboat* Dauntless *on the Great Harbor.*

and confectionery" were sold daily. In mid-June the Misses Chadwick left a "generous dish of ice cream" for the staff of the *Journal*, which declared they had "never tasted better cream in [their] life and this is the verdict of all who try it."

The house on Orange Street at the north corner of Martins Lane, which had been run continuously as a boardinghouse for at least a third of a century, set out on a new career in 1879 when the heirs of Adeline Fanning sold it for $475 to Charles A. Burgess, formerly on Union Street. Burgess gave it the name it was to be known by over most of the next score of years, the American House. In mid-May of 1880 the newspaper noted: "The American House is open for the sea-son, and under its ample roof the weary traveller will find comfort and rest." Burgess offered to provide "meals at all hours of the day," as well as "carriages for the accommodation of boarders to any part of the island." In 1882 it was conducted by William G. Baglen, who was from the Quinobeauin House, Medway, Massachusetts; and the Josiah Gorham house, next door, was used as an annex. The following spring Burgess advertised the hostelry for sale, the price being "less than $3,000," and he added that if it were "not sold will reopen June 1." It reopened under G. C. Kelly, proprietor, who called the inn the Central House. But the old name, American House, soon was resumed, and Burgess again was in charge.

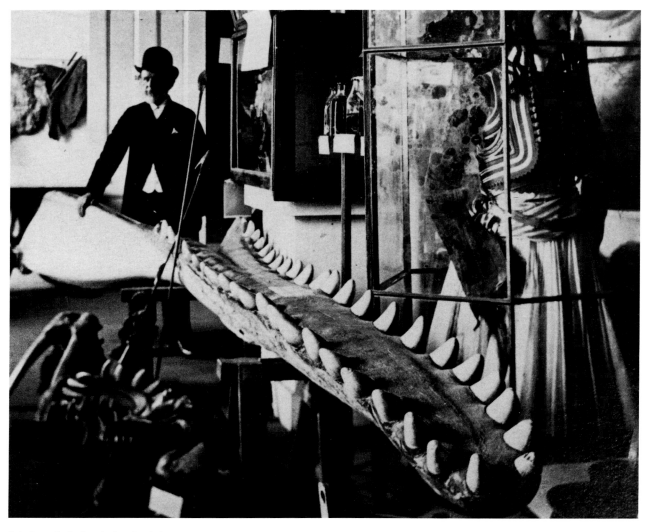

56 *Joseph S. Swain in the Atheneum museum.*

Across the street, the Sherburne House was under the direction of Thomas H. Soule, Jr., and doing so well that in 1883 Soule "secured the house of Mr. Lincoln nearly opposite the Hotel, in order to accommodate parties who desire nice rooms outside the Sherburne." In 1884 Daniel F. McKay assumed proprietorship, and Soule became the manager of Hotel Falmouth in the Cape Cod town of that name.

The Bay View House had a new manager in 1881 in the person of James Patterson, who had been "successful . . . as a hotel keeper both in New York and in Massachusetts," including the Lin-

coln House in Hyde Park. Patterson became proprietor of the Surfside Hotel in 1888 and again in 1891, and at the latter time he was running the south-shore hostelry, the Bay View House, and the Sherburne.

The noteworthy growth of an established Nantucket caravanserai during the early eighties was that of the Springfield House on North Water Street. Albert S. Mowry was running the three-unit complex in 1880. The main pavilion and Annex No. 1 across the street were owned by Elijah H. Alley, and the original Springfield House building (21) was sold on 7 May by Almon T. Mowry

57 *The New Springfield House, with corner of dining-room pavilion in left foreground.*

to Mary C. Mowry, a "single woman" of South Walpole, for $2,000. The downstairs of the building had been converted into the dining hall, and there were guest rooms above. On 1 November 1880 Albert S. Mowry paid $300 to Alfred Swain for the lot adjoining on the south side, which ran back to Beach Street. Here, in 1883, James H. Gibbs constructed what at first was to be known as the "New House." Soon it displayed a large sign inscribed "SPRINGFIELD HOUSE" atop the porch over the entrance steps, indicating its primacy in the hotel group.

The building was full three stories, of which the outer walls of the first two were clapboarded and those of the third shingled and slightly flared out at the bottom, giving the effect of a mansard roof, reflecting the look of the two pavilions at the north end of the street. The veranda across the five-bayed front and deck continuing along the right flank (shown covered in early engravings) also repeated features of Annex No. 1. On the first floor was a parlor (15 x 45 feet) at the

northwest corner, having three windows in the long wall and two in front, between which was a plate mirror from floor to ceiling. Opposite was a fireplace, with painted mantel panels that were hailed as "MORCEAUX IN ART." They were executed by W. Ferdinand Macy, and most of the subjects were appropriate to Nantucket. A description recalls: "In the centre is a transcript of marine landscape—sunset on the ocean. The sky is luminous, and the turbid sea, bearing a single floating spar, is full of motion. A lone gull swoops down from the upper air, giving the whole a vivid effect." Another panel depicted "a lovely ideal of eventide . . . prefigured in an agile female form with drapery, floating away from the golden crescent moon." Others were "ornamented with our island grasses, and lilies, peacock feathers, [and] the sentimental owl."* In addition to the parlor were "twenty-two spacious and cheerful sleeping rooms, each with a large closet." Water was piped to conveniences on each floor, and gas lit every room. Steam heating and gas fixtures were sup-

---

*Macy was born in New Bedford of Nantucket ancestry; he studied art in New York. This contemporary description is reprinted from Louise Stark's article "Early Nantucket Artists," in *Historic Nantucket*, October 1958, pp. 32 -33.

58 *The Veranda House, Step Lane, after 1885.*

plied by the C. M. Mowry Company of Springfield, the owner obviously a relative of the hotel proprietor. Plumbing was installed by a local concern, William Deacon & Company. Masonry was by J. S. Appleton II and painting by Henry Paddack. Steam heating permitted the inn to stay open all winter. A pleasant follow-up to the hard work involved in constructing the building was the gay New Year's party given by landlord Mowry at the close of 1883. The guests were the artisans and workmen and their wives. "At the close of the feast a few felicitous remarks were indulged in by the host, Henry Paddack, Esq., responding in behalf of the guests."

The Springfield had a nearby rival called the Veranda House. The nucleus of the building is said to have been made from parts of the William Gayer house of 1684, formerly facing Centre Street and taken down to make way for the Peter Folger house built in 1765 but described as a "new

dwelling house" when Edwin Coffin sold it to Joseph Pease in 1850 (according to a brochure produced by Thomas J. Devine entitled "Veranda House and the Overlook Hotel," n.d.) The Veranda House belonged to Nathan Chapman, who purchased it in 1881 and turned it into a boardinghouse. It faced Step Lane, which the proprietor began calling Chapman Avenue, though the name was not generally accepted and did not survive. The hostelry was described as being "located near the shore of the harbor on elevated ground, a short distance from the steamboat landing. . . . This house has been newly fitted with eighteen large, airy rooms, and three spacious verandas on each of three sides of the house, where patrons may enjoy the benefit of the sea breezes." Other patrons enjoying sea breezes detracted from the privacy of those having rooms sheltered by the verandas. Rates were "$9.00 to $11.00 per week . . . $2.00 to $2.50 per day. . . . Children under 10 years $4.00 to $7.00."

In 1883 Chapman purchased the home of the Springfield House contractor, James H. Gibbs, at what is now 20 North Water Street, and had a connection built between it and the original building, the Gibbs house serving as an annex. Another residence, known as the Joy house, was standing at the street intersection, and it was moved to the south side of Step Lane. Its former site was terraced and used as a recreation ground for guests. In 1890 the north wing was added to the Veranda House.

On 10 July 1883 Nathan Chapman of Nantucket was granted U. S. Patent No. 280,796 for a bread cutter. It consisted of a board with uprights to hold the loaf and guide the knife in cutting slices of uniform thickness. The apparatus adjusted to the size of the loaf, which was held firmly by means of a spring, and grooves in the bed permitted the blade to pass through the whole loaf. Undoubtedly the apparatus was used advantageously in the kitchen of the hostelry.

Edward K. Godfrey compiled the first modern guide book entitled *The Island of Nantucket* and subtitled *What It Was and What It Is*, published in New York in 1882. Godfrey covered every aspect of Nantucket that would be of interest to visitors—from its bathing facilities to how the islanders lived. He listed the nine hotels with their addresses and proprietors:

Ocean House, Broad St., J. S. Doyle
Springfield, No. Water St., A. S. Mowry
Sherburne House, Orange St., T. H. Soule, Jr.
Bay View House, Orange St., J. S. Patterson
Veranda House, Chapman St., N. Chapman
American House, Orange St., W. C. Bayley
Ocean View House, 'Sconset, L. S. Coffin
Atlantic House, 'Sconset, Eliza Chadwick
Wauwinet House, A. W. N. Small

A revised edition of the Godfrey book published two years later carried no indication that it was a revision, but it included an advertisement for the Old Colony Railroad that gave the 1884 schedule; two hotels are added to the list:

Surfside Hotel, C. H. Moore
Nantucket Hotel, J. S. Doyle

Just as the Surfside Hotel was moved from Rhode Island, two parts of the Nantucket Hotel on Brant Point were moved there from town. The center pavilion was the old Friends meeting house on Main Street, subsequently the straw-hat factory and then Atlantic Hall, lately serving as the Nantucket Roller Skating Rink. The east wing had been a domicile on Orange Street. The owner-designer of the hotel was George F. Hammond, a Boston architect. During the spring of 1883 he purchased most of the old Philip H. Folger marine railway site, below Easton Street on Brant Point, on which to place the hotel. In July, having decided on a different location, Hammond bought three house lots on the north side of the peninsula between John Street and the U. S. government property, facing the new jetties. The lots were to the east of land that Thomas H. Soule II (of the Sherburne House) had gotten for a similar purpose, which was not to materialize. Hammond's undertaking involved a complex agreement with Henry Coleman, who not only sold Hammond the land but the dwelling on Orange Street, which Coleman was to take down, transport, and set up on the easternmost lot in a form as similar as possible to that of a cottage already standing on the westernmost lot on Brant Point. Coleman agreed "to build and furnish a Hotel on the said estate in accordance with plans submitted," and "within ten days from the completion of said Hotel" he was to receive $5,000, with a balance to be taken out as "Shares of Stock in said Hotel . . . to the amount of four thousand dollars, to be computed upon the actual cost of building and furnishing the same." The old meeting house must have figured in the "plans submitted," as by mid-September we find the notice: "The demolition of Atlantic hall, which is to be re-built as a hotel on Brant Point, is progressing rapidly." The name proposed at that time was Hotel Driftwood, and in November the newspaper reported that "Hotel Driftwood is daily growing and is now a very prominent landmark." A month later we find: "The name Hotel Driftwood

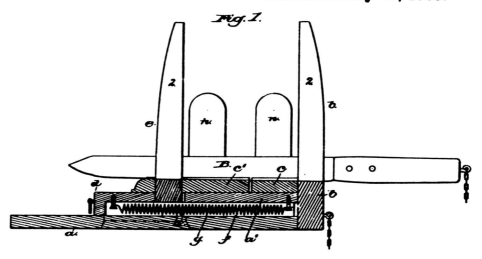

(Model.)

N. CHAPMAN.
BREAD CUTTER.

No. 280,796.

Patented July 10, 1883.

Fig. 1.

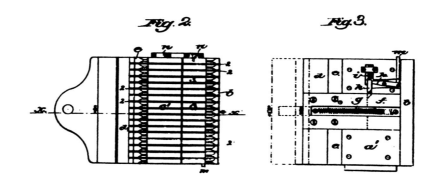

Fig. 2. *Fig. 3.*

Witnesses.
Inventor.
Nathan Chapman

59 *Nathan Chapman's patent for a bread slicer, 1883.*

60 *The Nantucket, Brant Point.*

has been changed to Hotel Nantucket." Work moved ahead, though probably halted during much of the winter, and by the middle of February 1884 the exterior of the building was being painted. A month later Folger & Brock contracted to paint the interior.

The Nantucket was indeed a landmark of unprecedented size on the island, and it must have looked impressive to passengers on the *Island Home* as the boat entered the harbor. The hotel stretched 200 feet along the beach a short way back from the water. The middle section of five bays was two full stories with third and fourth floors under the roof, and it was flanked by three-and-a-half-storied wings of four bays each. These forms of nearly equal height were crowned by two open gazebos, one with a reverse-curved and the other with a pyramid roof, connected by a roofwalk bearing the name, "THE NANTUCKET," in six-foot, cut-out letters on the railing. Identical letters were repeated in the upper part of the taller, central part of the ground-story porch that spanned the entire front,

including the outer, semi-detached pavilions, which were two-and-a-half-storied. A deck surmounted the middle part of the porch, and balconies punctuated the adjacent forms. The detailing, including the plainness of the deck, balcony, and roofwalk railings and the combination of gabled, hip-roof, and Dutch dormers, lacked visual interest, and old sixteen-paned sashes in the main part with new two-paned sashes elsewhere left much to be desired architecturally.

The main part of the building housed "the dining room, office, barber's shop, baggage and gents' toilet room" in the first story. The dining room measured 45 by 65 feet and was furnished with imitation mahogany tables and chairs. Chandeliers were of "tasty pattern," and fluid for them was manufactured by a "Springfield Gas Machine Company's apparatus." In an ell were the kitchen and room for the boiler, the latter supplying steam for cooking as well as for heating the dining room and parlor; and a steam pump filled a large water-storage tank in the garret. Lodging rooms in the wings were furnished "with

61 *The grand parlor of The Nantucket.*

sets of lakeside [Eastlake] pattern of imitation mahogany." Others of the 100 guest rooms were similarly furnished.

Directly above the dining room and of equal size was the grand parlor. Its ceiling was "supported by large trusses." The ceiling and the walls were papered and wood floors were polished and partly covered by rugs; furniture here was mostly wicker. A door opened on the deck in front, and a circular void at the back framed an elevated "alcove . . . utilized for the presentation of parlor theatricals, or for the use of the orchestra whenever it may be desired." Windows were "hung with shades and gracefully arranged portieres." Stairways were at either side of the dining room and grand parlor, and passageways beyond led to chambers in the wings. Electric bells in guest rooms connected with the office, where J. S. Doyle, formerly of the Ocean House, presided. A detached building behind the main block contained a "billiard and bowling salon and bar" and

the help's quarters. Later in the summer a bathhouse building was built.

In the spring of 1886 a part of the building again was on the move. The east, or Orange Street, wing was shifted to the rear of the hotel by a Mr. Dunlap of New Bedford, and a larger, three-storied addition was built by James H. Gibbs to take its place. New furnishings were brought from Boston.

Roller skating had become popular in Nantucket after the conversion of Atlantic Hall for that purpose. With the removal of the building to Brant Point in the fall of 1883, that form of social recreation was missed, but was provided with suitable shelter again two years later. The Island Roller Skating Rink, built by James M. Gibbs, was a huge barn-like structure at the north corner of Sea and North (now South) Beach Street. The roof required 120,500 shingles and its floor 8,000 feet of boards. The rink was opened by manager G. E. Schofield on the evening of 2

July 1885, the hall decorated with Chinese lanterns, sun shades, and colored streamers, with music provided by the local Mechanics' Band and Teague's Orchestra, the latter permanently employed for the season. As a special treat, Jessie LaFone, the "prima donna of skates," performed. "Her handkerchief trick showed her perfect control of the rollers, and the imitation of a locomotive was superb." General skating followed. A decade later the building was taken over for the electric plant.

Edward K. Godfrey's *Island of Nantucket*, which gave the list of hotels recorded, identified the proprietors and locations of twenty-three boardinghouses in existence in 1882:

David Bunker, Gay St.

George Chadwick, Vestal St.

Charles Dunham, Union St.

Mrs. Avis M. Enas, Union St.

George G. Fish, Broad St.

Peter Folger, Centre St.

William C. Folger, Fair St.

Timothy M. Fisher, Union St.

Mrs. Lydia C. Holway, Broad St.

Mrs. Elizabeth A. Hussey, Centre St.

Mrs. Laura A. Hinckley, Fair St.

Charles Luce, Orange St.

Charles L. Swain, Darling St.

Thomas G. Nickerson, North St.

Judah Nickerson, Union St.

Mrs. Caroline Swain, Summer St.

William T. Swain, Broad St.

Charles E. Smalley, Orange St.

Mrs. Throckmorton, Centre St.

62 *A view from Steamboat Wharf, ca. 1890. The Veranda House is between the second and third catboat masts. The New Springfield is seen between the fourth and fifth masts (with dark top story). Hayden's Bathing Rooms at water's edge at the right. The Island Roller Skating Rink (with three cupolas) is beyond.*

63 *Mrs. Riddell's boardinghouse (large house at right) on Gull Island, off Centre Street.*

Mrs. Temple, Pearl St.

Mrs. E. A. Waitt, Pearl St.

Robert B. Coffin, 'Sconset

Oliver Folger, 'Sconset

The number of boardinghouses was not increased in the later edition of Godfrey's book, as had been the case with hotels. Several known through advertisements in newspapers following the first publication are:

I. S. Riddell, Gull Island (1882), which became Mrs. H. L. Riddell's in 1895 and carried on into the twentieth century.

Mrs. Stephen S. Gibbs, 33 Milk Street (1882).

Mrs. S. B. Soverino, Orange Street, two doors below Silver (1883).

Albert Easton, 25 North Water Street (1884), was run by Mrs. Easton after 1898; Easton added a portico of his own design in 1903, and the house was taken over by Mrs. Frank B. Mayhew in 1908.

A number of out-of-town inns sprang up during the early 1880s, mostly in connection with cottage-lot developments (see chapter four). A. M. Norcross's Weston House at Quidnet (north of Sesachacha Pond) preceded Ellen Round's

activities in that area. When advertised in 1881 the Weston House claimed already to be "widely known for its advantages for Perch fishing, Shark fishing, etc.," utilizing both pond and ocean. It offered to serve "First-class shore dinners . . . at any time." Beginning in 1884, Norcross and his brother ran the Wauwinet House for about a decade.

There had been an attempt to purchase and "build a wharf and make other improvements, with a view of having a pleasant summer resort" on Tuckernuck Island by "certain New York gentlemen" in 1872, but nothing materialized at that time. Ten years later M. W. Dunham built and operated the East End View House there. It was "tastily fitted up," and it offered "Clam-bakes, Fish Dinners & c., for any number." Dunham was "also prepared to take a small number of boarders."

Nearby on the main island, John R. Sandsbury could take several boarders at his place "a few steps from the shore of Maddaket Harbor, on reasonable terms."

Also in 1883 a nameless innkeeper sought "A FEW SUMMER BOARDERS" to be "accommodated on a farm . . . 2½ miles from town, and within 100 yards from the shore of the Inner Harbor."

64 *The Cedar Beach House, Coatue.*

A hostelry of some consequence was the Cedar Beach House on Coatue. It was begun in 1883 by A. W. N. Small, formerly of the Wauwinet House, and served meals at all hours between 8:00 a.m. and 11:00 p.m., specializing in shore dinners. It was accessible by steam-yacht *Coskata* from town and had the "Best bathing, wading, and air on the island. Free from all insects." The Coatue Land Company was offering its 275 lots at that time, and it sold the whole project in 1890. The Cedar Beach House continued under the direction of C. F. Hammond. It then boasted "quite a large bathing establishment . . . with a toboggan slide, swings and other features . . . and hundreds of children enjoyed the exhilarating sport of a rapid shoot through the atmosphere, terminated by a plunge into the Atlantic." The Cedar Beach House was abandoned a few years before its destruction by fire at the end of August 1908.

Construction under way at Squam Head during the early 1880s created an island mystery.

Some of its materials were bricks from the old Citizens Bank building that had been at the corner of Main and Washington streets, recently demolished. First completed was a large stable, and work was progressing on a sizable two-and-a-half-storied building. It had the form of a typical New England residence of five bays, with pilastered doorway and corners, clapboarded in the first story and shingled in the second. The main block, which was two-rooms deep, had a bracketed gable roof crowned by a hip-roofed cupola pierced by arched windows. There were bay windows on the flanks, and attached was an awkward, flat-roofed wing of two stories at the back. Connected with the mystery house was the name of William H. Chadwick, who a few years before had succeeded William Mitchell as cashier at the Pacific National Bank. Chadwick's recent operations in real estate had attracted attention and prompted comment, but it was believed generally that he was acting as agent for "parties abroad." The worst of

65 *Chadwick's Folly, Squam Head.*

rumors declared that the building under construction was to be a gambling casino, and wharves were to be provided below for the yachts of wealthy patrons. The 17 January 1885 issue of the *Inquirer and Mirror* made the facts public. The headline read: "OVERDRAWN. A BUBBLE OF EXCITEMENT CAUSED BY THE ACCOUNTS OF THE CASHIER OF THE PACIFIC NATIONAL BANK."

The story began: "About a fortnight since, the assistant cashier of the Pacific National Bank detected in the accounts figures that were puzzling and startling, and hurriedly informed the president and vice president of the discovery." Chadwick, the cashier, who had a reputation for being "a man of excellent business abilities" had "overdrawn his account to a small amount." It also was discovered that he had been tampering with other accounts over the past two years and had appropriated between $10,000 and $15,000. Col. Daniel Needham, a national bank examiner, was called in and found that through making "several false entries" and "over-increasing thirty eight shares of stock," Chadwick had extracted $11,500 from the bank. In addition, he had borrowed large sums from individuals on the island, estimated to bring the total amount to $50,000. Chadwick's father paid off the bank deficiency in

cash, and the personal debts were smoothed over in various ways. The cashier lost his job and was sentenced to five years in jail. The house at Squam, which was being "fitted up in the most approved manner with modern conveniences," was auctioned off on 13 August 1894. It spent most of its existence, ending in 1956, in neglect and abandonment, the windows boarded up and clapboards and shingles falling off. The hulk was known as Chadwick's Folly.

Like the Ocean House forty years earlier, the hotel that was to become the grandest and most spacious, and would be situated on the island's choicest site, was anticipated two decades before it was realized. During the summer of 1868 an essayist had noted that if Nantucket had sufficient accommodations for "four or five thousand visitors . . . they would leave from fifty to seventy-five thousand dollars at least among us every year." Large seasonal hotels had proved to be lucrative ventures "at Niagara, and Cape May, and Old Point Comfort, and surely would pay here." The proper place for it, he continued, was the Cliff, where "The view is perfect; if there is a breath of air, it blows here. We doubt not that eventually some enterprising person will see the advantages of the locality, and that a spacious, verandahed hotel will crown the bluff, with its flight of stairs down to the shore, with its row of bathing houses, with its boat houses for those desirous of sailing, fishing or rowing, and with its bowling alleys, billiard salons, and base ball and croquet grounds." The idea was tossed around for years, with some people being for and some against it. In 1872 a correspondent signing himself "E." declared: "We must *have* it," and concluded by asking "who will subscribe the first hundred dollars, towards the building of the Cliff House?" Three years later there was a serious attempt to realize such a hostelry, but at the end of the summer it was reported: "The project for a new hotel at the Cliff has been given up for the present, as the desired piece of land could not be obtained."

Almost nine years were to elapse before the promise of such a hotel becoming a reality presented itself. In the spring of 1886 the New Bed-ford *Standard* carried an announcement that was repeated in both island newspapers: "Robert H. Slade, architect, had prepared plans for a new hotel to be built at Nantucket, the work of which will be in progress the coming season." It was to be built by Charles H. Robinson and "after its completion will be sold to a lady now keeping a boarding house." The hotel building was to be 115 feet long on the front, with an extreme width in the center of 70 feet. On the main floor were to be the entrance hall, parlor, and dining room; on the floors above some forty sleeping rooms, and in the basement the laundry, smoking, and billiard rooms. Wide piazzas were to be on two sides. It was noted that: "The old house which now stands on the site will be built on to the main building at one end, and will be used principally for kitchen purposes. The hotel will be finished on the exterior with ornamental shingle work." The article in the *Inquirer and*

66 *The Sea Cliff Inn (1887), North Street (Cliff Road).*

67 *Reception Hall of the Sea Cliff Inn.*

Mirror appended a statement by Robinson to the effect that the report was partially inaccurate (prompting deletions from the passages here offered). Two months later the paper reported that the hotel was to be sited "on the Obed G. Coffin lot, North Street [Cliff Road] for Mrs. C. W. Pettee," that the building was "being framed in Maine" and the parts were to be "brought here by vessel." Construction was carried out over the next six months, and in May of 1887 the official announcement and description read:

"THE SEA CLIFF.—this is the name by which the new hotel on North street is to be known. Mr. Charles H. Robinson . . . has about completed the contract, and the house . . . is one of the finest

buildings on the island for hotel purposes. It . . . stands on the lot next west of Capt. Charles C. Mooers' residence, and is three stories. The dimensions have before been referred to and will be unnecessary here. The first floor is devoted to parlor, dining room, office and kitchen. The parlor occupies the street corner on the west, and is of fine proportions. It has a bow window on the front, in which is arranged an upholstered seat. A handsome mantel and fireplace also add to its attractiveness. It is directly off the office. This latter apartment is arranged with every convenience for the transaction of the business, and is also ornamented with a handsome mantel. The clerk's desk is at the rear, and [nearby] . . . are doors leading to Mrs. Pettee's private rooms, which overlook the water. The dining room is a spacious room, extending from front to rear, 72 x 36 feet. . . . Side boards, drawers, shelves, etc., are just where they are needed. . . . The serving room opens directly into it, and here also is evidence of careful planning for the greatest convenience. The kitchen and pastry cook's rooms are handy and well arranged. A handsome staircase leads from the office to the second floor, where are rooms for guests. They are large, airy apartments, well lighted, and command on every side a pleasant prospect. The same may also be said of those on the third floor. In the basement is a billiard room 30 x 21 feet, a large laundry and furnace room, store-rooms, and sleeping apartments for the servants, arranged with all necessary details. The house is to be supplied with gas, and the mains are now being extended for the purpose. Large piazzas on the rear and front offer an attractive retreat for shade and comfort. The sanitary arrangements have been looked after with the greatest care. . . . All in all, the Sea Cliff is a superior hotel, and there is every reason to believe it will prove a success for the enterprising lady who has had it erected."

The Sea Cliff was an irregular pile in the "Queen Anne" style, its walls mostly clapboarded in the first story and shingled above, the base line of the shingles staggered for a rustic effect. Veranda piers were shingled and bracketed or arched, and railings were of lattice pattern. Roof variations included gables, hips, and gambrels, and even the pre-existing kitchen pavilion at the south end of the building (a "typical" or Nantucket Quaker house type) was ornamented by a double-pitched gable added at the center. Fenestration consisted of single, double, triple, flat-topped and arched windows, bay windows, and several dormer windows, each one different. The Sea Cliff made the first use of the Queen Anne style for a Nantucket hotel. It ushered in a new era, though the principal manifestation of the mode was in later additions to the Sea Cliff itself.

The year 1887 was to witness a number of changes in the personnel of Nantucket hotels. After the death of Joseph S. Doyle, who had presided over the Ocean House since 1879, Mrs. Doyle assumed responsibilities as proprietress, and she was to continue until the 1890s, when Hibbard and Hutchins became managers of both the Ocean House and Ocean View House at Siasconset. In 1887 Charles H. Mowry assumed charge of Springfield House following the death of his father. John Thomas took over the American House in July, succeeding Charles Burgess. The Bay View House was leased to Miss Bessie Appel, of Hartford, Connecticut, who conducted it herself. Daniel F. McKay remained proprietor of the Sherburne House, and the Veranda House was being run by S. C. Davenport.

In the fall of 1888 the Elijah H. Alley homesite and adjoining lots on the north side of Easton Street, opposite Springfield Annex No. 1, were purchased by Charles F. Folger, of the Nantucket family but then living in Philadephia. His intention was to erect a "building, where he will carry on a first-class restaurant next season." The restaurant did not materialize in 1889, and when building was begun on the land in the fall of the following year, it was for a hotel to be called the Point Breeze. Perhaps the name attempted to compensate for its location in town, though there is no denying that it was at the base of Brant Point, where it got not only the breeze but, from many of the rooms, views of the harbor. The Point Breeze was framed by Edwin R. Smith, masonry was laid by John C. Ring beginning late in 1890, and the building was pushed to completion during the spring of 1891. Plumbing was by James Y. Deacon. Its conveniences included an electric signal system, which required its own generating plant, and telephones, such as recently had been installed in the Springfield. Preston Nason did the work. A long sign atop the porch roof over the entrance steps was lettered "POINT BREEZE" by M. F. Freeborn.

The Alley house was retained as an annex providing ten guest chambers, and the hotel proper was built close to its east side. It was a building of three full stories over a high basement, with additional rooms in the garret lighted by dormer windows; a slender, square, four-storied turret with steep pyramid roof was at the southeast cor-

68 *The Point Breeze, Easton Street, late nineteenth century.*

ner. A plain porch ran across the front and left flank at first-floor level. The building measured 40 by 62 feet and contained forty rooms. In the basement were the billiard and smoking rooms, toilets, porter's, and store rooms. On the first floor were the office, parlor, two dining rooms, and two sleeping apartments. The kitchen was in a separate pavilion. Bedrooms were on the upper floors of the main building. H. Pennypacker was engaged as clerk and George Thomas as steward.

Although in more restricted quarters and not so stylish, the Point Breeze could accommodate more guests than the Sea Cliff, for which the following year it was determined to build a second and larger pavilion. Ground was broken for it at the beginning of December 1892 and Mrs. Pettee was in town looking after the work, which was being executed under the supervision of E. T. Carpenter of Foxboro. The addition to the Sea Cliff provided a new guest parlor and several smaller reception rooms, an imperial staircase in the entrance hall, another ample stairway at the end of the long passageway running through the rear wing, a large room for guest entertainments in the basement with a seating capacity of 300 persons, and seventy-five bedrooms. The building was wired for electric lights.

The new part of the Sea Cliff was much larger than the old building, being four-storied in front, though not as wide as its neighbor, and its wing was full three-storied with a flat roof providing a deck, entered from the stairway turret at the back. The two buildings were set about thirty feet apart and connected by an enclosed passerelle (called the Midway) from the original rear veranda (which had been enclosed) to the rear of the new grand parlor, which connected with the stairhall and front veranda. The 1893 pavilion had a higher basement, and there were steps, under pedimented end wings, at either extremity. Piers supported arches. While maintaining its identity, the new building reflected certain design elements of its predecessor: walls were shingled, floor levels were revealed by horizontal strings to which walls slightly curved out, and there were similar roof and fenestration treatments. The long rear wing, with its flat top, might have been a monstrous pile were it not relieved by a series of equally spaced buttresses, whose caps served as pedestals for the deck railing, and there were subtle differences in the handling of windows. Bargeboarded gables to right and left of the facade, prominent roof-ridge cresting, and great high chimneys flared out at the top provided a monumental crowning to the building. Even the iron fire escapes affixed in 1894 failed to mar seriously the building's attractiveness.

While the Sea Cliff was prospering, the Point Breeze was suffering adversity. In March of 1894 the equity of the Point Breeze was sold at public auction for $100 to Richard E. Burgess, and Folger's furniture in the building went to Capt. William T. Swain for $400. The debts must have been considerable, as a month later the hotel was at auction again for a second mortgage. Swain, who had purchased the furniture, was the proprietor when the Point Breeze was opened about the twentieth of June. He adulated the rooms as being "airy and spacious, nearly every one looking out upon the water, and [the beds] are furnished with solid hair mattresses with inner wire springs." Connected with the establishment was "a large play room for children and grounds for tennis courts." Later in the summer, William T. Swain installed a duplex recorder giving the exact time and temperature on a large dial; and Mr.

69 *The Sea Cliff Inn, showing 1893 addition (far end).*

70 *Mrs. Hooper's boardinghouse, Broad Street.*

Mowry of the Springfield and Major Tupper of the Nantucket had similar instruments put in their houses shortly thereafter. In the spring of 1895 Swain advertised the Point Breeze for sale, and at the beginning of the 1896 season the new manager was Bracey Curtis.

Many new boarding and lodging houses were in Nantucket Town during the later 1880s and 1890s.

In 1888 the "Newly and tastefully furnished rooms" of the Academy Hill Apartments at "Academy Avenue [Lane] and Westminster Street" were available through application to William A. Cavannah.

W. Clark Myrick was conducting a boardinghouse on North Water Street, perhaps continuing that of W. H. Myrick (1876).

In 1889 Mrs. W. C. Smith opened Franklin Cottage on North Street (Cliff Road). After 1903 Mrs. Smith also conducted the Oneonta on North Street.

Also on North Street the Island Home House furnished "Excellent table, airy rooms," at "moderate prices" in 1889. It was run by Mrs. E. B. Harps, who in the mid-1890s could accommodate thirty guests and rented out a ten-room cottage. At that time her house was advertised as "new" and "Nearly opposite the Sea Cliff inn." Perhaps her cottage across the road, which commanded "an excellent water view" was the original Island Home House. Mrs. Harps later relinquished the name to the home for the elderly infirm on lower Orange Street.

In 1890 Mrs. G. W. Hooper offered "large

pleasant lodging rooms" on Broad Street, "next to the Ocean House and Nesbitt cottage." It later was called The Gables, the Greek revival house built for Edward W. Gardner shortly after the Great Fire of 1846, now 23 Broad Street. After Mrs. Hooper's regime ended in 1905, dormer windows were added on the west slope of the roof. This side was extended in the early 1970s.

In 1891 Mr. and Mrs. John D. Nesbitt let "A first class cottage of six rooms, thoroughly furnished—gas and bath." This must have been the Eben Allen cottage, adjoining the Ocean House, on lease, which the Nesbitts purchased six years later. The Nesbitt House proper, next east of Mrs. Hooper's, was built about 1878 by Charles H. Robinson for William T. Swain, who was mentioned as having a hostelry here in Godfrey's *Island of Nantucket* (1882) and who was to conduct the Point Breeze in 1894–95. Swain sold the building to Charlotte W. Pettee (first matron of the Sea Cliff Inn) in 1888, and she resold it to the Nesbitts in 1895. The house in similar style, just beyond, was built for Andrew Hunt after his purchase of the lot at the end of 1877, and after changing hands twice was acquired by John D. Nesbitt in 1896. The two buildings were connected by a covered way. They were run by Mr.

71 *Eben Allen Cottage, Broad Street.*

72 *Nesbitt House, Broad Street.*

Nesbitt until he was incapacitated by Bright's disease (from which he died several years later—in 1913), then by his wife, Mary B. Nesbitt.

Boardinghouses that were first advertised in 1891 include those of Amelia F. Brown, no address; W. T. Worcester, 139 Main Street; Miss M. P. Ayers, 45 Pearl Street (north side of India Street, halfway between Centre and Liberty streets); and Mrs. Rachel H. Austin, northeast corner of Centre and Pearl streets. The last was owned by Dr. David G. Hussey and contained "3 connecting parlors, 17 lodging rooms, servants' quarters, dining room seating 75, large serving room, large kitchen. . . ." The house was "lighted by gas [and had a] Smith & Anthony heating furnace." The building was sold at auction on 20 May 1896 to John Roberts, who reopened it on

25 July, thus beginning its long career as the Roberts House.

During 1894 Wallace Cathcart had a boardinghouse at 21 Liberty Street, which was listed as being continued by Mrs. Cathcart in 1896. At some point Mrs. Cathcart moved to 71 Pearl Street, and in 1903 she removed to 36 Hussey Street. The old stand on Pearl Street continued as a boardinghouse.

Two neighboring guest houses on Gay Street were opened under the same management in 1894. One was newly built and called The Hillside, located on the south side of the street east of the old silk-factory building. It was a two-and-a-half-storied shingled cottage with gable toward the street and bracketed eaves, and it provided "Excellent rooms with or without board." The older counterpart was The Summit, the east half of the former silk mill, and W. A. Searell's Waverly during the 1870s. The Summit's table was "unexcelled," and both houses had "electric lights and sanitary plumbing," soliciting patronage from "June to October." The Hillside was put up for sale in April of 1896, and when it was opened in June it was "under the supervision of Mrs. W. C. Smith, of New Haven" (formerly of Franklin Cottage). The property was owned by Nathaniel P. Gray during most of the Searell regime, and beginning in August of 1876 through the balance of the century it belonged to Edward H. Holbrook. It was taken down in 1940.

T. C. Pitman had a boardinghouse at the north corner of Centre and Quince streets in 1895, fur-nishing meals with or without lodging. This was in the old William Brock house built in 1788. After 1900, Mrs. T. C. Pitman had a boarding-house at the north end of the block on Centre, corner of Gay Street, which was to be enlarged as an annex to the Ocean House a dozen years later.

Calvert Handy's Central House, commencing in 1895, also was on Centre Street at the north corner of Lily Street. It had been J. B. Swain's boardinghouse during the late 1870s, and it tem-porarily was given the name Brattleboro House. Handy had run the Old Colony restaurant on Steamboat Wharf before plunging into the hostel-ry business. He kept the Central House function-ing all winter. After the turn of the century, it was conducted by Thurston C. Swain, and Calvert

73 *Mrs. Austin's, or the Roberts House (after 1896), Centre at Pearl (India) Street.*

74 *The Hillside, Gay Street, ca. 1914.*

Handy was running the Waverly House at the corner of Gay and Westminster streets.

The 25 April 1896 issue of the *Inquirer and Mirror* printed a map of Nantucket by Henry Sherman Wyer, photographer and author of a number of picture books on the town and island during that decade, and on the map identified as "Publisher and Manufacturer, LOCAL VIEWS AND SOUVENIRS." The map extends from the harbor to beyond Gardner Street, and from Plumb Lane to about the site of Hinckley Lane on the Cliff. Shaded squares indicate recent summer cottages on the Cliff and in the Brant Point area, certain public buildings downtown, and hotels and boardinghouses. Forty-five historic structures and hostelries are identified by number. Boardinghouses mentioned above include: Central House (Centre Street), The Hillside (Gay Street), Nesbitt House (Broad Street), Pitman House (Centre Street), "Mrs." Ayers (Pearl Street), and Mrs. Harps (North Street). Names that were on the Godfrey list of 1882 and repeated on the map are: Mrs. Fish (Broad Street), Mrs. Enas (Union Street), Mrs. Swain (Summer Street), and Mrs. Waitt (Pearl Street). Also indicated are the two bathing beaches: Hayden's, north of Cliffside, and the larger Cliff Shore at the jetties.

The Wyer map notes seven hotels as being in the area, but the listing is not complete. Nantucket's first directory came out in 1897, and establishments omitted from the map but given there were those of W. Cathcart (Pearl Street) and Mrs. H. L. Riddell (Gull Island). A newcomer on the list was Miss E. L. Fisher, 3 Water Street. But even the directory did not cover the field, as we find in the newspaper during the spring of 1897 a notice regarding rooms for rent by Mrs. G. L. Flagg (no address). In 1899 Mrs. Jane L. Folger let rooms at 51 Fair Street, evidently continuing the practice of William G. Folger begun in 1871. Elizabeth M. Folger had a boardinghouse on Cliff Road. Another lodging-room keeper, who barely got in under the wire of the nineteenth century, was Mrs. F. E. Holdgate on West Centre (West Chester) Street. The site of the Bay View House is not included on the Wyer map, and the inn is not listed in the 1897 directory, by which we assume that it had stopped taking guests.

An old inn on Orange street underwent alterations when it acquired a new owner in 1895. It was the building on the north corner of Martins Lane, lately owned by Charles A. Burgess and called the American House. Purchased by Charles H. Robinson, in his characteristic manner he added bay windows on the front, in balance on either side of the centered entrance, and running up three stories. Otherwise the exterior was broken by horizontal levels of clapboards and shingles. Robinson changed the name of the house to Holiday Inn and E. M. Jewett was the proprietor. In 1901 W. D. Carpenter, of the Ocean House, became the manager.

Out-of-town retreats for visitors during the last decade of the century were mostly in the village of Siasconset, being the cottages on the bluff. One of them had been the old fisherman's shack that stood on the east side of Broadway, called Woodbine before its removal to the corner of Grand Avenue south of the gully in 1881 and afterward called Thornycroft. In 1889 it offered "TABLE BOARD" by "Miss Yonge, late of the Town and Country Club, New York City."

Another boardinghouse in the village was Orr Cottage, with "Dinners furnished on application," conducted by Mrs. I. F. Orr. This was the former Atlantic House.

75 *The William Brock house (1788), later T. C. Pitman's boardinghouse, Centre at Quince Street.*

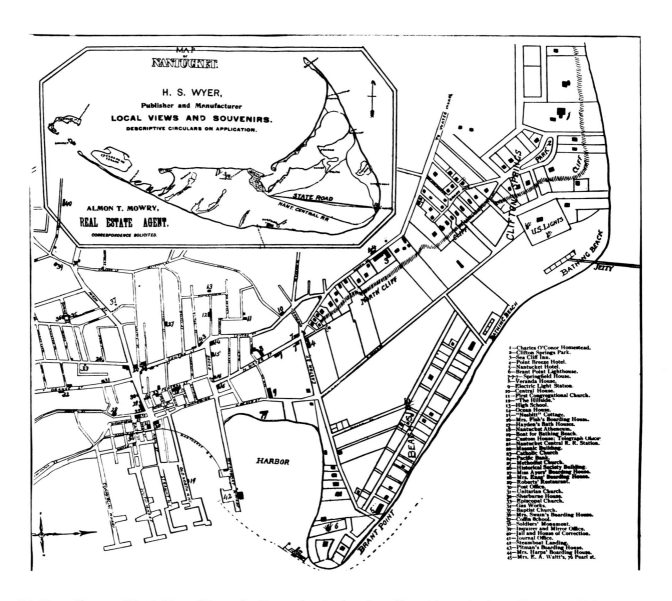

The legend on the map reads:

1—Charles O'Conor Homestead.
2—Clifton Springs Park.
3—Sea Cliff Inn.
4—Point Breeze Hotel.
5—Nantucket Hotel.
6—Brant Point Lighthouse.
7—Springfield House.
8—Veranda House.
9—Electric Light Station.
10—Central House.
11—First Congregational Church.
12—"The Hillside."
13—High School.
14—Ocean House.
15—"Nesbitt" Cottage.
16—Mrs. Fish's Boarding House.
17—Hayden's Bath Houses.
18—Nantucket Athenæum.
19—Boat for Bathing Beach.
20—Custom House; Telegraph Office.
21—Nantucket Central R. R. Station.
22—Masonic Building.
23—Catholic Church.
24—Pacific Bank.
25—Methodist Church.
26—Historical Society Building.
27—Miss Ayers' Boarding House.
28—Mrs. Eno's Boarding House.
29—Roberts' Restaurant.
30—Post Office.
31—Unitarian Church.
32—Sherburne House.
33—Episcopal Church.
34—Gas Works.
35—Baptist Church.
36—Mrs. Swain's Boarding House.
37—Coffin School.
38—Soldiers' Monument.
39—Inquirer and Mirror Office.
40—Jail and House of Correction.
41—Journal Office.
42—Steamboat Landing.
43—Pitman's Boarding House.
44—Mrs. Harps' Boarding House.
45—Mrs. E. A. Waitt's, 76 Pearl st.

76 Henry Sherman Wyer's Map of Nantucket Town, showing location of hostelries and points of interest, 1896.

In 1891 a Siasconset spa providing professional health care was Rest-Haven, "A GROUP of cottages situated on a bluff overlooking sea and moors" that was run by Mary F. Mann, M.D., and M. Ella Mann, M.D., who were of the New York Medical College and Hospital for Women, a homeopathic institution. The Manns were specialists in "Nervous Diseases and Diseases of women and children." In 1903 Rest-Haven was

moved to Quidnet, and several years later to town.

In 1897 G. H. Brinton could provide "A FEW LADIES" with "pleasant rooms" and "first-class board . . . near the ocean, fine view." Brinton had been conducting the boardinghouse "on the Heights" successfully for some time, and during 1897 he "leased for a term of years the Atlantic House," which had been closed since having been struck by lightning and damaged on 12 August

1895. Early in the twentieth century, Brinton was to build and manage a fine new hotel in Siasconset called the Beach House.

At the west end of the island, in 1892, a lone reminder of the grandiose scheme of the Nantucket Sea Shore Enterprise of twenty years earlier, was the Great Neck House, which was available "after July 18th for Clam & Bluefish Chowders and Lobster Dinners." Patrons were requested to make reservations a day in advance. A "Notice left at Cornish's grain store . . . [would] be promptly forwarded."

Two years later, in the vicinity, a Mrs. Ramsdell conducted the Maddaket House, which she had to close early in the season due to having injured her ankle.

A few matters pertaining to late nineteenth-century summer life, though having little to do directly with hostelries on the island, are in order. The first is the Tourists' General Registry Agency, begun by F. L. Patterson in 1883 at 2 Orange Street. It was defined as "A Bureau of Information where everybody goes to learn where everybody is." For a small fee visitors registered there could be found by friends or for the delivery of telegrams or express packages. On hand for their use were files of New York and Boston newspapers, railroad guides and timetables; and "Whitman's Phil [Philadelphia?] Confectionery, Sheet and Band music, Elegant Stationery, Art Novelties . . . [and] Cigars" were for sale.

In 1885 a subscription was gotten up for the erection of a bandstand on the square, where the Mechanics' Band, organized the previous year, would perform during summer evenings. It was set up in front of their headquarters, and concerts here became an annual attraction. The bandstand was carted off each fall and brought back in the spring.

During July of the first year of the downtown musicals a stranger to the island, looking for a

77 *The Cliff Shore bathing beach.*

78 *Former American House, remodeled and enlarged in 1895 by Charles H. Robinson as the Holiday Inn, Orange Street at Martins Lane.*

place to stay, approached a pleasant-looking building on lower Orange Street "under the impression that it was a hotel. He liked the location and water prospect, and the keeper . . . [appreciating the situation, conducted] the man around the house that he might select an unoccupied room . . . the latter's suspicions becoming aroused he inquired where he was and learned that he was in the almshouse."

In 1886 Nantucket received its first telegraph/telephone equipment, and its heretofore charming streets began to be disfigured by posts and wires. Billy Clark had the "honor" of setting the first pole, which was planted on 20 April near the B. G. Tobey residence on the east corner of Main and Gardner streets. One line from town

went to the station on Smith's Point, and Albert S. Mowry obtained permission from the chief signal officer to use it to contact his cottage at Great Neck on condition that he would report wrecks occurring in its vicinity. Mowry was one of the first to install an electric annunciator (intercom) system, which was in the Springfield House. In 1887 a telephone connection was made between H. S. Sweet's store on Federal Street and the post office in Siasconset. The Wauwinet House was given a line to town the same year. Communication wires were joined by others carrying electric current for lighting in 1889. Generators went into operation on 17 August, when the hotels Nantucket, Veranda House, and Springfield House were the first places illuminated. The last installed its own electric power plant in 1891.

On 5 July 1887 a hundred Talmadge Pilgrims visited Nantucket under the leadership of the pastor himself. "The redoubtable Clark was on hand with flags, horn and bell, and presented Dr. Talmadge with a handsome bouquet of flowers and picture of himself on duty. Prior to the departure of the train he enlivened the time and amused the passengers by parading up and down the platform modestly shouting. 'I'm the man who drove the first and last spike on the Nantucket railroad and set the first telegraph pole!' It was a jolly crowd that went to 'Sconset, though their mirth was exceedingly ill-timed . . . [contributing] to the terror of an already frantic horse at the Orange street crossing, as there were ladies in the carriage."

During the last decade of the century proposals for a new convenience for summer visitors caused a great furor and considerable talk, but the furor was short-lived. The proposed project was a street railway system, and two factions were in competition. At the 9 October 1889 meeting of the selectmen a petition was received from Thomas G. Macy of Nantucket representing "a company of New York capitalists." The document outlined a rail line through town and out Brant Point, "to be operated by animals, electricity, or other motive power." As there was not a full board present, the selectmen tabled consideration to the following week. By that time a second petition had been presented by Joseph A. Grant of Everett and P. A. Underwood of Cambridge, Massachusetts, spokesmen for a group interested in the new electric company, which favored electric power for the cars. This one proposed continuing the line to Siasconset. Both companies claimed priority on the grounds of having been "working quietly" for some time. The selectmen held informal hearings to learn more of the matter, and a public review was slated at Town Hall on 3 December. Meanwhile, because *Inquirer and Mirror* editor Roland B. Hussey was involved with the second group, in the 30 November issue the newspaper published a picture of "A Car on the Revere Beach Electric R. R. Co." to acquaint Nantucketers with how an electric car looked, most of them never having seen one. A second town meeting was held on 18 December. Allen Coffin appeared at both as attorney for the two natural

79 *The beach under the Bluff at Siasconset.*

80 *William D. Clark, Town Crier, 1892.*

foes of a new transportation system, the Nantucket steam railroad and the public-carriage drivers. A ballot vote taken at the later assemblage turned down the petition by a count of 222 to 191.

However, the issue was not settled. The selectmen were accused of accepting the hospitality of the electric company at the Springfield House, and in any event they granted a franchise. Difficulties immediately arose over the route, regarding streets to be used in town and Milestone Road to Siasconset in the country. The other group, entitled the Beach Street Railway Company, resubmitted a petition in March of 1890, and it was given the official nod in July. A

month later the company was organized with Harvey Pratt as president, John F. Simms as treasurer, and Thomas G. Macy as clerk. The electric railway got no further than implanting a line of stakes and plowing up a half-mile strip as an experiment. But the horse guard charged ahead by engaging Jesse B. Snow to make a survey, importing twenty laborers from New Bedford to install tracks under the direction of Charles H. Cox, and ordering materials. Town crier William D. Clark was invited to drive the first spike, and this act was about the only aspect of the proceedings to please the townspeople. The system made its initial run on 20 September and consequently was of limited duration the first season.

The Nantucket Beach Street Railway ran two "bobtailed" or single-horse carriages. Its tracks extended from the corner of Main Street up Federal to Broad, east to Beach Street, north to Easton, and out the Brant Point Road to the Nantucket Hotel. Passengers for the bathing beach were transferred from the rail cars to horse-drawn barges on Easton Street. The bobtailed cars ran a total of about ten blocks. The company sought to extend its line out Main Street and through Pleasant Street to Atlantic Avenue, thence to Surfside and circle around the east end of the island, using electric-powered cars. Another year it proposed taking its tracks out Washington and Union streets to Siasconset, but nothing came of either proposal. The system built endured only three summers, and the tracks embedded in the streets remained a nuisance until the last of them were taken up in 1898.

The steam railroad, though persevering, was experiencing vicissitudes. The Surfside boom was not working out as expected, and the Surfside Hotel had changed hands several times. In 1889 the hostelry was purchased, with certain parcels of land, by Francis Doane of Boston, and at that time Almon T. Mowry was trying to give away house lots on presentation of proof of building a cottage. In 1890 Daniel McKeever assumed a mortgage on much of the property, and the following year he sold out to William H. Gwynn of Cohoes, New York. Improvements in 1890 literally shortcircuited. The Nantucket Electrical Light

Company was called in to illuminate the hotel and also to erect eight arc lights on the road to Surfside. In mid-September, "lightning freaks" split some thirty poles along the road, put transformers at the hotel out of commission, and caused a blackout on Milk, York, Pine, and Orange streets in town. Landlord Spooner had managed a successful season, but it was his last. In 1891 James Patterson, who had run the Surfside Hotel three years earlier and at that time was managing the Sherburne House and Bay View House, was named proprietor. He put his son, Frederick, in charge of the hostelry on the south shore. Charles H. Robinson built a bowling alley adjoining the hotel and laid a mile-long plank walk to the lifesaving station. He might have included a nursery for little Freddie Patterson, who arrived on 25 August, the first child born at Surfside. Family and structural additions of the summer were counterbalanced by subtractions in the fall. In September James Patterson and Son made an assignment to Allen Coffin for the benefit of their creditors, their liabilities amounting to $2,500; and the gale of 23 October leveled the Surfside depot and one of the bath houses connected with the hotel.

Owner William H. Gwynn took on the proprietorship of the Surfside Hotel in 1892. He set out to improve its image by scheduling dances to which gentlemen came in full evening dress, and he led the grand march in person. On the evening of 27 August the lawn behind the hotel was brightly illuminated, and guests were entertained by the trapeze performance of Ella Lheurany, "Queen of the Lheurany family of Paris." Afterward, tableaux were presented "in the spacious parlors of the hotel, under the management of Mrs. Appleton," and at the conclusion refreshments were served.

A severe storm on 21 August 1893 was more devastating to enterprises on the south shore than that in October1891. The train had made its morning run to Siasconset before the wind peaked at 59 miles an hour, taking up and turning over large sections of the track, so that the *Dionis* and her cars were stranded at the east end of the island. The damage was such and business so poor that it was not economically feasible to repair the road—either for the balance of the season or following year. Only the little engine *'Sconset* shuttled between town and Surfside during the summer of 1894. On 4 October the railroad was sold at a mortgagee's sale to John H. Fairbank, trustee under the mortgage, for $10,000. The Nantucket Railroad Company had come to an end after fifteen years. The Surfside Hotel was

81 *Horse-drawn barge and "bobtailed" rail cars at North Beach Street and Brant Point Road.*

82 *The Surfside Hotel, partly collapsed, December 1899.*

abandoned. It deteriorated, and during the last year of the century it was battered down by winter storms and ceased to exist.

Train service to Siasconset was restored in 1895, but by a different company, called the Nantucket Central Railroad. It ran directly from town to the village, with only the two stretches at the beginning (from Steamboat Wharf to the fairgrounds) and at the end (from Tom Nevers Pond to below the bluff) remaining intact. The shore route had proved too much of an expense and a headache. The rails taken up were reused in the new road, and the rolling stock remained the same. Delays in the work schedule prevented the train from running until mid-August. After that, and for the balance of the century, the operation of the island railroad was fairly routine.

The farthest point out from town served by both systems was also the site of the annual Agri-cultural Society fair, mentioned earlier as having acquired permanent grounds in 1859. Stock shows and various contests were held there, and booths were gay with edibles and vendibles, but the vegetable displays remained in the upper hall of the Atheneum, where arts and crafts were also shown. Prizes were awarded according to the adjudged merits, though they were seldom more than a dollar or two in cash, and the money was provided by the Commonwealth of Massachusetts. In 1885 the shows were moved to the skating rink in Atlantic Hall. Tables were arranged along the west wall, and the gallery served as an ice-cream saloon. Meanwhile, a new event had been introduced at the fairgrounds proper that made use of the half-mile course, formerly limited to livestock displays. In the account of the fair in 1868, the editor of the *Inquirer and Mirror* commented on the wholesomeness of limiting interest in horses to fine physique, saying: "We are grateful it has not been *horse-racing,* which was so deprecated by . . . [our] late venerable Ex-Governor Lincoln. . . ." The cause of the editor's gratitude was not long to last. In only four years (1872) the horse show was accompanied by a trotting match, in which participated Dr. C. D. Marsh, John W. Macy, and J. P. White. Few people witnessed the outcome of the race, as a cloudburst precipitated the spectators to shelter—undoubtedly to the gratification of a certain editor and others of like mind. The grandstand at the race course, which was covered by a roof, must have been built in 1894, as for the first time in that year a fee of 10¢ was listed for a seat in it. That was in addition to the 40¢ charged for transportation to the grounds via teams (from Main and Centre streets) or steamers (at the foot of Main Street), and it included the entrance fee. The two-day fairs each year closed with a Grand Ball: "Gent and Ladies, $1."

Back in town, as has been mentioned, Charles H. Mowry had taken over the proprietorship of the Springfield House in 1887, following his father's decease. Charles was newly married then, and on the evening of 20 April 1891 he and his wife had a few friends in to celebrate their fifth wedding anniversary. At about ten o'clock "the company was invited to the dining room where a beautiful collation of ice cream, cake, confections and fruit was served." Afterward they repaired "to the parlors to enjoy a little music." The newspaper reported that "Mr. and Mrs. Mowry were recipients of many testimonials of esteem from friends at home and abroad, including articles of furniture, books, silverware, etc. One gift, a cider pitcher and funnel, of a pattern of two centuries ago, attracted special attention, and Mr. Nason's testimonial and accompanying note created much merriment." Preston Nason recently had installed the electric plant. At the Mowry's wooden-anniversary party the guests enjoyed passing to and from the scene of the collation by a new covered way that had been built in the bracketed

83 *The race track at the Fairgrounds.*

84 *The New Springfield House, showing the covered way built during the spring of 1891 joining it to the Dining Room House.*

style and connected the principal building and dining-room pavilion. Also, an "archway entrance to the grounds of the Springfield on Beach Street" was a new feature and was said to have been "a handsome one."

The arched gateway directly east of the main building was a symbol of the new orientation of the hotel. In 1892 the Beach Street side of the lot was tripled in size through purchase of F. C. Sanford's land to the north. The combined lots became an extensive lawn, and with the building taller on that side due to the downward slope of the terrain, the facade toward Beach Street made an impressive new front. It provided easy access to the skating rink on Sea Street where all sorts of social events and entertainments took place, such as the german, or cotillion, given by Springfield guests on the evening of 14 August

1894, or the ball featuring the Jolly Three of the Nantucket Hotel a week later. At that time a carousel was operating nearby on Easton Street, a diversion which, the following year, was conducted by W. C. Brown.

Putting the new front of the building toward the east involved constructing a porch across that end, overlooking the lawn. At parlor level, the porch floor was 10 feet off the ground. On Monday evening, 30 July 1894, an entertainment at the Springfield for the benefit of the Merry Workers' Fund was well attended, and at its conclusion some of the guests improvised a dime-museum show on the piazza. When the crowd surged out into the open, a girder gave way at the inner side and a section of the porch floor tilted downward, precipitating twenty-five or thirty people into a jumbled heap at the base of the wall. "For a moment everyone was panic stricken, but cool heads quickly regained their self-possession and willing hands soon extracted the unfortunate ones from their predicament." Doctors Grouard and Williams came to the assistance of the few who were injured: a Boston woman suffered compound fractures of one leg and dislocation of both ankles, a Scranton man dislocated an ankle, several others sustained sprained ankles and back injuries, and Preston Nason hurt his hand. It was stated that Nason was acting as "correspondent for several publications [and] had started to take notes of the entertainment. He had written but a single line when the catastrophe occurred and he found himself on the ground with his hand maimed, his coat nearly torn off, and note book and pencil vanished." The journalistic endeavor seems rather remote from his role of installing electrical equipment. The accident was reported to have been caused by improper fastening of the girder, which was only "toe-nailed" against the sill of the house. This and other structural shortcomings were corrected.

Those injured in the mishap were unable to attend either of two events at the Atheneum later in the week. On Thursday evening Cyrus Weekes presented nearly a hundred "magnificent and thrilling illustrations of BEN HUR, A Tale of the Christ." Scenes included "the great chariot race, and the most vivid picture ever given of the crucifixion, and the principal events preceding it." Admission was 25¢ and 35¢, all seats reserved.

On the following evening Frank Lincoln, "THE WORLD RENOWNED HUMORIST," presented at the same place a performance called "Lincoln & Laughter," subtitled, "Musical Travesties and Social Satires." His presentation must have been funny as some of his "Press and Personal Commendations" read: "'I never laughed so much in my life.'—The King of Siam. 'Your imitations are simply wonderful.'—The Prince of Wales. 'You compel laughter.'—The Rt. Hon. W. E. Gladstone. 'Sanctified humor.'—Henry Ward Beecher. [and] 'A mimic of startling fidelity.'—The Czaro-witch of Russia." Tickets were 50¢ and reserved seats 75¢.

The momentous summer event toward the close of the nineteenth century was Nantucket's Centennial-Bicentennial Celebration of 9–10 July 1895. It commemorated the one-hundredth anniversary of changing the town's name from Sherburne to Nantucket and the two-hundredth

anniversary of the founding of the county. The downtown section was ornamented by several triumphal arches and red, white, and blue streamers. It was a homecoming for Nantucketers living abroad, and the arch at Steamboat Wharf was lettered: "WELCOME HOME" and "SHOULD AULD ACQUAINTANCES BE FORGOT." The principal arch at the intersection of Main and Federal streets was composed of two towers connected by a latticework bridge and festooned with tricolored bunting. On the north side was the motto: "ETERNAL HONOR TO OUR ANCESTORS," and on the south was the inscription: "SHERBURNE 1795 NANTUCKET." The arch at the head of Orange Street proclaimed: "ALL'S FISH THAT COMES TO OUR NETS," and the opposite side: "AS GOOD FISH IN THE SEA AS EVER WERE CAUGHT." The arch at Centre Street proffered: "OUR SPECIALTY—REST" and "PRIDE IN THE PAST, HOPE IN THE FUTURE." Two signs along Main Street were lettered: "PUBLIC SPIRIT THE TRUE BASIS OF PROSPERITY," and "A LONG PULL, A STRONG

85 *Triumphal Arch on Federal Street at Main, erected for Centennial-Bicentennial Celebration, 1895.*

86 *Alvin Hull, Town Crier, on Main Street during the Centennial-Bicentennial Celebration.*

PULL AND A PULL ALL TOGETHER." At the bottom of the square the Pacific Club's building was "modestly decorated" and bore an inscription: "SHIPS DARTMOUTH, BEAVER, BEDFORD, 1773–1783." The first two were Rotch vessels that figured in the Boston Tea Party and the third was the first ship to carry the Stars and Stripes on a commercial voyage to London.

Festivities on Tuesday morning began at 7:00 o'clock with an hour-long ringing of bells, booming of cannon, and screeching of steam whistles. "This was followed by a band concert from 8 to 9 by [the] Nantucket band on the Upper Square, a temporary stand having been erected and gaily decorated." Boat races came next, consisting of a five-mile catboat contest and a dory run. There was to have been a whaleboat race, but of the two entries one objected to the prescribed route and dropped out. The remaining boat "pulled over

the course in 12 minutes and was awarded the prize of $20."

"Meanwhile musical and literary exercises . . . held in the North Congregational church . . . opened at 9:30 a.m., with music by [the] Nantucket band. Allen Coffin, Esq., presided and read a cordial address of welcome prepared by Mr. Wendell Macy, president of the Centennial Committee, who was unable to be present." The program consisted of prayer by the Rev. D. C. Ridgeway; addresses by the Rev. Christopher C. Hussey, "The Social and Religious History of Nantucket in Its Palmy Days"; Anna Gardner, "The Antislavery Phase of Our Island's History"; and Alexander C. Starbuck, "Historical Matters Leading up to both the Centennial and the Duo-Centennial." Two poems were included: the Rev. Louise S. Baker's "Our Island Home" and Elizabeth Starbuck's "Centennial Ode." A selection by the Harmonic Quartette closed the morning's exercises.

The afternoon meeting opened with music by Martland's band of Brockton, which had arrived on the noon boat. The Hon. Charles Carleton Coffin spoke on "Nantucket's Position in History." Mrs. Caroline Earle White talked about "The Physical Characteristics of the Island." Mae Coffin read Dr. Arthur Elwell Jenks's paper on "The Energy and Hardihood of the Ancestors," and Dr. S. Sidney Mitchell talked on "Nantucket Abroad." Dr. Mitchell mentioned well-known Nantucketers and their activities in various parts of the world and concluded: "But I am sure from what has already been said that you will quite agree with me that had Nantucket been a little larger and a little more populous it would have dominated the whole United States." Allen Coffin read a poem written by the Rev. Walter Mitchell, beginning: "Come back, ye children, to your mother's feast."

"During the literary exercises in the church a band concert and baseball match between Middleton and Nantucket were taking place at the fairgrounds. The island's nine was made up from summer visitors." The newspaper did not deem it worth mentioning which side won.

"The grand banquet at the Rink took place at 7.30 o'clock in the evening. The rink was brilliantly lighted and tastefully and profusely decorated, and the long rows of tables handsomely spread and beautifully laden presented an inviting appearance." At the west end was the bandstand draped with flags and bunting and bearing a tablet on which were the names of the ten original purchasers of the island. The repast was succeeded by a "feast of reason and flow of soul." Henry S. Wyer was toastmaster, and several parties were called upon to pay verbal tribute to the island. Their testimonials were "interspersed with vocal and instrumental music to which the audience invariably" showed "their appreciation by hearty encores."

Wednesday events took the form of an outing to Wauwinet. Following the bell-ringing and band-concert hours, approximately 1,500 people were transported by boat to the head of the har-

87 *The Golf Club House at Siasconset.*

bor. A bicycle race also got under way in town and ended when John Killen arrived at the finish line forty-four minutes and fifteen seconds later. A clambake was held at 1:00 o'clock, costing 15¢ per plateful with the plate thrown in as a souvenir. The repast was followed by a 100-yard dash and a swimming match. The advertised greased-pig attraction failed to materialize, as the porker had been left on the wharf in town. The life-saving drill proved "very interesting to everybody and barring a slight accident, entirely successful. After one exhibition and while the buoy was being hauled off a second time, the flagstaff of the Sea Foam House, to which the hawser was fastened, gave way and came down with a crash." The return to Nantucket began at 4:00 o'clock.

"From 7.30 to 9 there was a reception at the rink which was thronged." It was an informal affair and highly enjoyed. Meanwhile there was a band concert on the Square during the evening.

The bicycle race from town to Wauwinet in July 1895 points out a special mode of transportation that attained enormous popularity during the last decade of the century. Bicycles were ridden by types of people who never had ridden before (or would again), including the matronly and elderly—up to ninety years of age on Nantucket. The clumsy high-wheel style had been succeeded by a model with two wheels of equal size that was easier to manage. The local newspaper made a practice of inserting the names of bicycle purchasers and makes of their vehicles. Bicycles were rented, sold, and auctioned. On the evening of 4 September 1896, the Eagle Bicycle Inn "was thronged . . . when twenty-eight wheels were sold by auction . . . for $17.00 to $47." In that year the cycle path to Siasconset was laid out, at least as far as Philip's Run, and it was completed the following summer. The steam roller, brought over to improve Milestone Road in 1894, was employed.

In 1897 a golf course was projected near Maxcy's Pond on Cliff Road in the Wannacomet section. The property belonged to the Williams family, John Williams having purchased it from the land developer, Charles C. Myrick, in 1875.

Dr. Harold Williams and a group of summer residents promoted the golf venture. A clubhouse was built on the links in 1899, opening with a social attended by 300 persons on 15 July. The building was provided with a porch in 1902, and a tennis court was constructed just west of it a year later. The Williamses owned the golf course until 1926.

A golf club was organized at Siasconset during the summer of 1898, John C. Grout and Charles Rich being its chief promoters, and the former becoming the club's first president. They "secured land privileges for the links north of the village," toward Sankaty, but whether near to the grounds of the present Sankaty Head Golf Club (incorporated in 1921) nobody seems to know. Fees were set at $2.00 for regular members and $1.00 for honorary. Within a fortnight after the first announcement, or by early in August, it was said that golf had "struck the town [i.e., Siasconset] with a vengeance," and the "'Sconset Notes" column in the newspaper declared that experts proclaimed "the 'Sconset golf moors . . . the ideal links in this section of the country."

In the following year Siasconset gained another golf course. It was on the land of Levi S. Coffin at Bloomingdale, west of the village on Milestone Road. For several years it had only nine holes but later was expanded to eighteen, which it maintained until just before World War II. (It is still known as Siasconset Golf Club—still owned by the Coffin family, and back to nine holes.) While it was under construction during June, the comment was made in the newspaper that the village would be "splendidly equipped for this popular sport very soon." At the end of the 1899 season, John C. Grout was quoted as having said that he hoped to incorporate his group as the "Sankaty Golf Club of the Siasconset Golf Moors, with a gilt lighthouse . . . for the members' insignia." He expressed the hope of building a clubhouse and installing two tennis courts the following year in order to make it "a real country club." The branch north of the village was referred to as the Sankaty Golf Club in 1900, but it seems not to have endured much longer.

88 *The auction sale of the old mill, Main Street, 4 August 1897.*

In 1899 a nine-hole golf course was established at Wauwinet. This being the third at this end of the island, the *Inquirer and Mirror* remarked that: "The east-enders are not to be outdone at the present time."

The auction of the old windmill on the morning of 4 August 1897 was primarily of local concern, but would have an effect on island visitors in that the mill was acquired by the Nantucket Historical Association and opened as a public museum. There had been five windmills on high places around Nantucket Town. The round-top mill (1802) on New Lane was demolished and its millstone used as the foundation for the Civil War Monument on Main Street at Milk, mentioned at the end of chapter two. The four other mills stood on Popsquatchet Hills to the southwest and dated from the eighteenth century. But by late in the nineteenth century one had been torn down, one burned, and one had been purchased by the town and blown up to test the

"practicality of gunpowder to demolish a building." The survivor had been sold for $20 in 1828 to Jared Gardner. If it had been a smock mill then, as at present, it would have been less than a quarter of a century old. Gardner found the oak framework sound, and restored or remodeled it to its current form. John F. Sylvia bought it for $1,200 in 1866, and thirty years later his heirs, Lewis Francisco Cordona and Jose Alexandre Marques of the Azores, ordered the mill sold. As was customary, a notice was inserted in the newspaper for four consecutive weeks, and the auction was held by Charles E. Mooers at his establishment on lower Main Street. The mill was knocked down to Miss Caroline C. W. French for $885 and presented to the Nantucket Historical Association. The association then was in its third year, and acquisition of the mill provided it with its first major structural exhibit. The group could feel that it was keeping up with private ventures, as the Jethro Coffin House, purchased several years earlier by Tristram Coffin of Poughkeepsie, was renovated in 1897 and opened to the public for inspection. The Historical Association was to acquire the Coffin House in 1923 and refurbish it before the close of that decade.

The last few items discussed—the Centennial-Bicentennial, the golf courses, and the old mill purchased to be put on display for visitors—are significant in illustrating an island trend. The first was a homecoming, a sort of Coffin Family Reunion magnified for the whole Nantucket community. It brought back those who had moved away, cementing their relationship with the old home place and giving them an intimate, nostalgic experience. Activities were indispensable to such a meeting, but it is significant that organized sports were not taken as seriously as they would have been elsewhere. The whaleboat "race" turned into a mere demonstration, the baseball game had no residents participating, and the greased-pig contest failed to transpire because its means had been left behind. As slogans on the various triumphal arches downtown revealed, interest was centered on local matters: on the island, on the town, and on the people who settled here, with emphasis on their being ancestors of the current participants. Mitchell's speech on Nantucketers abroad, poems, and testimonials all bore evidence of an insular orientation. Informal socials were favored, and it can only be guessed how the conversation coursed. But considered in depth, the natives had learned something about how to enjoy themselves from outsiders. The structure of their celebrations contained elements of mainland fairs and the sorts of recreational endeavors summer visitors liked to indulge in on Nantucket. In providing pleasure for vacationers, the hosts had grasped ways of pleasing themselves. The laying out of the golf links was an enterprise by both on- and off-islanders; and both were to use them, though undoubtedly the preponderance was with the latter. The mill and Coffin house museums were in line with the theme of the Centennial-Bicentennial, as being Nantucket antiquities well worth preserving and inspecting, a source of local pride. They set the pattern for festivities, recreation, and sightseeing attractions in the upcoming twentieth century.

VI. SUMMERING FROM 1900 TO WORLD WAR I

NANTUCKET entered the twentieth century fully aware of its role as island host to mainland escapees, but at the same time it was innocent of how visitors would alter the island. Maintaining its identity was the natives' nostalgic hope, and something of an economic necessity, yet catering to the demands of tourism produced inevitable changes which came about too gradually to be noted while in process. Half of the century was to roll by before cognizance was reached and steps taken on the matter. By 1900 a new look had befallen the town by the addition of various excrescences to houses for guest accommodations; this was accompanied by a gradual skinning off of white clapboards and their replacement with rustic gray shingles. Not only buildings but streets also were in transition. At the turn of the century the steam roller used to lay macadam on the Massachusetts State Highway (Milestone Road) and bicycle path to Siasconset began to be employed on streets in the town. Cobblestones on Pearl (India), Fair, and Orange streets were covered over. Difficulty in blending the bituminous material with the old paving resulted in such defects as a hump at the head of Orange Street, subsequently repaired. The opportunity was taken of making improvements in the sewage system while the streets were torn up, as along Centre Street; and here the sidewalks were widened two feet. Cement walks were laid, like that until recently in front of St. Mary's Church (1896) on Federal Street, the last of the cement sidewalks in the core district to be converted to brick. Mail boxes were placed at various points in town, and the first collection was made on 21

June 1901. Utility poles and overhead wires continued to propagate like seedlings in a nursery, and the greater the number of uprights and suspended lines, the more they spoiled the appearance of the streets.

Unforeseen when horseless carriages began coming to the island in 1900 was the subsequent takeover of the town's lanes and roadways by cars. The first automobile from the mainland was imported by two Nantucketers. In May, Arthur H. Folger and his son George brought over a Stanley Steamer (Turner, *Argument Settlers*, p. 69). It was a small, quiet, wire-wheeled car such as the Stanley brothers had been making for three years. In July, Samuel Howe of Ithaca, New York, came with his Locomobile, which was a steamer manufactured by the company that had bought out the Stanleys' design rights in 1899. Before the Locomobile had been on the island a week it frightened a horse, which precipitated its carriage against a tree in front of the Hadwen and Barney candle factory (now the Whaling Museum) on Broad Street. The driver was thrown out against the curbstone, sustaining a head injury. Howard Willets came in August with another steamer, which also frightened a horse, though the resulting accident did no harm to humans. Early cars were looked upon by the natives as curiosities: whether from conservatism or economic reasons they had little to do with them. Soon they were to get an Auto Exclusion Act passed by the state legislature.

By the turn of the century theatre people were already patronizing Siasconset, and their

89 *East side of Centre Street from the corner of Liberty (modern photograph).*

influence was to be felt during the early decades of the 1900s. Their presence prompted recitals, presentations, and performances, which were given in Union Chapel and at the railroad station. A group banded together to erect a building for such activities. It called itself the Siasconset Casino Association, and William J. Crittenden was made treasurer. In the summer of 1899 the

sum of $1,200 had been subscribed, $800 paid, and a site promised. In September John Collins was asked to furnish a design for the casino. C. C. Taber was superviser of construction, and Horace L. Gibbs was in charge of the work. The casino was located on the south side of New Street near the east end. The sprawling building was shingled and covered by a low-pitched roof capped by two louvered square cupolas. A plain bracketed porch spanned the front and continued part way along the east flank, terminating at a closed pavilion projecting beyond the west end.

Following an informal dance in mid-July, the official opening of the Siasconset Casino was an entertainment on stage presented the evening of 4 August 1900. It was attended by "the largest and most select audience ever before gathered under a public hall roof on the island, the returns proving an attendance of 820 persons." Tickets were $1, 75¢, and 50¢. The audience came in twenty-three "large pleasure wagons," by single teams, bicycles, and on a special train from Nantucket, arriving at 7:30 packed to capacity. "When the doors were thrown open the crush was something to be remembered. It was a scramble for points of vantage. Women and even men lost their heads in their eagerness, while attendants at the doors shouted themselves hoarse endeavoring to hold

up the push and convince the people that there was room enough for all ticket holders." But, continued the report, when everybody was seated, "the picture that the splendidly lighted auditorium presented was one of animated beauty, the ladies' toilets being rich and in good taste." Lighting at the time was by kerosene lamps, exchanged for gas some years later, and electricity in 1914.

The "Dramatic and Musical Entertainment" was under the management of Mary Shaw, an actress of the Ben Hur Company. The program began with an overture played by the 'Sconset Hungarian Orchestra, followed by a piano solo by Lucy Drake. Next came a skit by Julian Sturgis called "A False Start," with a cast of three, including Miss Shaw, Miss Percy Haswell, and Walter Hale. The orchestra played "An Innocent Young Maid," and Mrs. Walter Hale recited, unprogrammed, "When My Ships Come Home from Sea." A Spanish dance by Agnes Everett and Allan

A 7009   Casino, Siasconset, Mass.

90 *The Siasconset Casino.*

Rowe, in costume, called up an encore. Another unscheduled number was Mary F. Crittenden singing "Time Enough" and "A Rose Fable." Margaret Galvin—a young miss—recited "Seein' Things at Night." Percy Haswell appeared in "Monkey on a Stick," a song and dance from *The Geisha*; and Arthur Shaw performed a Negro song and dance. The Sunflower Quartette rendered "The Dummy, Dummy Line." The climax of the evening was Arlo Bates's play, *A Gentle Jury*, having a cast of thirteen headed by the octogenarian favorite of Siasconset, Mrs. G. H. Gilbert. This travesty of female character greatly amused the audience, which was treated to a surprise epilogue by Vincent Serrano in the reading of a long poem epitomizing the performance by Mrs. Dr. J. S. Southerland, "which came in for its full share of the cheering and handkerchief waving as the last line left the speaker's lips." Gross receipts from the performance were $635, net proceeds over $600.

Most participants were professionals and regular summer visitors. Mrs. Gilbert belonged to the Lyceum Company and was well known in both England and America; she was a guest of Mr. and Mrs. George Fawcett. George belonged to the Maude Adams Company and also appeared in movies, among them Erich von Stroheim's "Wedding March." His wife, Percy Haswell, was of the Otis Skinner Company. Agnes Everett, like Mary Shaw, was of the Ben Hur Company. Others in the early summer colony were Frank Gillmore and Regan Hughston, who had played opposite Percy Haswell Fawcett in Shakespeare. Gillmore was one of the prime movers in establishing Actors' Equity and a leader in organizing the Actors' March at New York in August of 1919, in which 2,000 participated. Frank Craven made his first hit on Broadway in *The First Year* and later played the Stage Manager in *Our Town*. Isabelle Irving played the leads in such frivolous drawing-room comedies as *Tyranny of Tears* and *The Liars*. Her husband, William Thompson, played in the Maude Adams production of *The Little Minister* and Anne Russell's *The Royal Family*. DeWolf Hopper had become famous for his *Casey-at-the-Bat* and appeared in many Gilbert and Sullivan

operettas, and he was accompanied by his fifth wife, Hedda Hopper. Lillian Russell visited Siasconset as Mrs. Alexander Moore after her retirement (Barnes, *Heyday*, pp. 18–23).

Behind the building and connected with the casino were two tennis courts that were used first on 25 July 1900. A third court was added in 1903, and three more—requiring the purchase of more land on the east—in 1919 (Heller, *Album*, pp. 14–15). Of all organized games, a tennis court inflicts the greatest defacement on an outdoor setting. Amateur baseball chalks off a diamond but allows vegetation to take its course after the season. Well-designed golf links are developed in sympathy with the terrain. The lawn tennis of the mid-nineteenth century rolled up its nets after a game and left no more year-long blemishes than did croquet. But tennis courts destroy vegetation permanently, and the bare, tamped earth, affording a few enthusiasts pleasure during the short summer, was an eyesore foreign to the Nantucket scene. A bowling alley was erected by the casino in 1909. Its position was shifted in 1916, and it was sold and removed in 1920.

In 1900 the *Inquirer and Mirror* emigrated from its old stand at Main and Milk streets to the new brick and glass building designed by Elliott B. Hussey, of Boston, at the rear of the Folger Block, corner of Main and Orange streets. The old office building was transported to the head of Steamboat Wharf, and the next year it housed Covil and Pease's carousel. Also in 1900 the last of the recently introduced prairie-dog colonies (near Siasconset) was exterminated, completing a program carried over from the preceding year. A handsome new drinking fountain was erected at Folger Lane on the Madaket Road by the Nantucket chapter of the Daughters of the American Revolution. A memorial to native Abiah Folger, mother of Benjamin Franklin, and for whom the chapter was named, it was designed by Sarah W. Smith. In anticipation of other parties financing the laying of Wannacomet Water Company pipes to this locale, for the time being horses passed a dry trough. It was not a scorching summer, but rather the reverse, and the gloom of the weather dampened the spirits of islanders and visitors

The Sconset Train.

91 *Engine No. 1 and closed passenger car at Siasconset.*

alike. During the second week of August the clouds dispersed, and Charles A. Chenoweth, proprietor of the Old Curiosity Shop on lower Pearl Street, is recorded to have remarked that "everybody went to the christening last Sunday—when Nantucket had a little sun."

The success of the first performance at the Siasconset Casino led to another the following year, a benefit for that institution on 14 August. Although not called a vaudeville until later, the character of the entertainment was established. Numbers consisted of an orchestra overture, the Sextette (actually a quartette) from *Floradora*, a humorous skit with George Fawcett and Mrs. Walter Hale called *A Bit of Diplomacy,* Percy Haswell singing "Rhoda and Her Pagoda" from *San Toy,* Henry Woodruff in a vocal selection billed as "One Side of Grand Opera," Mrs. Hale reciting "A Village Gossip," Margaret Crittenden's solo "Somebody's Coming," the Opery Quartette from Yaptown presenting "The Opening of the Chestnut Burr," Percy Haswell and Vincent Ser-

rano in a farce, *A Pair of Lunatics,* a song by Eloise McCrey, and "The Doll's Quadrille." Most of the performers had participated the year before. An exception was Henry Woodruff, a musical star who, besides rendering the "One Side of Grand Opera," appeared in the *Floradora* excerpt and (as "Hank" Woodruff) in "Opening of the Chestnut Burr." After acting in Honolulu the following season, Woodruff had a summer house built on Morey Lane in Siasconset. Called "Aloha," the dwelling had South Seas features, such as the living room upstairs. The casino variety show continued as an annual event.

Rail service to the village was greatly improved in 1901 and over the next few years by the introduction of a locomotive to replace the *Dionis*. It came from the Hinkley Locomotive Works in Boston, and had seen twenty years of usefulness on the Boston, Revere Beach and Lynn Railroad. Sporting the numeral "1" on its nose, the engine generally was referred to by that digit.

The summer focus on the community at the end of the line prompted and justified a new hostelry. It was sponsored by George Herbert Brinton, who had run a boardinghouse for ladies and leased the Atlantic House (after its being closed for a couple of years) in 1897. On 5 September 1900 he purchased the property of Alexander B. Lamberton at the corner of Ocean and Cypress avenues on Sunset Heights. Lamberton had obtained it from Robinson and Ellis in two installments twenty and fourteen years earlier, and he had a summer cottage built facing the Atlantic. Brinton's hotel was an irregular building, having a four-storied polygonal pavilion attached to the summer cottage with a square section beyond a third story within a gambrel roof. In the middle of May 1901 Brinton announced that it would be called the Beach House. Opening was set for 1 June, and it was to feature "New furniture. Finest location in 'Sconset. Unobstructed ocean view [and the] Dining Room was [to] seat 100." Those interested were invited to write for further information, which later took the form of a printed booklet. Brinton did well, and in the spring of 1906 an addition was made equal in size to the mansard section. It was an enlargement, or replacement, of the Lamberton summer cottage. The building was lighted by gas, having its own manufacturing plant. The new work was executed by Charles H. Robinson, which leads one to suspect that he built the earlier pavilion as well. Five years later Robinson was to make an addition to the Beach House farm building (formerly Spotswood) at Polpis.

The unique event of the summer of 1901 on the island was the visit of the U. S. Navy's North Atlantic Squadron. Battleships *Kearsarge, Massachusetts,* and *Alabama* and the tug *Potomac* dropped anchor in the outer bay on 9 August for a week of maneuvers on Coatue. The peninsula had become a separate island due to the opening of the Haulover in December of 1896 and thus was inaccessible from Nantucket proper by land. Major Doyer of the Marine Corps was in charge and kept the men busy all of the first night landing five-inch guns and ammunition. They established what was referred to as Camp City. Those

aboard the *Alabama* got off easy, as it was in quarantine for the first two days because of several cases of mumps. The exercises on Coatue followed those of a sea skirmish involving the condemned Lightship No. 19, which the tug *Potomac* towed to a position off Gay Head, Martha's Vineyard, where it had been sunk in 20 fathoms of water.

The aspect of the squadron's visit that most pleased civilians on the island was the concert given in the lower square on Saturday afternoon, 17 August, by the band of the *Kearsarge*. In addition to the music, the affair provided an impromptu collision between a startled horse attached to a surrey and a team belonging to George W. Dibble. Both vehicles were damaged, but the horses escaped uninjured. The accident was followed by a dog fight in the street that sent people scurrying to the sidewalks. To top the event a woman fainted. On the evening of the 23rd a farewell reception at the Sea Cliff Inn with a german—or cotillion—was tendered the officers by summer residents from the Cliff and Beachside.

Hostelries presenting their names to the public through advertisements in the 1 June 1901 issue of the *Inquirer and Mirror*, with their proprietors, were: the Sea Cliff Inn, E. P. Carpenter; the Ocean House and Holiday Inn, W. D. Carpenter; Veranda House, John M. Winslow; Central House, Calvert Handy; Nesbitt House, J. D. Nesbitt; The Gables, Mrs. H. M. Hooper; Roberts House, John Roberts; Pitman House, Mrs. T. C. Pitman; the Island Home House, Mrs. E. B. Harps; Franklin Cottage, Mrs. W. C. Smith; and the private boardinghouses of Albert Easton, Mrs. H. L. Riddell, Mrs. W. D. Appleton (Lyon Street) and Mrs. Elmer E. Ames. The Siasconset list was composed of the Beach House, George H. Brinton; the Ocean View House, Robert M. Powers; and Orr's Cottage (formerly the Atlantic House), Mrs. I. F. Orr. At Quidnet was Rest Haven, presided over by Drs. Mary F. and M. Ella Mann. Conspicuously absent were the Springfield, the Sherburne, and the Nantucket, the last apparently because it was not yet open for the season.

The Springfield recently had been managed by A. R. Williams, and it was under the proprietor-

92 *The enlarged Beach House, Siasconset.*

ship of W. H. Gooch when offered for sale in July
of 1901. It consisted of four parts, the New
Springfield (1883), otherwise known as the Main
House, the Dining-room House next door; the
Alley Hotel on the corner of North Water and

Chester streets (now Annex No. 1); and the building across the street (formerly Annex No. 1),
which had become Annex No. 2. Purchasers presented themselves later in the year, and the transaction was accomplished early in 1902. The new

93 *The Sea Cliff Inn from the north, early twentieth century.*

owners were Albion T. and Myron W. Brownell of New Brunswick, and the property was sold by Almon T. Mowry, guardian of Mary H. Mowry, an insane person, late of South Walpole. Besides the four buildings, the property included the Sanford Lot behind the main and dining-room pavilions. The sale price was $15,000, and on 6 February 1902 the Brownells made a mortgage deed to Mary H. Mowry for $12,500. One stipulation was that Gooch's lease should be honored until its expiration on 1 April. The next issue of the *Inquirer and Mirror* following that date announced the change of management and stated that the Brownells intended to have the plumbing overhauled by J. Y. Deacon, connecting it with the Brant Point sewer, and that the dining room was to be enlarged, elsewhere mention being made that it was to accommodate 200 persons. This last became the building located back from North Water Street, to the north of the "New"

Springfield House. W. H. Gooch took over the management of the Nantucket on Brant Point. In 1903, Frank Worth, late of the Point Breeze, became head clerk at the Springfield.

To keep up with the Springfield in the matter of improvements, its neighbor, the Veranda House, acquired a new porch on the east side during April. The Roberts House had had its portico on Pearl Street enlarged a month earlier. In June a piazza was added to the Swain House at Centre and Lily streets, and later in the summer Thurston C. Swain changed the name of his establishment to Swain's Inn. The following year Albert Easton set a portico before his door, next south of the New Springfield on North Water Street, that was described as giving "somewhat a colonial aspect."

The Sea Cliff Inn went into the hands of new owners early in 1902. Charlotte W. Pettee had died, and so had her administrator, Erastus P. Carpenter, both of Foxboro. The caravanserai on Cliff Road was sold by the latter's administrator, Henry J. Fuller, to the Nantucket Company, "a corporation duly created and organized under the laws of the State of Rhode Island . . . in the City of Providence." The Sea Cliff consisted of two parcels: (1) that on the east side of the road containing the inn itself, extending back to North Beach Street and bounded partly on the northwest by the land of Eastman Johnson; and (2) a tract with two cottages thereon across Cliff Road and adjoining the northeast boundary of property owned by John and Ella B. Harps. The Nantucket Company paid $56,750 for the property on 11 March and simultaneously borrowed $35,000 from the Nantucket Institution for Savings. Later in the month a contract was made with Wyer and Company to execute carpentry work connected with improving the dining facilities of the Sea Cliff Inn, including enlargement of the serving room and pantry. In the fall the same concern was engaged to make "alterations and improvements," and in November the hotel's "addition" was said to be "rushed to completion."

Whereas the Springfield and Sea Cliff Inn changed ownership and were improved in 1902, their rival on Orange Street, the old Adams-Sherburne House, ceased to operate. On 5 December 1901 the heirs of John Winn sold the estate to William Barnes, Jr., for $3,975. Barnes intended to make it his private residence and charged Charles H. Robinson with moving the main building back from the street about twenty feet. Other structures were disposed of, mainly consisting of the two houses down the bank on Union Street. They were sold to A. M. Myrick for $125 to be removed from the land. In connection with the shifting of houses in this locale, it may be mentioned that the former Elizabeth McCleave house, then owned by Charles H. Robinson and adjoining the Sherburne on the south, was sold and moved by David W. Gibbs across the street to the corner of Orange Street and Martins Lane, about where Irene Fisher's boardinghouse had stood. The evolving William Barnes, Jr., residence utilized the frame of the old hotel and became a building in the Colonial Revival style, with leaded fan

doorway and hip roof, wings projecting laterally, and a long porch across the rear affording a fine view of the harbor. Wyer and Company were responsible for the carpentry, Arthur Williams for the masonry, J. Y. Deacon for the plumbing, H. Paddack for the painting, and the house was furnished by W. T. Swain.

Several places serving meals of various sorts opened in 1903. During the spring appears the name of the Ocean View Cafe, which specialized in a "quick lunch," with Charles H. Carter as proprietor. The location of the Ocean View Cafe was Broad Street near the Steamboat Wharf, according to the Nantucket Directory for 1909, when Mrs. W. H. Arnold was in charge. John Roberts's restaurant and bakery were on Main Street, two doors above the post office. The proprietor apparently was not that of the Roberts House at Centre and Pearl streets, but very likely he was the John Roberts who lately had vacated the house on Union Street being run at that time by Mary E. Palmer.

Of greater moment was the introduction of establishments that had been prohibited on the island for a long time. In 1897, Thomas Lewis had applied to the town officers for a license to run a liquor saloon. His endeavor had been backed and an appeal on his behalf made by Richard S. Burgess, owner of the premises for the intended establishment, but they were turned down. Early in May of 1903, however, the newspaper announced: "For the first time in the town's history, liquor saloons of the first class are being conducted in Nantucket, those of Thomas Lewis and Andrew T. Backus opening on Saturday last under licenses granted by the board of selectmen." In 1904 Thomas Lewis initiated the construction of Progress Hall at the southeast corner of South Water Street and Old North Wharf. It was two-storied, with a bowling alley and pool room below and an entertainment hall above, and it was said to be the "largest building erected upon the island for business purposes by a private party in many years." The bowling alley was listed as Lewis's sole business in the Nantucket directory for 1909, and Andrew T. Backus is characterized as a fisherman, indicating that the liquor saloons did not last long.

Copyright 1905 by the Rotograph Co.

A 6904   Point Breeze Hotel, Nantucket, Mass.

94 *The Point Breeze, showing the new pavilion, 1903–4.*

In the fall of 1903 preparations were begun for an addition to the Point Breeze on Easton Street. The new part was to be on the east side, set back to about half the depth of the old building. It was designed by George Watson of Brookline and built by W. H. Wyer and Company of Nantucket. The piazza was removed from the original hotel early in October, as the addition was to have a frontage of 104 feet, with a porch spanning most of it, and a porte-cochère projecting out at an angle between the old and new. Framing of the Watson design was accomplished during November and early December. Like the parent hostelry, the offspring was three-storied and on a high basement, but it was in the Colonial Revival style, the walls painted a dark color (early tinted postcards showing them a barn red or olive green) with white trim. Pilasters embraced the upper sto-

ries (above porch level), supporting a full entablature crowned by a hip roof, and there was a projecting pavilion in the center with a Palladian window in the pediment. The New Point Breeze offered a sun parlor across the east end and a large social hall on the main floor, above which were private rooms in suite, with telephones and baths. Plastering inside was executed by Nathaniel E. Lowell and plumbing by Willard B. Marden. Bracey Curtis, proprietor since 1896, offered a free booklet on request when the enlarged hotel opened on 1 June 1904.

The long front porch on the New Point Breeze perhaps inspired Charles H. Robinson to add a piazza on the north side of Holiday Inn, and certainly it prompted the improvements made to the Ocean House during the spring of 1904. They consisted of a sun parlor measuring 50 by 15 feet on the east side; and the insignificant bracketed veranda across the front was removed to make way for a longer, taller, square-piered open gallery with balustrade on top, tying in with the sun parlor projecting on the left flank. It was a monstrous appendage to the old Jared Coffin residence, and the brick basement wall and shingled panels beneath the porch railing and conservatory window-sill level contributed to its grossness. The sun parlor was entered through the main office and front porch. The room was proclaimed "tastefully fitted up for social parties and lounging."

There were a couple of pleasant surprises for visitors downtown in 1904. One was on Federal Street, where cobblestones had been covered and leveled by the steam roller in June. The place in question was W. H. Sisson's The Old Nantucket Candy Kitchen, at the southeast corner of Chestnut Street. It offered "Kenney's Famous Salt Water Taffy (8 flavors) . . . Peanut & Popcorn Brittle, and Fresh Buttered Popcorn. Cottage City Popcorn

Bars . . . Carmels . . . Boston's Pride—the Molasses creams [and] Salted Peanuts." The other was the new bandstand on Main Street, which was octagonal and had a canopy top. Replacing the former four arc lights, illumination now was by twenty-three incandescent bulbs, provided gratis by the Nantucket Gas and Electric Company. The band gave nightly concerts. Sidewalks were crowded with people, and the square took on a lively appearance. The bandstand was moved away each year for the winter, a process that was simplified in 1908 when it was taken apart in sections that could be stored under shelter, requiring less refurbishing in the spring.

At 3:30 on Saturday afternoon, 20 August 1904, the band played at the bathing beach, but which of the bathing beaches is not specified— Hayden's Clean Shore in town or that at Beachside, or either of the two beaches adjoining under the Cliff. That to the east was the public beach, managed that summer by Clifford Folger. The

95 *The Ocean House, with porch and sun parlor addition of 1904.*

two together had "about 300 rooms," but demand was "frequently in excess of the accommodations," and "Mr. Folger" was contemplating "an addition to his structure before another season." The other, to the west, was the White City Bath Houses. It claimed to have been "Established in 1869 as the Cliff Shore Bathing Houses." As we have seen, bathing houses on the Cliff Shore were inaugurated by E. W. Allen, of the Ocean House, five years earlier. The proprietors of the White City, George W. Burdick and Son, recently had "purchased a new tract of land to the west of government jetty," and additional accommodations were under consideration.

Baseball was popular during the summer of 1904, the teams made up largely of hotel employees. Favorite fields were to the rear of the Springfield House and across from the Sea Cliff Inn.

The old squantum movement was revived in 1904 with the opening of Quidnet Inn on the Norcross property at Sesachacha Pond. T. G. Macy was proprietor, offering shore dinners.

The summer of 1904 was the last season the Nantucket Hotel on Brant Point was open. The building had suffered depredations during the spring, the front doors having been broken open and vandalism committed. W. H. Gooch, who had been running the Nantucket since leaving the Springfield in 1902, gave up its management and was replaced by A. R. Williams, assisted by Albert T. Ring. Although the following year was a good one for tourism on the island, the Nantucket remained desolate. In August Frank Sylvia was appointed watchman of the property, and it was offered for sale by the Citizens Savings and Trust Company of Cleveland, which held a $4,000 mortgage on the hotel. Its days of playing host were over. C. A. Chenoweth and Allen Smith bought the contents, and early in October they opened up the building and sold the furnishings during the day, whereas the linens were taken to the Covil and Pease store on Main Street and disposed of during the evening, the latter "bringing the women out in force." In November W. H. Wyer began razing the building. The newly organized Wauwinet Tribe of Red Men had purchased the main part of the building and engaged a contractor from New Bedford to move it to their site on South Water Street. Thus, the old Quaker meetinghouse from Main Street was brought back to town at the beginning of 1906. The Red Men were occupying the upper floor by the beginning of June. In 1907 the lower story became Smith and Blanchard's Moving Picture Show with "polite vaudeville." The cinema began to be called Dreamland Theatre as early as 1911, when it was being run by Folger and Hull, formerly showing pictures in the Burgess Market Building. It is assumed that the name came from one of the three famous amusement parks at Coney Island, New York, popularized through its theme song, "Meet Me Tonight in Dreamland."

Holiday Inn on Orange Street opened on 1 May 1905 under its new manager, J. Butler Folger. Folger was determined to begin with a bang and went in person to Steamboat Wharf to meet the boat that evening. He rounded up a group of businessmen and offered them free transportation to the inn. They accepted, "and the house started off with all but two rooms filled on the opening day." Little wonder that when the Holiday Inn closed on 23 September it had enjoyed its "most successful season . . . over 800 persons . . . [having] been entertained." The announcement was made at this time that the "May house [that of Josiah Gorham, 29], situated north of the hotel property . . . [was to be] joined to the main house as an annex." Enlarging the dining facilities was also proposed.

While the Wauwinet Tribe of Red Men was getting finishing touches applied to its new quarters in town, an addition was being appended to the Wauwinet House at the far end of the harbor. James A. Backus, who had run the Wauwinet House since 1897, in the spring of 1906 engaged Holmes and Pease to erect an addition on the north side of the existing pavilion. It was to house "a parlor and a few lodging rooms." The structure was two-storied, its doors and fenestration placed arbitrarily, and it fitted awkwardly against the old story-and-a-half form. A plain porch, upheld by slender square posts, was made to span the entire front. The effect was far from elegant, falling

96 *The enlarged Wauwinet House of 1906. The original pavilion is at the far end.*

short of the contemporary enlargement of the Beach House at Siasconset, but it looked the way a remote inn on a summer-resort island might be expected to look.

The Point Breeze Hotel had been in its full stride for three years. It had its own orchestra, which also played at the Siasconset Casino and elsewhere; and when the musicians left Nantucket early in September the newspaper noted that they would stay together, furnishing music at the Hotel Aspinwall, Lenox, Massachusetts, during the fall and at Magnolia Springs, Florida, throughout the winter.

Formation of the Nantucket Athletic Club evidently had been proposed during the early 1890s but remained dormant for some years. Through the efforts of William S. Kimball, Dr. Harold Williams, and others, it was organized in 1901 "to promote the general social and athletic interest of the town." Its clubhouse was opened on the harbor side of the south end of Beach Street on 5 April 1905, containing a reception hall, billiard room and bowling alley, a library, an "audience room," and other meeting chambers. Here, five months later, stragglers of the summer

colony put together a benefit performance for the town crier Billy Clark, who had become infirm. The featured artist was mezzo-soprano Margherita Hall. The function was so well attended that chairs had to be brought from the Atheneum to accommodate the audience. A tennis court was added in 1907, and another court and a gymnasium were built two years later. Dr. John S. Grouard was president and Richard E. Congdon was vice president.

The Nantucket Yacht Club came into existence in 1906 at the instigation of Paul G. Thebaud, a yachting enthusiast and long-standing member of the island's summer colony. Thebaud belonged to the New York Yacht Club and secured permission to establish a base here. It originally was designated Nantucket Station No. 11 of the New York parent organization. Thebaud purchased a building to house the club and had it moved to the end of Steamboat Wharf, equipping it and employing an attendant at his own expense. The purpose was to take care of all the needs of visiting club members (Wyer, *Sea-Girt*, p. 105).

With the bringing over of Engine No. 1 in 1901, the railroad gave exceptionally good ser-

97 *The Nantucket Athletic Club, South Beach Street, 1905.*

vice to Siasconset for several years. Once in 1905, toward the close of the season, the train failed to return to town because the coal procured could not be made to build up sufficient steam to turn the driving wheels. In mid-July the train came to a halt at Low Beach after leaving the hamlet, having settled between spreading rails. Teams were sent for to conduct the passengers to Nantucket, and work crews spent the night getting the vehicles back on the rails and the track repaired in order that the schedule might be resumed next day. The accident forebode an extended interruption of service.

Early in May of 1906 the announcement was made that the operation of the Nantucket Central Railroad over the ensuing summer was unlikely. The village had come to depend on the system for two-score years, and a return to the primitive means of horse and buggy—even over the improved Milestone Road—seemed dismal. A proposed alternative to rail transportation was running battery-powered electric omnibuses, such as had been used for sightseeing in Philadelphia

during the previous summer. The proposition was advanced by W. F. Codd of the island and John R. Bacon of the City of Brotherly Love under title of the Nantucket Traction and Auto Transit Company. Its application was presented in mid-May. The selectmen hesitated to pass on it and called a public hearing on the matter for the 23rd. The backers of the Auto Transit objected that there was not enough time for them to prepare a fair presentation, but the meeting was held without their being represented. The main local objection stemmed from the buses being automobiles, albeit powered by electricity rather than petroleum, and therefore subject to the exclusion laws. They were considered undesirable, and the Codd-Bacon proposition fell through.

It was optimistically imagined that some act of Providence would permit the railroad to run during the summer. At the electric-omnibus hearing George H. Brinton of the Beach House proved himself of this persuasion, as he "spoke happily of the railroad." Shortly afterward Capt. John Killen was reputed to have made an offer to purchase the railroad on behalf of nonresidents. This touched off a series of rumors regarding buyers, some of them undoubtedly real, such as one set of "capitalists" in New York and another of "parties" in New Bedford. There was even a headline in the 9 June edition of the *Inquirer and Mirror* stating: "Train Will Be Run. Syndicate Will Lease or Procure Railroad Property—Expect to Operate It by June 20th." But the date came and went without incident. The next issue of the weekly conjured up another mysterious would-be purchaser, who had "been in town this week making careful investigation, and left again to present his findings to those who sent him." Neither he nor any of the others was mentioned again in the press, where transportation matters were limited to the irrelevance of the automobile issue. People got to and from Siasconset mostly via horse-drawn barge in 1906.

The railroad finally found a taker during the following spring. Overtures were made by Thomas G. Macy, an old hand at Nantucket railroading through his role in the Beach Street Railway Company of the early 1890s. Late in May of 1907 the steam railroad to Siasconset was procured for $12,000, and a sum of $5,000 was earmarked for restoring the line. Thomas G. Macy became general manager and his brother Cromwell G. Macy II was treasurer. They kept the name of the Nantucket Central Railroad, though the new regime was referred to mostly as the Macy Syndicate. They issued bonds on the company, painted the depots at the terminals a terracotta color with dark red trim, and put the line in good order.

In October Treasurer Macy announced that the Nantucket Central was getting a gasoline rail car

98 *"The Bug" and "The Cage" of the Nantucket Central Railroad.*

99 *The* Nantucket *at Steamboat Wharf.*

for the Siasconset run. It was expected to be delivered later in the month, to be pressed into service immediately and continue throughout the winter. Here was a phenomenon that nobody could object to—rail connections with the east end of the island the year round—being sufficient to make anybody overlook the fact that the vehicle was an automobile. The little rail car was made by the Fairbanks-Morse Company at Three Rivers, Michigan, and it had a two-cylinder, twelve-horsepower engine. It arrived by boat on 26 November. Its appearance was unprepossessing, consisting of a shallow box nine feet long on four wheels, with glass windshield at the front and a top; its open sides and rear were equipped with roll-down curtains; it contained three benches, one facing forward, and the other two on either side, with the entrance at the back. The car car-

ried a driver and eight passengers, and its name, *Siasconset,* was lettered over the rear wheels. But it became known generally as the "Benzine Buggy," later shortened to "The Bug." Two trips were made each day, and the fare was 40¢ either way. In the spring a paneled body was built on the vehicle, with small glass windows at eye level, affording more protection. An open trailer was also added. Made on a similar chassis by Alfred Mann, its main purpose was to carry baggage, but it included benches and could accommodate five or six passengers as well. It acquired the sobriquet "The Cage." A ride on "The Bug" or in "The Cage" to the old watering place was a jerky and unique experience.

Rail-car transportation enjoyed a successful year, and in December of 1907 a twofold program was announced with regard to the railroad. One part had to do with improvements at the beginning of the line. Rails were to be lengthened out Steamboat Wharf as far as the freight house, and the station was to be moved to a point beyond the catboat basin. This would permit visitors debarking from the boat to board the train immediately. The second part had to do with new rolling stock. There were to be two vehicles, petroleum-powered like the *Siasconset* but looking very much like buses on tracks, with hooded engine at the front and seats for passengers behind the driver's closed cab. The work at Steamboat Wharf was accomplished early in June, as planned, but the proposed conveyances failed to appear. Replacing them was a single car, which had been manufactured at the Mack Brothers plant in Allentown, Pennsylvania, and it resembled a trolley more than a bus. The newcomer was the fulfillment of Thomas G. Macy's dream of more than a dozen years earlier, of expanding the horse-car system to Brant Point to include an interurban type of rail coach to Siasconset.

The new rail car arrived on 28 July. Its name, *Nantucket*, was emblazoned on an elliptical plate on each side. It was considerably larger than the *Siasconset*, 25 feet long and weighing 12 tons, with a capacity of twenty-three persons. It was a handsome design, with six slightly arched windows on either flank, entrances front and back, the ends curved, one an open observation platform, and having a clerestory over the center aisle tapered at the extremities. Its best performance was given on 16 August, when it pulled the old passenger coach loaded with fifty persons. The added weight delayed its regular trip time of a half hour by less than five minutes. It seemed too good for the Nantucket railroad, this ninety-horsepower, sleek rail monarch, and troubles soon overtook it. A journal box overheated from friction on the afternoon of its arrival, and the car was laid up for the rest of the day. On 2 August it derailed on an open switch at the foot of Main Street. The same thing happened on 17 August. On 2 September the car was put out of commission by an accident to the shaft and transmission gears, necessitating new parts sent from the factory. On 13 and 14 September it was again

out of service, no explanation given. After two months of bucking the uneven rails on Nantucket the vehicle showed signs of breaking down altogether. The manufacturer asked for its return, and on 8 October the namesake of the town, county, and island left on board the schooner *Helen* after a short and hectic career.

In spite of the mechanical faults that developed in the *Nantucket*, the Macy Syndicate kept Siasconset linked to town during its two years of management of the Nantucket Central Railroad. The village was holding up its end as island host in hotel, guest-house, and cottage accommodations. A new name had appeared in the latter industry, that of R. E. Burgess, who had ten furnished cottages to rent in Evergreen Park in 1907. The Siasconset Casino was open every weekday night, offering moving pictures from 7:00 to 11:00 o'clock. The bill included "Illustrated Songs" by J. W. Blair, a popular tenor from New York. Programs changed every Wednesday and Saturday, and seats were 10¢.

Back in Nantucket Town there were altogether four exotic shops in 1907. In addition to the established Jacob Abajian's Oriental Bazaar and A. D. Zorab's shop on Centre Street, two Japanese stores opened on Main Street. Also that summer, W. B. Brown conducted a skating rink in Progress Hall on South Water Street.

The Sea Cliff Inn, which had been owned and operated by the Nantucket Company of Providence over the past five years, again changed hands in May of 1907. The new owners were Clifford Folger and W. D. Carpenter. Folger, who had become manager of the bathing beach in 1904, hailed from South Framingham, Massachusetts, and served as the Sea Cliff's treasurer. Carpenter had managed the Ocean House over the past seven years, which post he kept along with a similar one at the Sea Cliff. The new feature publicized at the Sea Cliff Inn during the first season following the changeover was its private kindergarten, conducted by trained personnel with special equipment, largely outdoors and on the beach.

Mrs. William Chauncey Smith, who in the preceding chapter was mentioned as running

100 *The David Nevins summer house (1895), Cliff Road, later Nevins Mansion (modern photograph).*

Franklin Cottage for guests in 1889 and who had undertaken Oneonta as well in 1903, had another house on the cliff in 1908—Nevins Mansion at 11 Cliff Road, originally the summer home of David Nevins, built in 1895. Mrs. Smith claimed that it was "The finest estate and the best location on the island, with a magnificent ocean view, and every convenience for the comfort of guests. . . . Large commodious dining-room running the length of the house . . . cuisine unexcelled. Spacious lawns on the west, with fine view of the old town. Grounds beautifully terraced on the east. Rooms in suites of two and three with private baths. Open from May until late Autumn." In 1910 Mrs. Smith opened "The New Hill Crest . . . on the crown of the hill on Cliff Road."

Other changes in the boardinghouse business of the time included: Mrs. J. Butler Folger, wife of the man who assumed management of the Holiday Inn in 1905 and herself the recent manager, opened her own Folger Inn, which, if in her husband's home, was at 150 Main Street; Mrs. Calvin Handy, who with her husband had run the Central House (Swain's Boardinghouse) on Centre Street at the turn of the century and then the Waverly House on Gay Street, undertook to conduct her own boardinghouse at the corner of Broad and North Water streets, lately that of Mrs. George G. Fish. Mrs. William H. Arnold managed the house at 3 Broad Street, and Mrs. Eleanor E. Brown offered rooms at 24 Broad. Mrs. Henry W. Brown was at 10 North Water, and Lydia B. Gardner let rooms at 2 Chester Street. Other boardinghouses included those of Mrs. Mary A. Ames, 4 Fair; Mrs. A. L. Fisher, 40 Centre; Thomas D. Herrick, North Liberty; A. G. Harvey, 6 Step Lane;

Frank C. Lamb, 17 Quince; Mary Waitt, 38 Pearl; Mrs. W. H. H. Smith, 20 Federal; and J. B. Staples at Quanato Terrace, 1 Quanato Court off Orange Street. Familiar to us from former references are Mrs. H. L. Riddell's Gull Island House; Mrs. Ellen B. Harps's 32 Cliff Road, the Misses Ide's Cliff Cottage, 21 Cliff Road; Mrs. Mary E. Palmer's Palmer House, 20 Union Street; Dr. Mann's Rest Haven, 9 Pine Street; and Imogene F. Orr's Orr's Cottage on Main Street in Siasconset. Mrs. Orr had purchased the Atlantic House from Mrs. Eliza Chadwick in May of 1901, involving a mortgage of $3,500. In May of 1909 she lost the property through default of payments to Mrs. Chadwick's heirs, one of which was Frederick S. Chadwick, who had operated the Atlantic House during the early 1890s. In the fall of 1910 the heirs sold the old caravanserai to Louise Streeter Warren of Detroit for $4,000. The inn continued in business for a few years longer under its former name, the Atlantic House.

The names of a few establishments that more properly were boardinghouses were scattered among the list of legitimate hotels given in the Nantucket directory for 1909. Those named, with their proprietors (some of which are supplied from other sources), were: Beach House, G. Herbert Brinton, Siasconset; Cathcart House, Wallace Cathcart, 30 Pearl; Cottage Content, Mrs. W. B. Gurley, 4 Easton; Easton House, Mrs. Frank B. Mayhew, 17 North Water; The Hillside, Miss M. C. Townsend, 8 Gay; Holiday Inn, M. M. Harris, 31 Orange; Nesbitt House, Mrs. Mary B. Nesbitt, 23 Broad; Ocean House, W. D. Carpenter, 29 Broad; Ocean View House, Robert W. Powers, Siasconset; Pitman House, T. C. Pitman, 46 Centre; Point Breeze Hotel, Bracey Curtis, Easton; Roberts House, John Roberts, Pearl at Centre; Sea Cliff Inn, W. D. Carpenter, Cliff Road; Springfield House, Willard H. Gooch, 19 North Water; The Gables, Mrs. Harriet M. Hooper, 23 Broad; Veranda House, John M. Winslow, Step Lane; Wauwinet House, James A. Backus, Wauwinet; and Waverly House, Manuel J. Sylvia, 10 Gay Street. In 1908 the Pitman House acquired a "commodious piazza," and the Ocean House had

101 *Mrs. G. G. Fish's boardinghouse, at the east corner of Broad and North Water Streets.*

102 *Cottage Content, Easton Street.*

a 20-by-40-foot addition built on the dining room and the annex remodeled. An unpleasant incident of the year was that twenty minutes before a proposed auction at the Springfield House on 3 September, the sheriff placed an attachment on the property against a $500 debt for paint and labor recently incurred.

An out-of-town loss was the burning of the Cedar Beach House on Coatue, which occurred on 28 August 1908. The Cedar Beach House had been in operation for twenty-five years, and it had closed for the season only a few days before. Those who went out to examine the ruins found a man's newly made footprints on an otherwise smooth beach, leading one to suspect a willful act of arson.

The railroad played a prominent role in island affairs in 1909. The breakdown of the *Nantucket* had discouraged the Macys, and in May of that year they were dismissed from the picture by the United States Circuit Court of Boston, which appointed a receiver for the company. It had failed to pay interest on its $17,000 bonds, and it had $18,000 in stocks outstanding and other debts amounting to $13,000. For a while the matter of train service looked hopeless, but a corporation made up of men from New York and New Jersey purchased the line. Ira L. McCord was president, Ten Eyck R. Beardsley, vice president, Edgar J. Hollister, treasurer and Julian F. Fleetwood superintendent on the island. They dropped the "Central" from the name, reverting to the original, Nantucket Railroad. The first major undertaking was replacing the old track with new and heavier rails and ties. The process began with the procuring of materials and workmen, and early on the morning of 22 June a select group was hauled by Engine No. 1 to the east end of the line, where a 50-foot section of the old tracks was taken up. Fifteen new sleepers were set in place and two shining rails laid on them. Capt. John Killen drove the first spike, of gold, for one rail, and G. H. Brinton of the Beach House drove a second, of silver, for the other. The laborers then took up the task and by nightfall had replaced a half mile.

A month after the event at Siasconset, on 23 July to be exact, the work train was starting out from Nantucket when the engine and tender suddenly jumped the track, and the former keeled over on its side at South Beach. Engineer Hendricks showed quick presence of mind by throwing the throttle before he leaped from the cab. The cause of the accident was failure to bolt the fishplates holding the rails together. The same negligence was found elsewhere and remedied. The locomotive was hoisted back on the track

and the fire started; but it was blowing steam and required the services of a party of boilermakers from New Bedford to put it in serviceable condition. The summer was well advanced before railway service was provided. The closed passenger coach of 1885 was renovated and painted a brilliant carmine, and on the new and heavier rails it provided the smoothest ride to date.

But, as so often happens when things are running smoothly, a change was in the offing. For the Nantucket Railroad it was the acquisition of new rolling stock. It consisted of two cars manufactured in Wilmington, Delaware. One was a combination baggage and passenger coach and the other was entirely for passengers. They were painted a light vermilion. Their mobility was provided by a little bogie engine made in Richmond, Virginia. It was out of scale with the carriages and

103 *The Pitman House, with its "commodious piazza" of 1908.*

104 *The wreck at South Beach, 23 July 1909.*

looked like a goat hitched to an elegant landau intended for horses. Although at the time of its arrival the critics managed to squeeze out a compliment for the first engine made expressly for the island system, after a while they began referring to it as the "toy locomotive." The trial run was made on 2 June 1910, and the train went into operation five days later. It left Nantucket at 11:00 a.m., 1:15, and 7:15 p.m., and it came back with departures from Siasconset at 5:45 a.m., 12:00 noon, and 5:00 p.m. daily. Fare was 30¢ one way or 60¢ round trip. On the whole, service was excellent.

The noteworthy event of the summer of 1910 was not on the route of the railroad but at Wauwinet. The community at the Haulover had imitated Siasconset in the addition of new summer features, even to attracting thespians. It had its own casino, a building that had been moved near to the hotel and set on the site of the later casino (of 1934). There were a complete stage and dressing rooms. The event considered was held here on the evening of 9 July. Following the pattern of entertainments in the Siasconset Casino, it was a vaudeville, presided over by Tom Bell. The difference lay in its being impromptu, and the performers were guests. The Wauwinet Casino was crowded "to the doors, even standing room being at a premium. . . . Promptly at eight o'clock Miss Mary Horne opened the performance . . . [with a] piano solo, Tschaikowsky's Barcarolle 'June, which she played with a delicacy and sympathy that won for her . . . many compliments. . . . She was followed by J. W. Peddie, with two baritone solos, after which Messrs. Keep and Stackpole perpetrated an act of 'Refined Repartee,' funny enough to justify their immediate engagement on the Metropolitan stage." A skit by "The Three Morleys" depicted them as a lion and two hunters in Africa, in which cameras, guns, and morphine were employed to capture the king of beasts. Vocal numbers included plantation songs by Al Reeves, accompanying himself on the guitar; the "Fearless Quartette," composed of Messrs. Keep, Stackpole, Bell, and Peddie; and then Ruth Waring sang "Florian's Song" and "When Love Is Kind," the last an old Irish melody. Dances in costume consisted of a sailor's hornpipe by Ruth Waring and Mary Horner and a barn dance by Carolyn Chester and Esther Waring, who also performed a Spanish dance. "The Human Bird" was a number by Mr. Briggs in which he whistled solos from Italian operas. Tom Bell recited several childhood verses by Charles Follen Adams and Eugene Field, then imitated a Georgian preacher of color sermonizing on "The Ship of Faith." The entertainment concluded with a duet on violin and guitar by Dudley and Reeves. At 9:45 the floor was cleared for general dancing.

For a good cross section of visitors' social amusements on Nantucket during the summer of 1910, a selection from the "Here and There" column in the *Inquirer and Mirror* for 23 July supplies the following items:

"Ball game this Saturday afternoon on the new grounds at the rear of the Springfield House. Oak Bluffs will cross bats with Nantucket.

"An exciting game of baseball was played at the Fair Grounds on Monday afternoon between the 'Nantuckets' and the 'Independents.'

"The Sea Cliff and Point Breeze hotels are holding weekly dances this season for the entertainment of their guests—the former every Saturday evening and the latter every Wednesday evening.

"For a bit to eat, don't forget to visit the Chanticleer, Siasconset." The last was a paid advertisement, such as occasionally was inserted in the column. The "Independents" mentioned in the second item was a baseball team made up of islanders while the "Nantuckets" were summer visitors.

The bandstand on Main Street was the butt of comments again this season by reason of its shabby appearance. A couple of the comments ran: "The band-stand is certainly a mighty poor specimen of Nantucket architecture. . . ." and "Something ought to be done towards building a structure that will be a credit to the town and not an eye-sore." Concerts began on 1 August. Two weeks later there was a general feeling against them because of the damages caused. Listeners leaning against the buildings had broken two panes of glass, one in Burgess's Market and the other in Wing's Store. At this same time the open-air song services, formerly held on the grounds of the Congregational Church, were transferred to the bandstand following Sunday afternoon

105 *Engine No. 2 and the new cars of 1910, on the Goose Pond causeway.*

concerts. On 17 August a special program of Civil War songs was given for surviving members of the Grand Army of the Republic. The veterans solved the eyesore problem by covering the pavilion entirely with flags and bunting.

The building adjoining the Roberts House on Centre Street, which had been built in 1850 as a meeting house for a group of dissident Friends and later served as a Baptist church, was acquired by John Roberts as an addition to his boardinghouse. He engaged Holmes and Pease to convert it into a dining hall during the spring of 1911. In noting the changes, the newspaper ended with the statement: "The building has now lost all semblance to a church, with a piazza in front and a kitchen at the rear."

New names in the hostelry line appearing in 1911 include those of the Widgeon Point House on Hummock Pond and the Garden Tea Room (the Old Homestead Garden) at 22 Union Street.

The old iron posts for gaslights, long unused because of the newer hanging electric street lights, were removed from Main Street and taken over to adorn the village of Siasconset.

Entertainments were being presented near the waterfront in Nantucket. The Dreamland was offering four reels per show. At the beginning of the season the two features on the same bill were "Her Mother's Wedding Gown" and "The Return of Iowa-Wa," the latter described as "a fine Indian picture." Vaudeville was included on Wednesday evenings, when the admission charge was 20¢.

A few blocks away, the Athletic Club was the scene of a variety of diversions. On 27 July and again on 2 September, George Spink, a theatre person staying with his wife at the Sea Cliff Inn, presented a "musical entertainment in two acts, 'A Japanese Romance,' for the benefit of the Nantucket Hospital fund." The Nantucket Cottage Hospital (to be located on West Chester Street) had just been organized at the beginning of June. The Spink production had for leading characters Omona San (a Japanese damsel played by Ellen Tate Spink) and James Bowen (a young American businessman, Kenneth S. Webb), who at the opening of the play are about to celebrate their

wedding. Three of Bowen's friends appear bringing the news that he must come away with them on urgent commercial matters. As a Japanese wedding takes three days to complete, the bride's father is incensed. He dismisses the groom-to-be and forbids his daughter to see him. The young couple plans to elope, but the plot is apprehended by the Japanese parent. The rather unromantic ending to A Japanese Romance is that the father becomes reconciled upon hearing that Bowen has made a million dollars on the current venture. He decides to permit the nuptials and accompany the couple to America. There were twelve title characters and a similar number of atmosphere supporters in the cast. Two songs made a hit, these being "Charge It Up to Profit and Loss" and the toast, "To the Country and the Girl I Love."

The annual masquerade of the Athletic Club, after having been postponed for three days because of inclement weather, took place on the evening of 31 July. Over 250 persons participated.

The 'Sconset Carnival occurred during the first week of August in 1911. On Monday (which fell on 31 July) the contest for electing a king and queen came to a close with Mrs. Joseph Jefferson receiving 14,000 votes for queen and Frank Gillmore over 7,000 for reigning monarch. As soon as the results were announced, "the crowd went to the hotel of the queen-elect, . . . and . . . her Majesty was taken in an improvised sedan chair to the king's abode, where he awaited and welcomed his consort in a delightfully happy vein, and made his subjects at home on the spacious lawn. Cottagers, storekeepers and the hotel people . . . made the old village and its suburbs gay with decorations." The five days of activities consisted of tennis matches every morning; a croquet tournament on Tuesday afternoon and push pool and bridge in the evening; a baby parade Wednesday afternoon and a meeting of the royal court and a parade of floats at night; a kite-flying congress on Bunker Hill Thursday afternoon and a bowling contest in the evening; a dog parade Friday afternoon and a children's masquerade and the coronation ceremony Friday evening; on Saturday, water sports during the late morning, a golf tournament in the afternoon, and a parade of decorated bicycles, wagons, and carriages at night. There were prizes for all events.

A good deal of summer people's amusement is derived from watching each other. The following three excerpts are offered as samples of occurrences during the season of 1911:

"A woman and a large tiger cat furnished amusement to bystanders on the wharf Monday noon [26 June]. The cat somehow escaped from a basket on the woman's arm, and, scratching and spitting, was perched high on a pile of furniture, completely ignoring his mistress' appeals to come down and get into the basket again, that she might go aboard the boat. Finding pussy stubborn, however, the lady mounted the back of a chair and pulled her pet down from its high perch, but it seemed to object to being jammed into the basket again. Gentle slaps were followed by some not quite so gentle, and the cat finally received a good sound spanking before it was landed in the basket and the cover tied on. And through it all not a soul made any attempt to assist the befuddled woman—probably through fear of pussy's claws—but lots of people looked on and enjoyed the scene."

"An interesting sight Wednesday noon [30 August] was the couple which hastened down the plank walk onto the wharf, the woman carrying an umbrella over her head, while behind her came 'hubby,' in one hand holding a chain to which was attached a fractious dog, while with the other hand he was endeavoring to hold up his wife's skirts. And worst of all, the water was dripping from his wife's umbrella right down the back of his neck. We know the water 'tickled,' from the way he kept screwing up his face, that he was between two fires—if he raised one hand the pup would escape and if he raised the other his wife's petticoats would trail in the mud—so the poor fellow set his teeth and bore the ordeal like a martyr."

"Charles W. Barrett took his last salt water bath of the season on Wednesday [20 September], falling overboard from the pier at the cliff beach. After donning a suit of dry clothing he rinsed out his trousers and turned them through the "wringer' at the bath house. To his consternation he then discovered that his watch had been left in one of the pockets and had gone through the machine—to its sorrow."

Improvements to Nantucket hostelries in preparation for the 1912 season included new fences and an extension to the Beach House Farm at Polpis made by Charles H. Robinson in September of 1911; an addition to the Sea Cliff Inn, the work of Holmes and Pease over the winter; and the installation of a new electric-lighting plant in the Sea Cliff during the spring. W. D. Carpenter having acquired the Pitman property, on the south corner of Centre and Gay Street, in May had a third story added to the house to increase its capacity to twenty-one guest rooms, and it afterwards was used as an annex to the Ocean House.

The agreeable summer atmosphere on Nantucket was due no more to the resident proprietors of the hotels and guest houses than to the seasonal help hired from abroad. Many of them were here on a sort of paid vacation. Waitresses at the Beach House in Siasconset were students at Mount Holyoke College. Those at the Sea Cliff Inn were young teachers from various places. On 20 July 1912 the "guests" of the Sea Cliff "crossed bats" with the "employees" (probably *not* the waitresses) in baseball, and the former won with a score of 16 to 8. On 1 August 1912 the help of the Point Breeze was treated by proprietor Bracey Curtis to its annual evening sail up the harbor on catboat *Lillian.*

In the spring of 1912, "Driftwood," built next to the old lighthouse on Brant Point for Isabel Morris in the mid 1890s and since 1898 the residence of Henry Bigelow Williams, was sold. The building in the "Queen Anne" style contained a spacious living room and other family rooms and glass-enclosed verandas downstairs, plus eight masters' and four servants' chambers above, and there was a large stable on the three-acre premises. The property was purchased and became a guest house run by H. C. Gardner and family of West Medford. The old name was kept.

106 *The Sea Cliff Inn, showing additions of 1911.*

Not far away, this same year, Mrs. Charles Winslow (perhaps the same who had run "The Winslow" on Pearl Street) took over the former Olympian Cottage on North Beach Street, calling it Ye Olde Olympia Inn. She offered rooms and/or board consisting of "the best of home cooking."

At this period, the gasoline-powered vehicle was back in the news, gaining a toehold in island affairs foreshadowing the problem of automobile traffic that was still a few years off. In 1912 a gasoline-powered chemical fire engine was brought to Nantucket on trial. The dread of fire was an uppermost consideration here, and any instrument that could more readily combat it was highly desirable. The fire engine was manufactured by the Knox Automobile Company in Springfield and carried two chemical tanks, ladders, and 200 feet of hose. It was priced at $5,900, and as its trial

107 *View of Brant Point from the end of Old North Wharf. Driftwood is in the center (above man in boat). Cottage Content is the next large house to the left.*

proved satisfactory, the machine was purchased. Its acquisition meant that every Nantucket taxpayer owned a share in a horseless carriage.

The *Siasconset*, otherwise known as "The Bug," crawled back in the limelight after having been overhauled in a garage on Martha's Vineyard during the fall of 1911. In May of the following year it was put into full-time service on the Nantucket railroad while Engine No. 2 was being refurbished. Engine No. 1 was completely out of the picture, and it is said to have been buried at the junction of Washington and Fayette streets. At the opening of the 1912 season a local mechanic, Jeremiah W. Diamond, undertook to put the miniature trolley in shape for another year. Diamond worked on its mechanism for three weeks; then he invited three friends to accompany him on what turned out to be a record-breaking run. "All the way out the little car fairly flew over the rails." It chugged up Tom Nevers Head and skimmed down to Low Beach; and when "Diamond thought it time to shut off the power, in order to run up gracefully to the 'Sconset terminal, . . . he found the brakes would not work and he could not stop the engine." The only alternative was to jump into the beach sand. His friends preceded him, and "Diamond was the last, for he stuck to his post like the Jim Bledso of old, and not until he saw death staring him in the face did he desert 'The Bug' and make his famous leap for life, which the eyewitnesses stoutly maintain was most thrilling." The next moment "The Bug" squashed itself to death against the rear of the locomotive standing on the track. The remains were gathered up, and two days later they were brought to the edge of town and interred in the Clay Pits west of Orange Street. Conductor William I. Sandsbury read a poetic memorial composed by himself.

108 *The chemical fire engine of 1912.*

109 *Clinton S. Folger's "Horsemobile" leaving town for Siasconset, 1913.*

The third automobile item has even less to do, directly, with the summer life on Nantucket than the other two. It concerns a five-passenger Overland brought by its owner, Clinton S. Folger, in the fall of 1913. Folger ran a hack service on the island and had a contract with the government for delivering and collecting the Siasconset mail. Folger favored the summertime exclusion of cars and brought his vehicle over after season. He and the selectmen differed on the proposition of driving cars after season, and Folger was given two tickets for driving in Nantucket Town. He then proceeded to accrue wide publicity by driving his "Horsemobile." With signs on front and rear of the Overland lettered "U.S. MAIL," the car was attached to a dumpcart pulled by a pair of horses and thus was taken from its garage to the post office, and thence to the edge of town. Here it was unfastened and proceeded under its own power to Siasconset and back. The team and dumpcart waited to tow the mail car to the post office and then home. Folger's defiance of the court dragged on into 1914 and ended before the Committee on Towns at the State House in Boston, where he was shown his signature on an automobile-exclusion petition circulated in 1912. He had no case. However, several times over the next four months Folger used his car to rush doctors to emergency calls, which seemed to give him status on par with the fire engine. Otherwise he had to obey the Special Act of Excluding Automobiles, which came to a vote of the town on 18 June, and passed with a 142 plurality out of 610 votes cast.

A business and residential directory gotten out for Nantucket in 1914 included a list of the hotels and their locations and proprietors:

Beach House, Siasconset
J. Herbert Brinton

Cathcart House, 30 Pearl St.
Wallace Cathcart

Colonial Inn, 17 No. Water St.
Mrs. H. S. Ross

The Hillside, 8 Gay St.
Brainerd T. Jenkins

Nesbitt House, 19 Broad St.
Mary B. Nesbitt

New Springfield, 19 N. Water St.
Edward S. Tirrell

Ocean House, 29 Broad St.
W. D. Carpenter

Ocean View House, Siasconset
Robert M. Powers

Phillips House, Siasconset
H. R. Phillips

Pioneer Inn, Madaket

Pitman House, 46 Centre Street
T. C. Pitman

Point Breeze Hotel, Easton Street
Bracey Curtis

Roberts House, Pearl corner Centre Sts.
Mrs. John Roberts

Sconset Cottage Club, Ocean Ave.
Siasconset, Isaac Hills

Sea Cliff Inn, Cliff Rd.
Clifford Folger

Squam House, Squam Head
Mrs. H. E. Dunbar

The Gables (rooms), 23 Broad St.
Mrs. G. H. Hooper

Veranda House, Step Lane
John M. Winslow

Wauwinet House, Wauwinet
James A. Backus

Waverly House, 10 Gay St.
M. J. Sylvia

Boardinghouses listed (omitting those repeated from the hotel roster) were:

Mrs. Mary A. Ames
4 Fair St.

Mrs. William D. Appleton
6 Lyons St.

Mrs. Eva B. Chase
(rooms, 21 Union St.)

Cliff Cottage (the Misses Ide)
21 Cliff Rd.

George A. Dunham
6 School St.

Timothy M. Dunham
64 Union St.

Arthur B. Enas (rooms)
7 Union St.

Mrs. A. L. Fisher (rooms)
40 Centre St.

Lizzie A. Folger
6 Darling St.

Lydia B. Gardner (rooms)
2 Chester St.

Gull Island House
Gull Island, rear of 82 Centre St.
Mrs. H. L. Riddell

Mrs. Calvert Handy
26 No. Water St., Worth House

Adelaide Hersey (rooms)
20 Pearl St.

Hillcrest Cottage
10 Cliff Rd.
Mrs. William Chauncey Smith

Mrs. Frank C. Lamb
17 Quince St.

Mrs. Anna Mooers (rooms)
1 N. Water and 24 Broad St.

Palmer House
20 Union St., Mary E. Palmer

Quanato Terrace
1 Quanato Ct., J. B. Staples

Rest Haven, Dr. Mann
Pine at Summer St.

Mrs. W. H. H. Smith (rooms)
20 Federal St.

Mrs. Kate Terry (rooms)
48 Centre St.

The directory listings are not complete. Charles H. Robinson's Holiday Inn, formerly the American House, north corner of Orange Street and Martins Lane, must have been in operation in 1914. The owner had purchased the Josiah G. Macy house, next door north, in 1911, and connected it to the hotel proper. Following Robin-

110 *The Ships Inn, Fair Street.*

son's death, his executor, William F. Codd, acquired the complex. After owning it for three years, he sold it to William F. Macy in 1920, with restrictions that the hotel building be demolished before 1 April 1921, and only a private dwelling could be erected on the land. Other establishments known to have been running during this period, but missing on the 1914 directory list, include: Atlantic House, Siasconset; Swain's Inn, Centre at Lily Street: Cottage Content, W. B. Gurley, Brant Point; Saratoga Cottage, T. D. Herrick, North Liberty Street; Mrs. William A. Arnold, 3 Broad Street; Mrs. Eleanor E. Brown, 24 (?) Broad Street; Ella B. Harps, 32 Cliff Road; Mary Waitt, 30 Pearl Street; A. G. Harvey, 6 Step Lane; Drift-

wood, H. C. Gardner, Brant Point; and Ye Olde Olympia Inn, Mrs. Charles Winslow, North Beach Street, all of which have been mentioned previously. Others to materialize over the next three years were: Clisby House (1916), Siasconset; the Weeweeder Inn (1915), Surfside; Mrs. A. B. Ayers (1916), 73 Main Street; M. C. Bacall's Ships Inn (1916), in the old Capt. Obed Starbuck house (1831), Fair Street at Mott's Lane; Tolovana (1916); Mrs. H. D. Hartley's The Moorings (1916); and Martha Allie Coffin's The White Elephant (1916), on Easton Street.

The season of 1914 was not a good one by general consent. By mid-July business was so poor at the Atlantic House that the proprietress seriously considered closing its doors. One would expect Siasconset to have had the best patronage on the island. Besides providing places for the sports and amusements already discussed, special events of the summer were the "'Sconset Follies," which opened on 14 August, and the "'Sconset Midway" of 20 August. That the lag was general is indicated by the Steamboat Company's proceeds for the months of July and August, which were short by about $12,000 in comparison to what they had been for the same two months in 1913.

The year 1915 got off to a dismal start when one of the most severe northeast storms in Nantucket's history hit the island on 13 January. The tide rose to its peak at 9:25 a.m., completely submerging the wharves, with the water advancing as far as the rear of Red Men's Hall (Dreamland Theatre). The railroad line in the vicinity was badly damaged, the turntable on Easy Street ruined to the point of having to be removed.

With adversity prompting Nantucketers to take stock of the situation, one feature they set upon to improve for the coming season was the bandstand on Main Street. It was larger than its predecessor and built by B. Chester Pease, painted by H. Paddack and Co., and wired for five 300-watt bulbs by Karl Brookseifer, the materials provided by the electric company. Contributions were solicited for the August concerts, and the Worcester Brass Band was engaged for these musical entertainments.

That history repeats itself is illustrated by the real-estate development attempted at Tom Nevers Head, recalling that at Surfside a third of a century earlier. The speculation to the east already had been projected in the fall of 1910, when the Nantucket Railroad considered putting a way station there and purchasing a second engine; but no justification for the expenditures materialized. At the beginning of 1916 the tract at Tom Nevers Head was sold by Edgar J. Hollister to Franklin E. Smith of Boston and Edgar C. Linn of Brookline, and they incorporated as the Nantucket Land Trust. The Tom Nevers Head tract contained more than 2,000 acres, with a frontage of about two miles on the south shore, extending westward from Tom Nevers Pond and having a northern boundary of more than two miles on Milestone Road. The railroad tracks cut across it diagonally, dividing it into two nearly equal parts, and a small depot was built not far from the north side. The building measured about 12 by 24 feet and sheltered a waiting room, baggage

111 *The White Elephant from the harbor, 1918.*

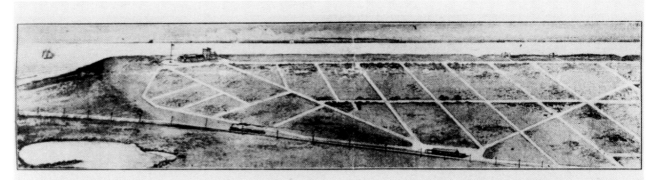

BIRDS-EYE VIEW OF "TOM NEVERS HEAD" TRACT—NEW "TOM NEVERS LODGE" ON THE HEADLAND.

112 *Perspective sketch of Tom Nevers Head tract layout, 1916.*

compartment, and ticket office. On the track side was a covered platform 44 feet long by 10 wide, with a sign beneath the eaves at either end inscribed "TOM NEVERS HEAD."

The street layout at Tom Nevers Head was more interesting than the monotonous grid at Surfside, in large measure due to the oblique cut made by the railroad tracks. Two avenues radiated from the depot to the southeast and southwest corners, with other streets parallel or perpendicular to the shore or the two radial lanes. On the "Head" itself, or southeast corner, was built Tom Nevers Lodge, an irregular pile in the Chicago or "Prairie" style of architecture, composed of a five-story square tower covered with a pyramid roof, encircled by an outside stairway to balconies at each level, and at the base were low wings reaching out in several directions, with gable roofs and simple open galleries, all with overhanging eaves. Featured were a rustic lounge and the "Lodge Cafe" with cobblestone ("peanut-brittle") fireplaces; and there were a "cozy writing room," guest rooms with hot and cold running water, and bathrooms, all lighted by electricity. Lewis Rice was manager. The advertising characterized it as 60 feet above sea level, twenty minutes by train from Nantucket, and close enough to take advantage of all the offerings of Siasconset.

Building lots in the Tom Nevers Head tract were disposed of through auction held each after-

noon at 2:30 from 19 through 22 July, to which free transportation was provided on the 1:15 train with return at 5:10 in the evening. In August special prices were set, ranging from $50 to $100 for cottage lots 50 by 100 feet in size. As at Surfside, no private summer houses appeared to keep company with the depot and lodge erected by the entrepreneurs themselves.

Whether from remembrance of the former hotel at Surfside or current success of Tom Nevers Lodge, in 1916 J. Butler Folger announced the addition of a "hotel" to his year-old Weeweeder Inn on the south shore. It stood on a twenty-five-acre parcel of land near Miacomet Pond inherited from Folger's parents in 1896. The Weeweeder Inn was a typical low-lying bungalow type, one-storied, hip-roofed, with a deep porch all around, its posts slender, square, and plain, and the rafters exposed. It was raised a couple of feet off the ground. No "hotel" joined it, but a structure similar to the original was constructed. The Weeweeder Inn was listed in telephone directories up to 1931.

Following the 1916 season, a Boston newspaper printed what purported to be a fire notice that had been posted in a Nantucket Hotel, though which one was not revealed. It instructed the person detecting a fire to: "Notify the desk at once. He will be asleep in room 72, just back of the office. Notify the proprietor. Notify the night watchman. He will be asleep as usual, somewhere on the premises. Return to your room and throw your trunk and clothes out of the window and you can repack them on the piazza or in the back yard. Now try to discover where the fire is. In ninety-nine times out of a hundred it will be some neighboring building; not ours. Don't forget to shriek all the time. It will be very soothing to nervous people."

In the fall of 1916 the war that had been raging in Europe for more than two years came the closest to the North American continent. The United States was neutral, and on 7 October the German submarine V-53 arrived at Newport, where the commander paid his respects to the admiral in charge of the United States naval station. The following morning the V-53 appeared in the vicinity of the Nantucket Shoal lightship, stationed 43 miles south of the island at the turning point for ships crossing the Atlantic. Here the American steamer *Kansas* was held up and her papers examined, after which she was allowed to proceed unmolested. But the British ships *Strathdene, West Point,* and *Stephano* and the Dutch freighter *Bloomersdijk* and Norwegian freighter *Christian Knudsen* were sunk. Each was given due warning, so that all on board could take to the lifeboats. The survivors were picked up by a destroyer summoned by radio from Newport, or made it to the Nantucket lightship. During the attack a German missile struck within 100 feet of the American lightship.

In the spring of 1917 Nantucket looked optimistically at the coming season. "Sure!" declared the 24 March issue of the *Inquirer and Mirror*: "The Nantucket Railroad will be operated, the hotels will be open as usual—and the people will come to Nantucket just the same. A little thing like an international war will not upset the regular order of things down here." But on 6 May the United States declared war on the Central Powers. The European holocaust thus was brought directly to every American family. There was the draft, and those who went to fight and die; there was Red Cross work for those who strove to render comfort and relief; and for all it was a road of scrimp and blood and toil. Vacationing was taboo. Nantucket's chief industry was stifled. Its summer was a fizzle.

The nation's chief executive, President Woodrow Wilson, and the First Lady, on a semi-vacation aboard the yacht *Mayflower*, visited Nantucket on 13 September. They came to see their daughter who had a cottage in Siasconset. The train had been put to rest for the winter, and during the carriage ride to the village Mr. Wilson remarked that it was good to be behind a horse once more. The slow pace on the island did not deter many of her sons from being rushed through induction into the army at Barnstable next day.

113 *The railroad depot at Tom Nevers Head, 1916.*

"TOM NEVERS LODGE"

Constructed for the interests of the community. Has limited number of Rooms, Hot and Cold Water, Electric Lights.
Rest Piazzas and Attractive Cafe under refined and capable supervision. Charming view. Quiet recreation.

114 *Elevation drawing of the Tom Nevers Lodge, 1916.*

Nantucket's great loss of the year was the old Alley Hotel, for a long time the main pavilion of the Springfield House, lately Annex No. 1. In February the town had voted to purchase the property at North Water and Chester streets and have the building removed, as it was considered an obstacle to traffic at the corner. The owner was Edwin S. Tirrell, manager of the Springfield since 1911. The property sold for $3,500. Early in October the building proper went at auction to Dr. E. B. Coleman for $95, and in the middle of May of the following year the land left over from the widening of the street was knocked down at another auction to Dr. J. S. Grouard for $1,000. On 15 September 1917 Tirrell leased the North Water Street portion of the Springfield to the government for a navy barracks, in conjunction with which also was taken over the Harbor View on Salom Street. They also were referred to as a dispensary, denoting medical usage. It is said that the buildings were badly treated. Edwin S. Tirrell sold the New Springfield and adjoining dining-room house to Harriet S. (Mrs. Charles) Ross in 1920, and she and her husband ran them as Crest Hall along with their own boardinghouse adjoining on the south. Tirrell disposed of the remaining Springfield building on the corner of North Water and Easton Street to Florence H. Breithut at the end of 1921. It retained part of its former name, going by the title of Springfield Lodge.

Nantucket's venerable inn was hardly uprooted before another major loss to summer operations was rumored. It concerned the railroad. The 1917 Christmas Souvenir Number of the *Inquirer and Mirror* contained an article on the history of the line, illustrated with pictures of the various trains. There also was a reprint of the poem "Lament for a Favorite Locomotive," originally published in the 9 September 1893 issue, when the *Dionis* was stranded at Siasconset all winter. In the news columns was another story on the railroad, this one divulging the imminent danger of its loss. The owners had been losing money in running it, because of poor patronage, whereas the iron in it had risen greatly in value due to wartime manufacturing. The course that they would take seemed inevitable. A side issue came forward as a consequence. Smith and Linn, owners of the Nantucket Land Trust, faced with the cessation of rail service, filed a bill in the Massachusetts Legislature on 11 January 1918, asking for the repeal of the Automobile Exclusion Act,

115 *Weeweeder Inn, Surfside.*

so that they might use cars to get prospective buyers to the Tom Nevers Head tract. By coincidence, the local stockholders of the Nantucket Railroad met on the same day. It was at the depot on Steamboat Wharf. The building was boarded up for the winter, and the people huddled in the most sheltered spot they could find on the porch. William I. Sandsbury read a report stating that the directors had authorized the sale of the railroad on 3 January, and the act needed the ratification of the stockholders. The benumbed group represented only sixty-two shares, which was below a quorum, and the meeting adjourned until 10 April.

"Junking of the 'Sconset road and selling it for tin may prove but a can opener to let the auto in," declared the *Brockton Enterprise* early in 1918. Three months later the truth of the statement was manifested at the hearing on repealing the Nantucket Exclusion Act at the Boston State House. Franklin E. Smith presented a thorough docket of arguments for changing the law. He asserted that the streets and roads of Nantucket were no less suited to automobiles than elsewhere in the commonwealth, and with the extinction of the railroad the use of cars would become a necessity. Smith noted that the railroad had operated on a $1,500 deficit during 1917, and it had gone into debt $3,000 for fuel. After due processing by the lawmakers, the automobile question was submitted to the voters of the island. On 15 May motor vehicles were admitted by a casting of 336 ballots in favor as against 296 against them. In the same issue giving these results was the notice that "J-u-n-k-e-d spells the fate of the little Nantucket railroad." The directors had not waited for the stockholders' ratification but had started the work of tearing up the rails in March. By the beginning of June the desolation was complete. The 1885 coach remained on-island, whereas the rails and the rest of the rolling stock were purchased by the "junk" dealers Thompson and Kelly of Boston; and the last remnants of the Nantucket Railroad were loaded on barges and taken to the mainland. (Lancaster, *The Far-out Island Railroad*, pp. 117–21).

VII. PROHIBITION:
THE ERA OF TEAROOMS AND SHOPS

THE ISLAND'S loss of the railroad during the early summer of 1918 had been a negative repercussion of the war in Europe. A couple of months later, Nantucket was to witness specific results, a reenactment of the German submarine V-35's attacks on allied merchant vessels of two years earlier. The difference was that the United States now was in the conflict, and Nantucketers were conscious of the Germans as serious enemies, because the victims of the attacks were actually seen, having reached their own shore rather than the lightship from which news of the episode was relayed to the island. On 10 and 11 August, German submarines operating from 100 to 220 miles off the Atlantic coast sent eight fishing schooners, the big British steamer *Penistone*, and the Swedish steamer *Syndland* to watery graves. Although the incidents were about 175 miles away, some forty survivors arrived on Nantucket. Assistance included a present of $20 to each of the nine rescued from the *Penistone* from a collection taken up by guests at the Sea Cliff Inn.

The two most noticeable changes on the island at the outset of the postwar period were the absence of the railroad and the arrival of the automobile. Nostalgia over the railroad revived in the fall of 1918 when a row of sleepers was found about a foot below the surface of Federal Street while a gas leak was being investigated. They were survivors of the short-lived (and not much cherished) Beach Street bob-tailed trolley line of a quarter of a century earlier. Eight weeks later, workmen filled in the steam-line crossing at the foot of Main Street, surfacing it with cobblestones; and the newspaper commented that "the

last vestige of the track of the lamented Nantucket Railroad" thus had disappeared. But the gap left there in the line of buildings was to be filled by a distinguished memento. The old 1885 passenger car, which had been left in the car house near Goose Pond, was brought out early in 1919 and hauled through Orange and Union streets to a position between the Pacific Club and store of Eugene S. Burgess. David W. Gibbs performed the moving, and Burgess put it in service as the "Pullman Lunch."

The replacement of the train by the subject of the auto-exclusion bill repeal was much in evidence. In front of hostelries the call of "carriage!" was replaced by that of "taxi!" At the peak of the 1918 summer season there were more than seventy cars on the island. An attempt to keep the menace in check was the imposing of an eight-mile-an-hour speed limit in town. Still, the vehicles were a nuisance on the streets. A new column was introduced to the *Inquirer and Mirror* in the 25 May 1918 issue, called "Automobile News." The second installment recorded that "Terry's Garage on Middle Pearl street" had become the center of the new fad, and that the public way in front sometimes was blocked by the congregation of machines. Perhaps the least objectionable cars were those making scheduled runs that replaced the former railroad. The Nantucket Land Trust acquired a nine-passenger jitney to serve the lodge, extending a passable road from the state highway to Tom Nevers Head. Clinton S. Folger purchased a Republic motor bus for regular runs to Siasconset, and even in the winter there were three trips a day each way, the last returning from

116　*The Old Pullman Lunch, subsequently Allen's Diner and currently the bar of the Club Car, Straight Wharf (modern photograph).*

the village at 4:15 p.m. Beyond the regular runs, Folger pressed his Ford into service. On the last Sunday in July 1918, it was near midnight when the car was wending its way homeward along Union Street and suddenly "gave two or three vicious chugs and then stopped." Its fuel tank was found to be "as dry as the desert of Sahara."

The humor of such an episode cannot atone for less innocent mishaps. On the same evening that Folger's cab stalled, six young people, work-ing at Siasconset during the summer, borrowed Horace Folger's touring car to go for a "pleasure ride." Their pleasure got a bit out of hand, as the vehicle met with an "unfortunate accident" near the third milestone on the state highway. One girl sustained a fractured collar bone, and anoth-er was taken to the Nantucket hospital "in a seri-ous condition." The island's first disastrous auto-mobile accident foreshadowed a recurrence of irresponsible driving here, with occasional com-parable consequences.

In 1919 Nantucket had 3,200 year-round residents, a summer population of 12,000, and the number of visitors that had come over by boat was 44,000. A handful more was transported by the new hydro-airplanes, which could land on the water. As these figures indicate, the far-out island enjoyed a successful season that year. In late July the newspaper announced: "Accommodations are rather hard to obtain in Nantucket at the present time. Hotels and boarding houses are about booked to the limit and those who rent 'lodging rooms' are reaping a harvest." Two weeks later the *Inquirer and Mirror* listed the number of cottages occupied by visitors.

(1) On the perimeter: Brant Point, about 30; Beachside, 22; Cliff Road (including Sea Cliff cottages and Hill Crest), 28; The Cliff, 33; Cliff Beach, 4; and North Road, 10.

(2) In town: Academy Lane, 7; Ash Lane and Ash Street, 3; Broad Street, 2; Centre Street, 16; Chestnut Street, 1; Chester Street, 5; Darling Street, 1; Fair Street (including Ship's Inn), 5; Federal Street, 1; Gay Street, 6; Gull Island, 1; Hussey Street, 8; Joy Street, 1; Liberty Street, 10; Lily Street, 10; Main Street, 17; Milk Street, 3; Mill Hill, 2; Mooer's Lane, 1; North Water Street, 6; Orange Street (including Quanato Terrace and Gorham's Court), 16; Pearl (India) Street, 14; Pine Street, 2; Pleasant Street, 4; Quince Street, 5; Ray's Court, 1; Salem Street, 2; School Street, 1; Step Lane, 3; Summer Street, 1; Union Street, 2; Westminster Street, 1; and Winter Street, 1. The Nantucket directory for 1919 alphabetized its hotels, with proprietors as: Beach House, Ocean Ave., Siasconset, M. J. Bulkley; The Breakers, Easton St., Brant Point, Mrs. Emily MacLaughlin; Clisby House, off Shell St., Siasconset; Colonial Inn, 17 No. Water St., Mrs. Harriett S. Ross; The Gables, 23 Broad St., George W. Hooper; Hillside and Summit Inn, 8 Gay St., Brainerd T. Jenkins; Nesbitt Inn, 19 -21 Broad St. George W. Burgess; Ocean House, 29 Broad St., W. D. Carpenter; Ocean Park (10 cot-

tages and dining room), Shell St., Siasconset, Robert M. Powers; Pitman House, 46 Centre St., Timothy Coffin Pitman; Point Breeze Hotel, Easton St., Bracey Curtis; Roberts House, 11 Pearl St., Mrs. Catherine M. Roberts; 'Sconset House, Ocean Ave., Siasconset, Isaac Hills, Jr.; Sea Cliff Inn, Cliff Road, Clifford Folger, treas.; Tom Nevers Lodge, Tom Nevers Head; Veranda House, Step Lane, John M. Winslow, mgr.; Wauwinet House, Wauwinet, James A. Backus; White Elephant, Easton St., Ralph W. Webb, mgr.

The first of two establishments missed on this roster is the Ocean View House at Siasconset. Since about the beginning of the century it had been owned and managed by Robert M. Powers (proprietor of Ocean Park, listed above), who sold it in December of 1917 to William F. Codd, the latter reselling it to Mrs. C. B. (Adelaide G.) Penrose of Baltimore in September of 1918. The second pavilion (1876) was moved southward on the lot and remodeled into a summer house, the balance demolished. Powers sold the Annex (1884) across Grand Avenue to Harry L. Burrage of Newton in July of 1919, and in the fall the building was razed to make way for a new house. The other inn missed is the Atlantic House, which, as we have seen, was purchased by Louise Streeter Warren in 1910. The hotel failed a few years later, and, due to unpaid taxes, it was sold at sheriff's auction to David Gray on 11 January 1922. The building was reduced in size, shifted sideways on the site, and became a seasonal cottage.

Several items in the hotel list were repeated among boardinghouses in the 1919 island directory. Others were listed mostly by proprietors' names:

Elmer E. Ames
4 Washington St.

Mildred G. Burgess
107 Main St.

Mrs. Calvert Handy
26 No. Water St.
(also listed as the Worth House)

117 *The Breakers, Easton Street, 1919.*

Corann Collins
87 Main St.

Lizzie A. Folger
6 Darling St.

Gull Island House (rooms)
to the rear of 82 Centre St.

Hillcrest Cottage
10 Cliff Rd.
Mrs. W. C. Smith beginning 1910

Holway House
24 Broad St.

Mrs. Anna Mooers
1 N. Water St.

Quanato Terrace
1 Quanato Ct., J. B. Staples

Ships Inn, Fair St.
Mabel C. Bacall, 1913–22, then
Ernest S. MacLaughlin

Mrs. Annie Smith
27 Union St.

Mrs. W. H. H. Smith (rooms)
20 Federal St.

As in times past, the local directory was not all-inclusive. Advertisements in the newspaper during late July and early August of 1919 listed rooms available at 35 Union Street, 16 North Liberty Street, 21 Lily Street, the Martin Box on Martins Lane, 12 Pine Street, and 8 Farmer Street.

The refreshment and food-service industry of Nantucket was undergoing changes at this time. In 1918, Walter H. Sisson, who had been running the Nantucket Candy Kitchen on Federal Street since 1904, took over the sweets stand adjoining the Atheneum on lower Pearl Street, presided over for at least the last ten years by Henry Todd, a seasonal resident. Sisson and his scions continued in business during the life of the little building through the 1950s, when its site was landscaped as the formal garden in front of the new library wing. A restauratrice was also shifting bases: Anna Ward, who had conducted the Grill Room at the Ships Inn on Fair Street (lately closed) reopened in the Old Wright Mansion at 94 Main Street (next door to the Hadwen House) in 1919, specializing in "Luncheon, Dinner and Supper Parties." In November Mrs. Ward bought the Walsh property, 61 Centre Street, and thereafter ran it as the Wonoma Inn. In 1922 she was advertising "Special Lobster and Chicken Dinners

to order, home made Cake, Jams, Doughnuts for sale and to order." Not far away, the Old Virginia Tea House and Gift Shop held forth at 3 Salom Street, now Whaler's Lane. (Lothrop's *Directory* for 1927 has it as "Salome," which may be a misprint, but an interesting one.) Also in the vicinity, Mlle. Aimee de Lagneau's Tricolor Tea Room was on North Water Street. Toward the close of 1919, L. C. Jewett, who had been chief steward at the naval barracks on Nantucket during the war, opened a restaurant called the Sea Grill Lunch Room in the stores of William Holland on Main Street. The 'Sconset House, with I. Hill II as manager, formerly the 'Sconset Cottage Club, took pride in its "Cuisine Par Excellence."

The big excitement for prohibition-headed Nantucket this winter revolved around the alleged robbery of a $3,000 store of wines and

118 *Quanato Terrace, Quanato Court (off Orange Street), 1914.*

We are Home Again

TODD, the Candy Maker, is back again for the season at the old stand, LOWER PEARL STREET, and for the next five weeks will make New Bedford's popular Old Fashioned Hard Candies such as your grandmother used to like so well.

Ye Molasses Candy Chewing Bars   Vanilla and Strawberry Bars
The Old Fashioned Horehound Squares   Lemon Drops   Molasses Peppermints   Sassafras Chops
Wintergreen Chops   Anise Drops   Cocoanut Squares   Clove Drops
Walnut Squares   Peanut Brittle   Peanut Bars
Also the famous Chocolate Cream Cocoanut and the N. B. Wafers, and many other kinds too numerous to mention.

THE LUCKY EGG--Each purchaser gets one FREE. ONE contains an order.

Our Specials for SATURDAY ONLY:

A fine mixed Chocolate Cream at 20c a pound. ·   The latest famous Coco Macaroons at 20c a pound.
Extra H. H. Marshmallows, usual price 50c, our price 22c.   ·   The Merry Widow Mixture 18c.
Todd's Immense Chewing Kandy 18c.   Try our Salt Water Taffy. ALWAYS FRESH.

119 *Todd's candy stand on Lower Pearl Street, 1908.*

liquors from the cottage of actor and playwright Robert Hilliard at Siasconset. The trial over the theft came up on 11 December, presided over by "a fair and impartial judge from another county." Nobody was proved the culprit, but "Nantucket" believed it knew who he was. "If it does," stated the newspaper editor, "it possesses information which Mr. Hilliard, his valet, three or four private detectives, a couple of lawyers, numerous federal officers, one caretaker, one chief of police, one sheriff, and several stenographers have not been able to secure." Nevertheless, it was highly suspicious that a general-store keeper of twenty-years' residence in the hamlet suddenly began illegally selling alcoholic beverages.

The national outlawing of intoxicants (the Eighteenth Amendment was passed on 16 January 1920) as a whole, made little difference to Nantucket with its natural propensity for being dry. Yet a few off-island proprietors of summer hostelries must have complained, because of the newspaper notice: "Some one asks what has become of the hotels that were going to close on account of prohibition? Well, at last account some of 'em are in great danger of getting closed up for profiteering." The end of the statement sounds like a persisting islander's dig at those who endeavor to make as much money as possible off visitors.

In Siasconset, G. H. Brinton constructed a "very attractive bungalow" at the foot of Brinton Road, which operated as the Green Tea Room during the summer of 1920.

At this time the Nantucket Athletic Club changed its name to the Nantucket Yacht Club. The island directory listed both athletic and yacht clubs, each with its own set of officers, in 1919. But a special meeting had been held, the proposed shift of appellations voted on, the matter duly announced in the local newspaper, and the change certified by the secretary of the commonwealth on 8 July 1920. An odd note is that a week before, announcement had been made about movies to be shown beginning on 2 July, at the Nantucket Yacht Club, meaning the building on South Beach Street. At the first annual meeting of the new yacht club on 14 July, Henry Lang was elected commodore. Lang recently had held that position in the old yacht club, founded by Paul G. Thebaud in 1906. Col. J. M. Andrews became vice commodore, E. W. Crosby secretary and treasurer, and Leeds Mitchell fleet captain; and none of those gentlemen had held former posts in either organization.

Later in the month, Tony Sarg presented a show with his famous marionettes at the yacht club to benefit the Nantucket Cottage Hospital fund. His marionettes were about 24 inches tall, had carved wooden heads, and were brightly painted and costumed. At 2:30 and 4:30 on the afternoon of 28 July performances were given of the "Marionette Vaudeville," and highlighted by the appearance of a juggler and an oriental dancer. In the evening at 8:30 Sarg gave his version of Thackeray's *The Rose and the Ring*. The latter was in three acts and eight scenes, complete with kings, queens, princesses, knights on prancing white chargers, and even a roaring lion. Spectacular stage effects included Porter Gruffanuff's disappearance through a door, until only his head protruded as the knocker, and Countess Gruffanuff's transformation, on stage, from an ugly dowager to a beautiful young girl. Eight persons were required to manipulate the figures, recite the lines, and change scenery and lighting.

Tony Sarg's instinctive showmanship once went unappreciated. He had come to the island early one summer to get the house ready for the reception of his wife and daughter, and, aware of their arrival on a certain steamboat, decided to give them a surprise welcome. He approached friends in the Coast Guard to transport him to meet the ship in transit. Tony's waving was unable to stop the boat, but a signal from the Coast Guard brought it to a halt. Its decks were crowded with cottage residents, many of whom were bringing their supply of bootleg liquor for the summer. Alarmed by what they thought was a Prohibition patrol, there was a general stampede to the far side of the vessel to dump overboard incriminating evidence before an impending search for illegal goods. They returned to see Tony Sarg's beaming face, just boarding and searching for his wife, who by this time had assessed the situation and removed herself from the mortification to the ladies room.*

Communal music was provided in 1920 by the setting aside of $1,500 for band concerts. The bandstand was "dressed up" and placed on the lower square "near the fountain, where the street is wider and there is less congestion from traffic." The first concert was presented by the Worcester Band on 2 August. The series lasted four weeks, after which the kiosk was hauled up to the jail yard for winter storage.

When the coal schooner *Allen Gurney*, a fifty-seven-year-old veteran of Long Island Sound and Narragansett Bay, was "laid up for good" at Nantucket toward the close of 1920, the owner, Capt. C. D. Huntley, sold it to two maiden ladies with protracted island connections. They were realtor Gladys Wood and Margaret Prentice, who leased a section of Steamboat Wharf and fixed up the

*The author is indebted to the late Mary Sarg Murphy for relating this anecdote.

120 *The Skipper, Steamboat Wharf.*

vessel to serve as a tearoom called the Skipper. The former *Inquirer and Mirror* printing office, which had been on Milk Street near Main and had been taken to the wharf to become a carousel shelter, lately serving as a steam laundry, became the galley. For the next thirty-five years the Skipper maintained the reputation of being one of Nantucket's best eating places. After the coal schooner deteriorated beyond repair, it was replaced by a built-up sham, since razed.

George H. Brinton had leased the "Beach House and Swiss Cottage annex" to Merwin J. Bulkley for $2,500 a year, beginning 1 January 1918 and to last through 1922, with an option to buy; but in the fall of 1920 Brinton sold Bulkley the Beach House and "all other buildings thereon" for $30,000, which included a $16,000 mortgage held by the Nantucket Institution for Savings.

It was in 1921 that Fred Allen took over the management of Burgess's Pullman Lunch, a step toward its becoming Allen's Diner. Harriet Wilson, of Chatauqua, New York, who had "had successful experience in managing summer hotels," assumed proprietorship of Tom Nevers Lodge. The former cook, Julia, returned, but otherwise Miss Wilson brought her own staff.

A new summer celebration was introduced in 1921 that was to become a biennial affair. Its purpose was to raise money for maintaining the Cottage Hospital. This institution had been organized in 1911 and opened for patients in several "cottages" on the north side of West Chester Street in 1914. We have noted the musical entertainment at the Athletic Club in 1911 and Tony Sarg's marionette show given for its benefit in 1920, besides which there had been a number of money-raising gatherings of a festive character. The first had occurred on 15 July 1913 at Mary E. Walker's, 34 Orange Street, and the adjoining yard to the north, where eatables, fancy and domestic articles, and flowers were sold, and tea was served to the accompaniment of the Sea Cliff and Ocean House orchestras. In 1915 and 1916 similar events were held at several of the large vacation homes on Cliff Road; and subsequent years saw them at the Athletic Club, the William Flanagan house and garden (Moor's End) on Pleasant Street, and the Barnes's boat house on Commercial Wharf.

Staged at the center of town in 1921, this was the first Main Street Fete. Advertised for Thursday, 18 August, rain postponed it until Friday. The street was roped off to traffic from Fair to Pleasant, and the historic houses on Main Street served as background for various groups. In front of the Frederick Mitchell house (69), Alfred D. Williams demonstrated the making of a lightship basket and William H. Chase the carving of a whale. Under a tree at the Charles G. Coffin house (78), several ladies were engaged in quilting; four others were knitting on the steps of the Benjamin Gardner house (85); and a girl was working a tape loom and another woman was hooking a rug in the yard of the Frederick Chase house (80). Elsewhere, people modeled old costumes. Visitors could look in some of the houses. Millard F. Freeborn circulated among them dressed as a town crier. Chester Pease drove a two-wheeled shearing cart in which three women in Quaker dress sat on rush-bottom chairs, in the appropriate manner. Walnut Lane, gay with Chinese lanterns, served as the midway with a wheel of fortune, the "Downfall of China," barrel-and-ball-throwing games, dish placing, a strong man, Siamese twins, "Human Monkey," wild man of Borneo, a balloon boy, clown band, and fruit and peanut stalls. Proclaimed one of the island's notable affairs, proceeds came to $10,160.58.

A long-awaited improvement to one of the important amusement facilities of Nantucket got under way in the spring of 1922. This was the renovation of Dreamland Theatre. Its owners, the Wauwinet Tribe of Red Men, had proposed the changes at the beginning of 1919 with hopes of having them carried out "before spring." They were to consist of lowering the front part of the auditorium to provide a sloping floor, moving

back the stage to increase the seating capacity to 600, furnishing new dressing rooms, and removing the pillared obstructions, substituting a truss system to support the lodge headquarters above. The estimate for this work, of $15,000, held up proceedings. The alterations finally began during the first week of March 1922. The new floor had a 4-foot declivity. Also, the projection booth was placed in an extension to the building. New seats and an improved system of ventilation were installed. The cinema reopened on 13 May with a showing of Mabel Normand in "Molly O." Shows were at 7:15 and 9:00 p.m., admission 25¢.

At the time of the Dreamland's reactivation the newspaper announced that the automobile count on the island had jumped from 198 in 1921 to 273 in a year's time. Of this number, 126 were of the "most popular make in the world, known as Fords, Tin Lizzies, or Flivvers." Other statistics regarding Nantucket's new look included the information that the yacht club now had six tennis courts, all heavily patronized. And below the 'Sconset bank there was a total of fifty-six cottages, about which the editor declared: "How the tribe has increased in the last two decades!"

Nantucket was treated to a return of Tony Sarg's marionettes, with three performances at the yacht club on 14 August 1922 and three at the Siasconset Casino the following day. Those at 2:30 in the afternoon were called "The Children's Hour," and those at 4:15 and 8:30 in the evening were Irving's "Rip Van Winkle." Admission at the club was $1.50 for the two afternoon sessions, and $2.00 for that at night. Each was 50¢ cheaper at the casino. The first performance at the two places was for children; and the last was given with the curtain screening the operators removed, allowing the spectators to see how the puppets were manipulated. As two years earlier, proceeds were donated to the Nantucket hospital fund.

In 1922, out-of-town room and board accommodations were provided at Edgewater Farm, on the shore of Hummock Pond. To the northwest of town, near the end of Cliff Road, Mrs. Latimer P. Smith's 19th Hole adjoined the golf club. In 1924

121 *The Chopping Bowl, Union Street.*

she sold it to Miss Jean Casilear Cobb (who had been conducting a gift shop there), and which in 1925 became the Shimmoah Tea House. Farther to the west, shore dinners could be had at Mrs. Jewett's Hithercot, near Madaket station. At the south shore, besides J. B. Folger's Weeweeder Inn, there was the Isla-Waters Tea House, giving "special attention . . . to Luncheon, Dinner and Supper parties." Across the Great Harbor, (A. B.) Tunning's-on-Coatue was located at the first point. Its shore dinners could be reached by boat from Old North Wharf from 10:00 a.m. to 10:00 p.m. On 4 September a masquerade ball was held there featuring Gus Bentley's Knickerbocker Orchestra. Four miles out on the Polpis Road was the Miriam Coffin T. House, supplying sandwiches and waffles; and farther on was Mildred's Tea Room, on the Wauwinet Road, specializing in chicken and waffle suppers

by appointment. In Siasconset, the Sign of the Chanticleer was in operation.

In Nantucket Town, Edward X. Ludwig's Chopping Bowl opened on 25 June. It was at 22 Union Street, and besides refreshment offered "Dancing and Exhibition of Paintings in the Garden Studio." A similar garden setting was provided by the Old Garden Gate, which opened on 15 July, in whose "shady nooks . . . ice cream and cake" were served. It was to be at 14 Pearl (India) Street for five years, then move to 6 Federal Street. Farther down Pearl Street, at 5, was the Ames Dining Room, presided over by Mary Ames.

An article in the *Inquirer and Mirror* in mid-July of 1923 publicized the lesser dispensers of sustenance, of course including some that have been mentioned: "In rambling around the island one sees many attractive tea room signs displayed, among which are: The Skipper, The Chopping Bowl, The 19th Hole, The Old Virginia, The Woodbox, Anchor Inn, The Blue Dory, The Bell Buoy, The Wild Fern, The Chanticleer, The Tavern-on-the-Moors, The Delft Tea Room, Miriam Coffin T. House, Weeweeder Inn, Isla Waters, Hithercot."

New items on the list begin with the Woodbox. It was and is on Fair Street, south corner of Hiller's Lane, an inn conducted by Maude E. Stovell, who purchased and combined the old George Bunker dwelling with the adjoining house in 1931. The Anchor Inn, at 66 Centre Street, was conducted by Marie Louise Miller. Mrs. L. S. Topham's Blue Dory was at 1 (now 3) Liberty Street, which became the Grey Gull, managed by Mrs. Nano G. Leahey, after the Dory moved to 94 Main Street (Wright Mansion) in 1924. Katherine Morris's Bell

Buoy Tea Room was on North Water Street. The Wild Fern was John C. Ayers's inn at 15 Liberty Street. The Tavern-on-the-Moors was on School Street, Siasconset. Minnie Nichols's Delft Tea Room, also in Siasconset, was on Shell Street.

Other new names appeared in 1923 in addition to the shifting of familiar names and proprietorships. Mrs. Deering now ran Jewett's Sea Grill at 37 Main Street, which was "open daily from 5:30 a.m. until an hour after arrival of the boat." "Home-made Delicacies" were available "At the ivy-covered red cottage near the Atheneum." In Siasconset, Minnie Nichols now offered gifts on Shell Street at the Essential Shop. Mrs. Albert Pitman conducted Ye Quality Tea Room and Gift Shop; and Mrs. Brown's dealt in pastries and ice cream on Broadway. Harriet E. Hollister had a tearoom at Quaise.

122 *George Bunker House (mid-eighteenth century), Fair Street at Hiller's Lane. Maude E. Stovell's The Woodbox during the 1930s and 1940s.*

We, today, may be a little taken aback by the quantity and variety of tea and gift places then in operation, but the Nantucket officials of the period were overwhelmed by them. Early in July, the selectmen instructed the chief of police to visit all of them and check whether they had the proper victualer and/or vendor license and were paying the proper taxes. The report, two weeks later, revealed that the "majority were being conducted by non-residents," some of which "had the required state licenses—some did not. Some had paid a local tax on stock-in-trade last year—some did not. None of the 'tea rooms' had taken out a victualer's license." The matter was investigated.

The investigation report affords us the names of a number of lesser emporiums. In Siasconset there were Marion E. Markham's shop carrying novelties and paintings; Margaret C. Johnson's Venture Inn, on the beach, selling men's and women's wear; Ellen Gardner's gift shop; Kate L. Dakin's gift shop; and Raymond Regan's 'Sconset News and Book Store, which, in addition to the goods mentioned in the title, sold "drugs, candy, tobacco, soda, etc." In Nantucket itself, Alfred P. Gould represented Jones, Peterson and Newhall; Gertrude H. Leonard was the agent for Leonard and Co.; Mrs. Coleman conducted a branch of Solov-Hinds and Co. of Boston; Mrs. J. L. Wiedman had the Jenny Lind Shop on Centre Street; and Helen Purdue ran a millinery shop. Bennett and Carroll, who had conducted an antique shop at 66 Main Street, in 1923 moved to Ivy Lodge, South Water and Oak Street.

As noted above, Miss Markham's shop and Mr. Ludwig's Chopping Bowl offered paintings for sale. This indicates that by the summer of 1923 Nantucket had become conscious of the art trade, especially in works by resident artists and depicting the local scene. A side issue that was to flourish was conducting art classes. Resident artist Wendell Macy had given art instruction on Nantucket during the 1880s and 1890s, but the first off-island teacher seems to have been Frank Swift Chase of the Art Students League in New York City. In July of 1920 he gave four weeks of lessons in landscape painting, and in August he presented an exhibition of his own landscapes at Marian

Sand's studio near the west end of Hulbert Avenue. The following summer, Michel Jacobs, director of the Metropolitan Art School of New York, conducted art classes on Commercial Wharf. Chase repeated his course that year, and at the end of August held an exhibition of his pupils' work at "the Brick Studio, Washington Street." During that season Lillian Gertrude Smith showed her work at the Auld Lang Syne studio in Siasconset. In 1922 Frank Swift Chase listed his address as 47 (now 1) North Liberty Street, which was Tony Sarg's recently acquired summer home. Emma H. Van Pelt taught watercolor classes, and Marion E. Markham held outdoor sketching classes for children, both at studios on Harbor View. Annie Alden Folger presented paintings, etchings, lithographs, drawings, and photographs for sale at the Barn Studio on Pearl Street. Nantucket photographs had enjoyed a steady sale since Josiah Freeman began working here almost sixty years earlier. The Candle House (former "Brick") Studio, south corner of Washington Street and Commercial Wharf, hung an exhibition of paintings by artists summering on the island, and it was open from the last week in July until September. In 1923 the Candle House Studio held another similar showing.

In 1924 this endeavor was taken over by the Easy Street Gallery in a building that was the old Hayden's Clean Shore bath house on South Beach Street and had been moved to near the head of Steamboat Wharf. The patron of the exhibitions at the Candle House Studio and owner of the new Easy Street Gallery was Florence (Mrs. Henry) Lang of Montclair, New Jersey, and Santa Barbara, California. Mrs. Lang herself painted, her subjects largely East and West Coast scenes, and she showed her work at the new gallery. She was a generous supporter of the arts, having sponsored the building of the Montclair Art Museum (1914 with additions in 1924 and 1931), was a benefactor of the Los Angeles County Art Museum, and a trustee of the Pasadena Art Association. In Nantucket at about the time she opened the Easy Street Gallery, Mrs. Lang began acquiring fish and scallop houses on the wharves (especially South Wharf), and other little buildings on the beaches

123 *Old Parliament House, Pine Street (modern photograph).*

of the harbor, had them fitted up as studios, and rented them at a nominal fee to artists and students. She purchased the old railroad depot, near her gallery, had it moved a few feet and gave it the title of "Choo Choo." During the summer of 1923 it served as Edith Allen Hall's shop for "linens, braided rugs and exquisite bags of Italian hand-work." Henry S. Eddy's canvases of Nantucket were displayed at his studio, Barnsite, behind what is now Cap'n Tobey's restaurant at the foot of Main Street. Group shows at the Easy Street Gallery became an important annual affair.

A residential development on Nantucket, offered in 1923, was devoted to artists. It was called Greenwich Village and was that part of Sunset Hill adjoining North Liberty Street. To obtain a spot there, one had to "do something clever, paint, write, sing, golf, ride, swim [or] play bridge." Blueprints of the layout could be obtained at 43 Pearl (India) Street. Lots were priced at $300 and $350, and houses, after the client's design, would be built for a total of from $1,500 to $2,500. It was promoted by "Ask Mr. Brock," and the first cottage in the area was erected in April of 1924.

Besides the Woodbox, which has been mentioned, establishments of the bed-and-board type recently inaugurated included: Mildred G.

Burgess's Homestead, Monument Square (west corner of Gardner); the Misses Ide's Cottage Inn, 17 Pearl (India) Street, successor to their former place on Cliff Road; and Miss Crosby and Miss Farrington's guest house at 11 Gardner Street, which moved to the Old Parliament House, 10 Pine Street, in 1924.

Whereas the flux of smaller guest houses, tearooms, and shops held the spotlight during the early twenties, the established hostelries continued to function, and they still accommodated the bulk of visitors to the island. They experienced changes too. At the end of the 1919 season the Point Breeze's roof was reshingled, and its walls—formerly green—were painted gray. James A. Backus made a "substantial addition to the dining-room of the Wauwinet House" in the spring of 1920. The Ocean House was acquired and henceforth supervised by Frank Worth early in August of 1921. In the spring of 1922 the Roberts House was repainted white by Joseph Larkin. An electric plant was installed at Wauwinet to light the hotel during the summer. That modernization or some other attraction prompted guests to linger late in the fall, as on Sunday evening, 17 September, sixty-five were served at dinner. At the end of the 1922 season, Ernest S. MacLaughlin leased the Ships Inn "for a term of years." The Veranda House, lately owned by John M. Winslow, was sold to Frederick M. Gardner. Fred H. Folger, of the Sea Cliff Inn, went to Winter Park, Florida, to manage the new Alabama Hotel during the cold months. A picture of it reproduced in the Nantucket newspaper showed it to resemble the Beach House at Siasconset.

Nantucket Town itself acquired several improvements at this time. In the fall of 1922 cobblestones were newly laid on the street in the upper square. The original stones had dated from 1837, to which additions had been made in conjunction with the widening of Main Street after the Great Fire of 1846. There had been a replacement of the cobblestones in 1889. The Electric Company, which up to this time stopped its generators at midnight, at the beginning of 1923 began to keep power flowing around the clock. The street lights hereafter would burn until dawn.

The "public settles" put on Main Street each summer were painted during March of 1923; but, at the middle of May, when they were to be taken downtown, it was found that the paint was still wet. This year, Nantucket had three drinking fountains. Those on Main and Orange streets cost the town $90 each for running water, and that on Madaket Road (the D.A.R.'s Abiah Folger Franklin memorial) $74. The street sweeper that replaced the old sprinkler when first put into operation turned its brush the wrong way; but "it was finally adjusted and showed the folks on Main Street that it really can brush up the dirt if given a chance."

The second Main Street Fete was held on 16 August 1923 from 2:00 until 6:30 p.m. in the same area as in 1921. The old residences again provided settings for costumed groups, some busy at ancient trades, and visitors could enter and inspect a few houses, such as Mrs. H. Linsley Johnson's "Brick," and Albert Reed's basement kitchen, with its fine collection of pewter. Chester Pease again drove the shearing cart, and A. F. Musgrave impersonated the town crier. Austin Strong was a returning sea captain of mid-century, accompanied by a Chinese wife (Miss Katherine Adams) and members of the ship's crew. Prints of Tony Sarg's drawing of the lower square were sold by his daughter, Mary; and also offered were antiques, toys, flowers, and refreshments. More than 4,000 persons attended, and the event netted $13,854.87. The afternoon peregrinations on Main Street were followed by a grand ball at the yacht club in the evening.

The annual Cattle Show and Fair was held on the two days following the Main Street Fete. Unlike the day before, 17 August did not provide agreeable weather, having rain in the forenoon; and interest in bovines had dwindled to practically nothing. The saving grace of the affair was the horse show and especially the races, with the grandstand packed on both days. An unscheduled attraction stemmed from the presence of "fakirs" with their "fruit and blankets and kewpie dolls, etc." They set up booths on the grounds and were beginning to operate when the appearance of the state inspector from the Department

124 *Scenes from the Main Street Fete of 1923. Marcella Smith and Lila McKnight in the portico of the Barrett House; shearing cart driven by B. Chester Pease; the "Returning Whaleman" with Austin Strong, Katherine Adams as his Chinese wife.*

of Public Welfare prompted the storing away of games of chance that violated the commonwealth's gambling laws. The problem was solved by "chance" methods becoming supplanted by those of "skill," as with darts and improvised targets, and baseballs and cake tins, visitors were permitted to try for the prizes.

For these events a new steamboat brought visitors from the mainland. It was the *Islander*, which made its first visit to Nantucket on 7 August under command of Capt. James O. Sandsbury. After arrival, the boat was open for inspection, and two days later it took over the runs of the *Gay Head,* which had been the Nantucket Sound conveyance over the past thirty-one years. The *Islander*, although only a trifle longer than its predecessor, was considerably wider. It could accommodate 2,000 passengers and twenty-five automobiles, and it was adjudged the "roomiest vessel on the coast." Built entirely of steel, it was equipped with a 1,500-horsepower engine of

four-cylinder triple-expansion type. The *Islander*, which hailed from Newport, had been deprived of its launching ceremonies because of the death of President Harding on 2 August.

The bathing beaches in or near town were undergoing turnovers. On 14 January 1921 Florence A. Hayden sold Nathaniel E. Lowell the old Hayden facilities, including the "Hot Water Bath House" property adjoining "the Nantucket Athletic Club" on Beach Street, and the "Upper Bath House" property. The latter had been purchased by Charles E. Hayden in 1880, half from Alexander E. Drew and the remainder from Henry Coleman, Charles C. Mooers, and Elijah H. Alley, developers of Beachside (see chapter four). It was located at the west end of Beachside, on the far side of Charles Street. Although shown as a "BATHING BEACH" on H. S. Wyer's map of Nantucket of 1896 (fig. 76), it is ignored in the 1897 and 1909 directories, and it is somewhat confusedly listed in the 1919 town directory, with an address of 3 South Beach—that of the Hot Water Bath House. Nathaniel E. Lowell, formerly a builder, conducted the bath houses himself following the purchase.

The lease for the Cliff Bathing Beach, which the town had had with Clifford Folger, proprietor of the Sea Cliff Inn, for the past twenty years at $350 a year, expired in the spring of 1924. Bids were invited, and a young clerk at the Pacific National Bank, Leon M. Royal, took it for fifteen years at $3,300, with the option for a five-year renewal. Besides conducting the bath houses, Royal had the privilege of renting chairs and "sun shades" (beach umbrellas), and of selling toys, tobacco, and refreshments. Royal purchased the building that Folger had erected for $10,792, and on 10 May 1924 advertised the opening of the "Cliff Beach Bath Houses" for 15 June. Before the latter date, a corporation calling itself the "CLIFF BEACH BATH HOUSES, INC.," with Clifford Folger as president, his son Fred H. Folger as vice president, and son-in-law H. M. Conrad as treasurer and clerk, purchased the Snow property "above and below the cliff" (west of the Cliff Bathing Beach) from Nathaniel Lowell, and offered all but the shore front for sale. They announced that they intended building bathing houses on it for the 1925 season. During the summer the Folger group filed an injunction against Royal on the grounds that the name was not included in the sale of the building. Royal launched a counter suit claiming that the Folgers were not a corporation. Hearings were held at Boston and Nantucket during August, concluding with the attorneys for the two parties coming to an agreement to suspend the hearings. Both relinquished use of the name "Cliff Beach." In 1925 the eastern beach opened on 16 June as "Royal's Bath Houses," and the western beach opened in July as the "Nantucket Bath Houses." The latter characterized itself as a "modern up-to-date bathing establishment, the result of our twenty years experience." H. M. Conrad was manager. The following year, it reverted to the name "Cliff Beach Bath Houses."

Clifford Folger went deeper into the bathing-beach business in 1924. He leased the "Upper Bath House" complex from Nathaniel Lowell for a ten-year period at $1,800 per annum. The contract mentioned an "old building" on the premises, containing eighty-nine rooms, and it gave Folger the right to add new structures, provided he assumed the resulting increase in insurance. When this facility opened for the season as the Beach Side Bath Houses in 1927, Mrs. E. H. Butler was manager.

In 1924 Nantucket had a bookshop. There had been bookstores here before, such as that of Andrew W. Macy, in the new Sherburne Block on Centre Street built soon after the Great Fire, which was run by the owner's sister, Harriet, when Andrew went in the Gold Rush to California at the end of 1848. But that had been more than three-quarters of a century earlier, and the new one was a unique phenomenon. Operating under the title of The Little Book Shop, located in the minuscule cottage at 2 Quince Street, it was the venture of Anna Kropp Barnes of Providence, Rhode Island, and Katharine Lord of New York City. The latter had a special interest in children, and she was the author of the *Little Playbook* and *Plays for School and Camp*. The proprietresses stocked the shop with unusual books and periodicals, the latter having to do with poetry, literature, art, and antiques, such as were not to be found on the shelves at newsstands. They also conducted a lending library and had the agency for Silver Box Sweets. During their first year in business here, they displayed a dummy of *Tony Sarg's Book for Children from Six to Sixty*, announcing that when it was published the author would autograph the first copy, which then would be auctioned to the highest bidder. The stunt sounds as though it might have been Sarg's own idea. The partners booked sixty prepublication orders as a result.

Automobiles continued to increase, and in May the *Inquirer and Mirror* presented the "New American song: Bumper to bumper and hub to hub, the cars are so thick that their fenders rub." Two weeks later the selectmen took up the matter of traffic rules and needs for the season. Among them were the prohibition of allowing more than two persons to sit on the front seat,

125 *The White Elephant, before rebuilding in 1962–63.*

removing the "hideous yellow" signs saying "Go to the Right," and painting a center line on streets in town and on the Polpis Road. One-way streets were not to materialize in this decade.

In 1924 Miss Helen Bartlett initiated a new tearoom, Drift Inn, on a knoll overlooking the head of Hummock Pond. Luckily it was elevated. Later, summer flooding caused a nearby structure to become dislodged, and it "drifted out with the storm." In town, Mrs. William Brown opened the Peter Rabbit Candy Shop at 22 Centre Street. The west annex of the White Elephant on Brant Point was connected to the main pavilion that year. In February, twenty-seven new dwellings were under construction on the island; and at the end of summer a minor boom was in progress at Pocomo. Places offering visitor accommodations appearing for the first time included: the Narwhal Guest House, Brant Point Road (28 Easton Street),

run by Arthur C. Putnam; the Reuben Joy Homestead (formerly Mildred G. Burgess's Homestead), northwest corner of Main and Gardner Streets; and 76 Main Street, the last under the direction of Miss Florence L. Swain.

The local chapter of the Daughters of the American Revolution, which had sponsored visits to old houses before in Nantucket, offered on 6 and 13 August, 2:00 to 6:00 p.m., a 50¢ tour to the homes of Mrs. Morgan, 2 Martins Lane; Mrs. Defriez, 15 Fair Street (home of Lucretia Mott); Mrs. Round, 5 Fair Street; Mrs. Cary, 25 Pleasant Street (built in 1745); Miss Walker, 11 Milk Street; Mrs. Dyer, 9 Milk Street; and Mrs. Folger, 16 Gardner Street, where the famous Folger clock (now owned by the Nantucket Historical Association) was to be viewed from 3:00 to 5:00. A comparable journey to the past was presented by the young ladies of the Congregational Church on the

126 *Fire damage to the Point Breeze Hotel, 1925.*

evening of 26 August. Their program consisted of old songs by a quartet, and lantern pictures were shown of Nantucket past and present.

Soon after the close of the season, on 18 September, a fire alarm was struck on box 36 at the Sea Cliff Inn. The auto-chemical fire truck responded. It was delayed in reaching the scene due to the congregation of cars left by people gathered to watch the excitement. The blaze was in a room over the kitchen and laundry at the south end of the building, where mattresses were being stored. One had caught fire and was soon extinguished. A follow-up occurred on 7 October. The Sea Cliff's gong started clanging and the automatic sprinklers working. They were noticed by passers-by and reported, leading to their being turned off. No cause for their being triggered was discovered.

At the beginning of 1925 a new "Iceless Soda Fountain" was installed in the R. G. Coffin drug store on Main Street. And in March a "large mov-

ing van" came over on the *Uncatena* with fixtures for the "new ice cream and confectionery store which is soon to be opened on Main Street by the Nicoletos Brothers." It was opposite the west corner of Federal Street.

In May, the Overland touring car, which Clinton S. Folger had brought to the island eight years earlier, achieving notoriety as the "horse-mobile" and which had changed hands three times since, went to its final rest at the Siasconset dumping ground.

The most catastrophic fire in a Nantucket hostelry was that which destroyed the old (1891) Point Breeze Hotel pavilion and seriously damaged the balance of the building. It began before 2:00 o'clock on the morning of 8 August 1925. The hotel watchman, Thomas McKeon, had just made his rounds and found everything all right; he was in the lobby when a guest on the third floor discovered the blaze. Hearing her, McKeon sounded the alarm, arousing Mrs. Hayes, the proprietress. The fire began in the kitchen, forming the rear ell of the old Elijah Alley house. By the time the fire pumper reached the Point Breeze, the entire west part of the building was burning. The hose connection pulled away from the nearest hydrant and it had to be attached to another farther up Easton Street. The firemen exerted heroic efforts, but the fire had a good start; the hotel was gutted and much of the old section collapsed. Fred Allen supplied doughnuts and coffee to the men during the ordeal. There was no panic among the guests, though many got out with only the night clothes they were wearing. There was some looting, and arrests were made. The hotel was insured for $30,000, but the loss was estimated at between $50,000 and $75,000. The remains of the west section were demolished. The later (1903–04) pavilion was rebuilt inside, and the Point Breeze Hotel reopened on 23 June 1926, with Frank Worth (also proprietor of the Ocean House) in charge. The management of the new Point Breeze was not remarkably different, as within a fortnight after the fire Mrs. Hayes had become Mrs. Worth.

The benefit for the hospital and third Main Street Fete was held on 13 August. It was similar to that in 1923, perhaps with a note of greater authenticity in costumes worn by the participants. An exception was the town crier, impersonated by a woman, Mrs. Davis Barnes, whose moustache fell off at an inopportune moment. The Tea Garden was a hit. It was on the grounds of the Henry Coffin house, the summer home of Mrs. and Mrs. George L. Carlisle. Here Jackie Perry's orchestra provided dance music for the young people. A dog show was held at the Coffin School on Winter Street. The fete brought in $21,355.51.

At the end of August the Nautican Realty Company announced a sale of "BRANT POINT SHORE PROPERTY." The items were the cottages on or near Harbor View Way, opposite the children's bathing beach. The houses were basically alike in plan and somewhat in form, the latter varied by different roof treatments. Each cottage had electricity and gas, modern conveniences (one full bath and a toilet), a living room, dining room,

kitchen, halls and six or seven bedrooms, some on the third floor. Fireplaces and screened-in porches, with water views from most rooms, were special features. The row of houses still exists, two of them being bed-and-breakfast establishments.

Nantucket gained three innovations in 1926. The first was the start of its deer herd. On 3 June 1922 a stag in an exhausted condition had been rescued from Nantucket Sound by a fishing boat and brought to the island. Four years later, in February, two does were brought from Michigan and liberated in the swamps near Squam. The original deer, known as "Old Buck," was hit and killed by an automobile on 24 July 1932. It was the second deer fatality caused by a car within a week's time.

The second advance was a mechanized ambulance for the Cottage Hospital. The old horse-drawn vehicle was taken to the mainland and returned mounted on a Reo chassis. The steamer *Uncatena* had to be pressed into service to bring it over, as the new ambulance was six inches too tall for both the *Islander* and the *Nobska*.

The third ornament was the lettering and installing of street signs in town. Some were attached to fences and many to the ends of houses nearest a corner. The project was meant to clarify the identity of streets, but that was not always the case. For instance, Fayette Street, due to the sign painter's error—or flair of originality—came out "LAFAYETTE" Street. Up to 1971 a correctly labeled board was at the west end, but its replacement at that time made both incorrect. The Nantucket designation of courts (a dead-end), lanes (short and without sidewalks) and streets (having sidewalks) began to be confused. Coon and Beaver lanes became Coon and Beaver streets, without justification. Martins Lane more appropriately might have become Martins Street. Academy Lane, which winds up the hill from Centre Street south of the Congregational Church, and at the top has no sidewalks, became Academy Avenue. In Nantucket, as we have seen in chapter four, this new term had been used initially during the 1870s for Bay Avenue, along the shore of Beachside, which, when the street was abandoned, was taken over by Hulbert Street, becom-

THE NAUTICAN REALTY CO.

as sole agents for the owners
announce a sale of

BRANT POINT SHORE PROPERTY

comprising a plot of land adjacent to a public park which will insure the buyer an un-
interrupted water view for all time. Four fully furnished summer cottages and also
four house lots suitable for the better class of summer residences. This kind of property grows harder to obtain year by year.

SAFEHARBOR

TIDEWAY

SHOREWORTH

LAURANELL

These cottages are attractively finished in the wood on the first floor and plastered
on the second floor except Lauranell which is plastered throughout. They are substantially furnished and have all modern improvements such as gas and electricity,

127 *Advertisement in the* Inquirer and Mirror, *29 August 1925.*

ing Hulbert Avenue. In 1881, the name of Surf-side Road was changed to Atlantic Avenue, as a matter of snob appeal, leading to the hoped-for cottage development on the south shore that did not materialize.

In the summer of 1926 Nantucket had two horseback-riding facilities. One was Hall's Riding Stable on Sea Street and the other was the Sherburne Riding School of W. H. Wyer, on Centre Street "near the Sea Cliff Inn."

This year, Elmer E. Ames built a bakery on West Dover Street and opened a retail store on Middle Pearl Street. Also on Pearl (20 India Street) was the Betty Bee Barn Studio, offering home-made candies, salted nuts, and coffee. At 26 Main Street the Anastos Brothers' Nantucket Spa sold "Choice selected fruits, nuts and candies, ice cream and sodas." Roger's, at 30 Main, the Modern at 40 Main (Nicoletos' ?), and Morris's Dairy Cot in Siasconset were ice-cream parlors. The Sunshine Shop, normally a gift and novelty store on Federal Street, now provided "Everything for your picnic or party." New tea places included the Cockatoo Tea Garden at E. S. McLaughlin's Ships Inn on Fair Street, and two in Siasconset, the Seamoor Tea Room on Ocean Avenue and Morey Lane and the Moby Dick on the south cliff.

In late summer exotic goods were made available at special auctions by two established Centre Street merchants. On Thursday evening, 26 August, Vartan Dedian presented "the largest and most beautiful collection of oriental rugs and Chinese carpets. . . . Mandarin coats, many rare antique Chinese . . . Armenian and Russian embroideries . . . [and] Russian and Indian brass." On the following Saturday George J. Khouri held a "Final Exhibition and Sale" in the Sea Cliff Inn reception hall, offering "Sicilian, Mosaic and Filet Fine Linens, Burato, Point de Milan, Point de Paris, Bincheaud Point d'Esprit Laces."

In 1927 Nantucket was connected with the mainland by regular air service to Boston. A Stinson-Detroiter first came over on 17 May, and regular flights began on 1 July. A landing strip, called Briar Cliff Field, was built by F. B. Maglathlin at Tom Nevers Head. The Boston Airport Corporation furnished a trip from Nantucket to Boston daily at 9:00 a.m., and a return trip at 5:00 p.m. One-way fare was $20.00, and the round trip (by the next plane) was $30.00. The biplane *Miss Nantucket* conveyed five passengers, flew at about 100 miles an hour, and made the trip in an hour and a half. Many of the early flights were delayed or canceled because of fog.

Live theatre passed a milestone in 1927, when Broadway playright Austin Strong conceived, played in, and helped produce the "Nantucket Follies," described as a "Vaudeville de Luxe." It was given at the yacht club on the evenings of 29 and 30 July. The entertainment was accompanied by the yacht club orchestra. The theme was local and largely reminiscent. It opened with a skit called *The Jolly Roger*, based on Roger's newsstand on Main at Federal Street. The proprietor was impersonated by Billy Russell, whereas the customers played themselves. It was succeeded by two dance numbers, little Florence Ingall in "The Hornpipe," and pupils of the Elizabeth Studio in "William Chase's Sailor Boys." A sort of master of ceremonies appeared in the person of Frederick Kitson Cowley as "The Quaker," providing a monologue for the tableaux. Two numbers based on Nantucket's past were "Admiral Sir Isaac Coffin, Baronet," with Gustavius Town Kirby as that illustrious gentleman, and "The Sailor's Farewell," the latter followed by a mimic of the scene as it would be performed in modern times at Royal's Bathing Beach. Tony Sarg appeared with a marionette and drew a caricature of his assistant, landscape-painting instructor Frank Swift Chase. Several songs were presented, including Mrs. Earle W. Cutler's "The Nantucket Cradle Song." Evidently considered the principal presentation was Austin Strong's play *The Captain's Return*, with Strong himself playing Captain Starbuck and Mrs. Cutler as Mrs. Starbuck, plus a supporting cast of twelve. The excitement of the homecoming, with presents for all, was enhanced by authentic costumes and set furnishings.

After an intermission came three dance numbers—the Charleston, a toe ballet, and a sailor's dance. Percy MacKaye gave an introduction to a scene called "The Dog Watch," showing Capt. B.

Whitford Joy (last square-rigger captain in the port of Nantucket) and crew on board the *St. Nicholas*, their various engagements punctuated by jokes, chanties, and a jig by an octogenarian. The ship's deck was especially realistic. Another skit, by Mr. and Mrs. Samuel Merwin and company of Concord, was derived from Gilbert and Sullivan, called "Pinafore'n'Aft." Then William E. Chamberlain appeared as "the magical man," assisted by Mary Sarg. An emotional episode was of Capt. Walter N. Chase, hero of the "Kirkham Wreck" of 1892, who was awarded a gold medal for bravery by the U. S. government for battling his way out to a shoal to save lives, a feat that lasted all of one day and into part of the next. The program ended with the "Pony Ballet," a dance by twenty girls directed by Mrs. Strong.

On the second (Saturday) night, when the orchestra started up the "Star-Spangled Banner" after the final scene, the audience shouted for Austin Strong, and when he put in an appearance, he was given three rousing cheers. After the audience dispersed, Strong threw a party for the participants and distributed presents, in turn receiving a ship model from the yacht club as a token of appreciation. Samuel Merwin came in conveying a "whale" filled with fruit (having a pineapple for a spout) and presented it to Mrs. Strong from the Concord group. With music playing and refreshments, the party was a "jovial affair and a happy aftermath to the final performance of the 'Follies.'"

On August 11th was held the fourth Main Street Fete. On that day, Main Street homes open for inspection were the Barney House, 96; the Varney House, 100; the Macy House, 99; and the Tobey House, 105. On the following day, another set of houses, farther removed, were available for the same purpose. They included the Eunice Brock House, Cliff Road; the Turner House, 86 Centre Street; the Peter Folger House, 51 Centre Street; Dr. Congdon's, 5 Orange Street; Miss Eleanor Smith's, Mill Street; and Moor's End, 19 Pleasant Street. Two new features at the celebration proper were the Fete Lunch Room, conducted at Mrs. J. S. Mitchell's, 77 Main Street, and the Story Tellers, in the Monnohanit Club's barn on Walnut Lane, suggested by the practice of such

entertainments in the Near East. There were games on "Frolic Lane" (Winter Street), a popularity contest (won by Mrs. N. H. Bokin), a dog show, candy and clams to eat, the usual display of old costumes, and many types of souvenirs on sale. Several hotel orchestras furnished music. The 1927 fete made $18,225.99.

As in 1923, the weather for the fete had been perfect, whereas that for the county fair on the 17th and 18th left much to be desired. The first day was rainy, and between the wet and the increased admission charge of $1, many people were discouraged from attending the second day. The "cattle show" was minuscule, and the agricultural produce was "so scanty that it was no more than one of the vegetable trucks carry on their daily trips from the farm to town." The fakirs plied their trades as usual, and there were vaudeville acts, acrobats, jugglers, and singers. The main interest centered around horses, the show, and races. The 1927 fair in no way came up to either the recent fete or "follies."

The Nantucket directory in 1927 listed twenty hotels and eleven boardinghouses—two more of the former and two less of the latter than in the 1919 register. Five titles and their proprietors remained identical, and five new listings.

Beach House, Ocean Ave.
Siasconset, M. J. Bulkley

The Breakers, Easton St., Brant Point
Mrs. Emily B. Gordon

Broadview Tavern, Lincoln Ave.
Mrs. R. S. Deering, Fred B. Folger in 1928

Crest Hall, 19 N. Water St.
was the "New" Springfield
C. C. Ross, prop. since 1920

The Gables, 23 Broad St.
George W. Hooper

Grey Gull Inn, 1 Liberty St.
(purchased in 1926 and conducted by Carl Stig)

Nantucket House, 1 N. Water St.
Mrs. Calvert Handy

Nesbitt Inn, 19–21 Broad St.
Mrs. George W. Burgess

Narwhal Guest House, 28 Easton St.
Mrs. Arthur C. Putnam

Ocean House, 29 Broad St.
Frank Worth

The Parker House, 11 N. Water St.
Mrs. Pearl Parker

Point Breeze Hotel, Easton St.
Frank Worth, mgr.

Quanato Terrace, 1 Quanato Ct.
Mrs. J. B. Staples

Roberts House, 11 Pearl St.
Mrs. Catherine M. Roberts

Sea Cliff Inn, Cliff Rd.
Clifford Folger, treas.;

Ships Inn, 11 Fair St.
Ernest S. MacLaughlin

Tom Nevers Lodge, Tom Nevers Head
Charles E. Kimball, mgr. in 1928

Veranda House, Step Lane
E. S. MacLaughlin

Wauwinet House, Wauwinet
James A. Backus

Weeweeder Inn, Surfside
J. Butler Folger

White Elephant, Easton St.
Mrs. Elizabeth Temple Ludwig

Wonoma Inn, 61 Centre St.
Thomas and Anna Ward

Worth House, 26 N. Water St.
Fred Allen (of the "Diner")

Two boardinghouses also listed were those of Mrs. Annie Smith, 27 Union Street, and Mrs. W. H. H. Smith, 20 Federal Street. Guest houses of 1919 that had ceased to exist were: the Hillside and Summit Inn, Gay Street; Pitman House, Centre Street; and the 'Sconset House in Siasconset. The Clisby House in Siasconset was in a state of transition, from which it was to emerge in 1928 as the Wander Inn, under the management of Sarah Folger. The Colonial Inn on North Water Street, owned by C. C. Ross, was conducted in conjunction with Crest Hall. Then in operation, but perhaps opened too late to be included in the directory, were Florence H. Breithut's Springfield

Lodge, 27 North Water Street, and Marie Louise Miller's Anchor Inn, 66 Centre Street.

The number of summer cottages, either owned or rented by their tenants, seemed to have increased over the past few years. The list of such places given in the local newspaper early in August of 1919 (tabulated by streets earlier) totaled fewer than 300. In the 1927 directory, following the names of permanent residents, the list of cottages comes to almost 700. These statistics are an indication of how more and more seasonal visitors were being accommodated on Nantucket during the period of prosperity a decade after the war.

Nantucket had a new boat in 1928. The *New Bedford*, built at that city along the lines of the *Nantucket* and the *Martha's Vineyard*, was launched on 22 May. She was assigned to regular service the following day, replacing the *Uncatena*, which had been making daily trips for twenty-five years. Capt. Francis J. Marshall, commander of the *Uncatena* during its entire life, took over the new boat. The *New Bedford* differed from its predecessor by having a screw propeller instead of paddle wheels. In this she resembled her sister ships, but varied from them in that the passenger gangway was farther aft, allowing more space for freight. The boat was 210 feet long and capable of a speed of 15 knots an hour. The first major breakdown was on 14 July when the shaft of the steering gear got stuck on pulling out from Nantucket. The *New Bedford* got through the jetties all right. The next five hours were spent in trying to remedy the trouble, after which it was towed back to Steamboat Wharf. Passengers finally were taken aboard the *Nantucket* at midnight to be returned to America.

In traditional manner, the summer of 1928 got started with the July Fourth celebration. This one followed the lately developed prescribed form, which featured a bonfire on the preceding evening. It was lit at the dumping ground, and the contribution of several hundred railroad ties doused with seventeen barrels of oil made the 1928 flame spectacular. The Nantucket band (augmented by a few musicians from New Bedford) was stationed on a hill to the east of the dump and played during the last hour before midnight. Spectators came from town on foot and by car, parking the vehicles along the Madaket and Hummock Pond roads.

Activities on the Fourth proper also were enlivened by the band. The parade of "horribles" petered out, as only two participants showed up. The main activities were sporting events for boys and girls held on Federal Street, and contests for grownups at the fairgrounds. The latter included trapshooting, horse and motorcycle races, and a basketball game. Silver cups were awarded the winners at the children's bathing beach preceding the fireworks display at night. The pyrotechnics were set off on the yacht club grounds, the club and town each having contributed $500 to the spectacle. The "grand wind-up . . . was more of a thrill than anybody expected, for it was a genuine bombardment, the bombs being sent up and exploding continuously for over five minutes, with the greatest racket Nantucket has ever heard."

The mechanized sightseeing tour got off to a start on Nantucket that summer. J. B. Folger devised a forty-mile trip around the island. The first was held on 1 July. Buses loaded in front of the Atheneum. Morning tours lasted from 9:30 to 12:30, and afternoon trips from 2:00 to 5:00 o'clock.

Renovation of the island's foremost historic monument was carried to completion in 1928. The Jethro Coffin house on Sunset Hill, built in 1686 for Tristram Coffin's grandson, and a museum since 1886, had been acquired in 1923 by the Nantucket Historical Association. Three years later, Winthrop Coffin of Boston offered to stand the expense of restoring it with the understanding that the work was to be supervised by William Sumner Appleton, corresponding secretary of the Society for the Preservation of New England Antiquities. After Appleton's preliminary work, Alfred E. Shurrocks, a practicing architect, directed the undertaking. The east corner of the eighteenth-century lean-to had burned and was replaced. William F. Macy, president of the NHA, spoke at the rededication ceremony on 30 July.*

There were two fires in 1928 damaging summer stands at Siasconset. The first, occurring on the night of 20 January, was the burning of the Ocean Park kitchen. The adjoining office was damaged, but the cottages escaped. It was thought that the fire was of incendiary origin. Also at night—or more accurately during the early morning hours of 5 August—the Tavern-on-the-Moors kitchen burned. Lately it had featured Jean Bats, of the Waldorf-Astoria, in charge of the cuisine. The building stood next to the fire station, and the 'Sconset fire volunteers, reinforced by the employees of the tavern, battled the blaze with two chemical tanks, eight hand extinguishers, and a number of water buckets. The fire house itself was seared. The flame started outside, presumably from a carelessly discarded lighted cigarette.

The high social event of the season was the Cabaret Fashion Show and Dance at the yacht club on 22 August. It was not held in the club's building but in the dining saloon of the night boat, the Nantucket, moored to the dock behind the building. Gustavius Town Kirby was master of ceremonies. The first number was Fred Marx performing sleight-of-hand tricks. It was followed by social dancing. After the 10:00 o'clock intermission, Gibbs Penrose entertained with a clog waltz to the tune of "Crazy Rhythms," for which applause called forth two encores. The first part of the fashion show was at 10:30, with a "display of some very exquisite evening, afternoon, sport and street costumes procured from Solov-Hinds Company of Boston," including some "original French models." The seven mannequins were accompanied by Tony Sarg in a sport suit and coat, "which he displayed with as much grace as the beautiful ladies." Social dancing resumed until 11:00 o'clock, when Polly and William Chamberlin performed "a pleasant 'Tango and Waltz.'" They were called back to repeat the number. Tony Sarg brought the voice of the "Governor of New York State . . . making his country-wide speech of acceptance," which was Al Smith on the radio becoming the Democratic candidate for President against Herbert Hoover. It was not the most acceptable presentation of the evening. Dancing prevailed until 11:30,

*Letters, drawings, and photographs pertaining to the house and its restoration are at the Society for the Preservation of New England Antiquities, Boston.

128 *The Jethro Coffin House, Sunset Hill, from rear, before the lean-to at the east end was replaced.*

when the balance of the fashion show occurred. At midnight, Mrs. John H. Kitchen sang two modern songs. She was urged to repeat one, called "Rain," and forgot the words, at which point she drizzled out of sight. Tony Sarg entertained with his marionettes in an "Oriental Fantasy," highlighted by a rajah laughing at a girl performing a "shimmy snake dance." Social dancing resumed until 1:00 a.m. Five hundred inflated balloons, large vases of hydrangea, and lighted candles provided a festive atmosphere for the "cabaret."

An organized theatre group appeared on the horizon. Calling itself the Nantucket Players, its career started with the controversial play *Salome*, written in French by Oscar Wilde in 1892 and under rehearsal with Sarah Bernhardt in the title

role when its presentation was halted by the Paris censor. It was published in English both in London and Boston in 1894, and was first given in that language in 1905. The Nantucket Players scheduled it at the Siasconset Casino for 15 August 1928, but due to rehearsal problems it was postponed twelve days.

The following year the group got off to an early start and held forth at the American Legion Hall on Washington Street in town, which recently had been given to the legionnaires by Mr. and Mrs. Henry Lang. The first production here was A. A. Milne's light comedy, *Belinda*, played on the evenings of 28 and 29 July. Seats were reserved and sold for $1.50 and $2.00. The second production was "an exhilarating comedy" featuring Olive Russell and Robert Ross, of the Civic Reper-

129 *Advertisement for the Tavern-on-the-Moors, 1927.*

tory Theatre of New York, under the direction of the latter. It was Roi Cooper Megue's play, whose title derived from the hit tune of "No, No, Nanette," here rendered *Tea for Three* (T43), billed for 30 and 31 August. But it was presented only on the latter evening as the director-actor got tied up in New York with the Eva Le Gallienne production of *The Sea Gull* and could not get back to the island.

Hostelries listed in the telephone directory for 1929 are about the same as those in the 1927 town directory, recorded earlier. Omitted two years before but included in 1929 are the names of the Misses Ide, 17 Pearl Street, and the Woodbox, 29 -31 Fair Street, both dating from the early 1920s; and Springfield Lodge, 27 North Water Street, formerly the Springfield Annex. Not listed were The Gables, the Worth House, Parker House, and Narwhal Guest House. The first three, at least,

were to continue under other names. The Gables was owned and being operated by Mrs. George W. Burgess in conjunction with the Nesbitt Inn. The Worth House was run by several ladies in succession under their own names; then in 1944 it became the Carlisle Guest House, Herbert S. Carley, proprietor. The Parker House was listed as the Stetson House in 1955. Crest Hall served as a school while the new public-school building was being constructed on Academy Hill during January to mid-September. A new name in the 1929 directory is Tashmoo Inn, on Main Street, whose title echoes that of a popular tonic and spring water of the period, but as an inn it seems to have quickly effervesced.

Dining places at the end of the decade included:

Kimball's Restaurant, South Water St.

Nantucket Spa, 26 Main St.

The Skipper, Steamboat Wharf

Shimmoah Tea House, Cliff Rd.

Worth's Ice Cream Parlor, 103 Main St. (between Macy and Tobey houses)

Christine's Refreshment Stand
Surfside Rd.

Hollow-by-the-Flare
Sankaty Rd., Siasconset (Mrs. A. V. Bennett, mgr., formerly of Ocean Park)

Dine-a-Mite, New St., Siasconset

Mrs. Etta Morris, New St.
Siasconset (ice cream)

Tavern-on-the-Moors
School St., Siasconset

The College Kitchen (at Chanticleer)
Siasconset

White Whale Inn (at Moby Dick)
Siasconset

Charles E. Kimball, proprietor of Kimball's Restaurant on South Water Street, Nantucket, and Tom Nevers Lodge, ran into difficulties this year by conducting his businesses without an innkeeper's or victualer's license.

The hospital fair of 1929 was held in town, but it broke away from Main Street and Nantucket's historic past. It took place on Easy Street and Old North Wharf on 8 August, having a background of the Great Harbor dotted with the "rainbow fleet" (catboats), and it bore the name of the Water Front Carnival. As it turned out, the principal interest centered around the visit of Gov. Frank A. Allen and the first lady of Massachusetts, who came over in the official suite of the *Naushon* (launched only three months before) from Woods Hole, escorted by Rep. Arthur W. Jones. A seventeen-gun salute was fired on the governor's arrival at 2:00 o'clock. Welcomed by a committee head-

T43 T43 T43 T43 T43 T43

"TEA FOR THREE"

A Comedy
to be presented by

"THE NANTUCKET PLAYERS"

On Friday and Saturday Eve'gs,

AUGUST 30th and 31st at 8.30 o'clock

at the

AMERICAN LEGION HALL

Tickets—$2.00 and $1.50.

T43 T43 T43 T43 T43 T43

130 *Advertisement for* Tea for Three, *1929.*

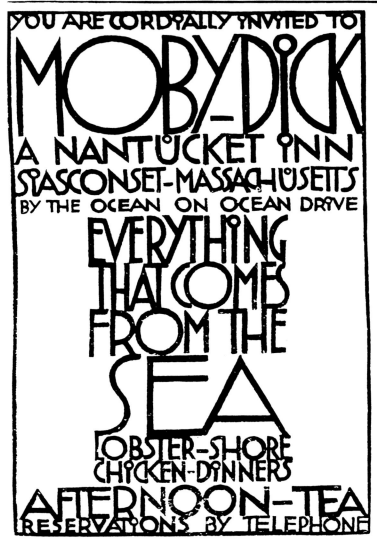

You are cordially invited to
MOBY-DICK
A Nantucket Inn
Siasconset-Massachusetts
By the ocean on Ocean Drive
Everything that comes from the sea
Lobster-Shore Chicken-Dinners
Afternoon-Tea
Reservations by telephone

Moby Dick

Siasconset

on Ocean Drive
overlooking Sea

A NANTUCKET INN
like an old English
coffee house.

AFTERNOON TEA

LOBSTER, CHICKEN
and
SHORE DINNERS

DANCING ON OPEN PORCH

Telephone 21-16.

131 *Advertisement for the Moby Dick Inn, 1927.*

ed by Everett U. Crosby, commodore of the yacht club and president of the Nantucket Cottage Hospital, Mrs. Allen was presented with a lightship basket by Mitchell Ray, and the party lunched at Austin Strong's boathouse on Old North Wharf. For this occasion the wharf was called "Frolic Lane," and after the repast the distinguished guests joined the throng, inspecting and purchasing from the various booths selling

flowers, toys and gifts, chowder, littleneck and cherrystone clams, hot dogs, ice cream, and soft drinks. Besides Easy Street's established landmarks such as the Skipper, the Easy Street Gallery, and the Napoleon willow (the parent seedling brought from Elba in 1842, the Easy Street tree sprouted from branches used for landfill), there was a new one for the occasion, a small-scale replica of the old mill, placed behind Dreamland Theatre.

A view of Easy Street and the harbor during the carnival. At the left appear three well-known institutions—Easy Street Gallery, the Napoleon Willow and "The Skipper." In the foreground is shown the interesting "Old Mill". In the distance the "rainbow fleet" had their sails flapping in the light breeze. At the right, with flag flying from mast-head, is Austin Strong's boat-house, where the Governor and Mrs. Allen were entertained at luncheon.

132   *"A View of Easy Street and the Harbor During the Carnival," Waterfront Carnival, 8 August 1929. The Napoleon Willow and the Skipper tied up at Steamboat Wharf are to the left and above the replica of the Old Windmill; Old North Wharf is to the right.*

Chances were sold on it or a $100 cash prize, and on a trip to Europe for two. The latter raffle netted $5,777.58, and the carnival as a whole brought in $25,584.10. Participants in the three former fetes missed the traditional theme and grudgingly admitted it was "something different." It made considerably more money, and everybody seems to have had a fine time.

At the end of the 1920s Nantucket reflected the nation in its economic and political outlook. Late in September of 1928 the *Inquirer and Mirror* repeated an article in which Henry Ford is quoted as having said that he could sell 20,000 cars a day, instead of only half that number, which were as many as his plants could produce. A bit over a month later, the presidential election destined Herbert Hoover for the country's top position (Nantucket's vote was 865 as against 395 for Alfred E. Smith). In March of 1929 there was a piece in the paper entitled, "Do They Gamble on Wall Street?" It affirmed in no uncertain terms that "they" do not. At the beginning of August it was noted that Nantucket's second-best summer month, "July [Was] Better than [the] Best August on Record," which was based on the quantity of tourists brought over on the boats and the flourishing state of local enterprises. This

was in line with an article assessing the President's first six months in office, which read: "Business is generally good over the country, and there is no reason to feel that we will be called on to expect anything but peace and prosperity during the next few years." In mid-October it was noted that "so fast is the old paper money going out of circulation that more than 180 tons are now stored in the Treasury-Department's storage vault at Washington." Taken altogether things looked bright and prosperous. But the bottom dropped out of the nation's economy with the plummeting of the New York stock market on 29 October 1929!

Except for an editorial comment on the proposed Empire State Building to be built in New York City, admonishing architects to "remember what happened to the stock market when it got too high," mention of the Wall Street crash was conspicuously absent from the island's journal. It had occurred after an extremely good season. Most people here were well heeled, and there seemed no reason to be concerned over a financial crisis in America at the time. Besides, bluefish had returned to the adjacent waters after an absence of fourteen years, and Nantucketers were preoccupied with their rods and reels.

VIII. THE DEPRESSION DECADE: THEATRICALS AND EXHIBITIONS

THE STOCKMARKET CRASH in the fall of 1929, however remote it may have seemed to the islanders at the time, created a grim economic slowdown that persisted through the nineteen-thirties. Due to the slack in vacation travel, especially during the early part of the decade, Nantucket's downtown streets were frequented by only a few more people during the summer than in the winter months. Proprietors of hostelries and restaurants struggled to remain afloat with little source of business buoyancy. After several seasons the pinch became acute, and some of them were forced to close their doors, a few losing their property and having to look elsewhere for a livelihood.

Under those trying circumstances two factors are to be noted. The first is the fadeout of the boardinghouse. We saw the beginning of the trend through comparing this species of inn between the 1919 and 1927 island directories. In that period the number of boardinghouses had decreased, whereas hotels had increased. But in the early 1930s the boardinghouse went out of existence. Some gave up feeding guests and became mere lodging houses; the very few that remained were reclassified as "hotels." The other factor is a recurring characteristic of Nantucket—that of withdrawing the vital energies back into the town. The older of the remote nineteenth-century inns already had come to grief: the Surfside Hotel before 1900, and the Atlantic House and Ocean View House at Siasconset at the time of World War I. Two exceptions to the trend were the Wauwinet House, which had begun small and grew, and the Beach House at 'Sconset, both of

which were—or virtually were—twentieth-century buildings. Even the quasi-remote Nantucket, on Brant Point, expired at the close of the 1904 season. The two hotels still running, farthest from Nantucket's Lower Square, were the Sea Cliff Inn and the Point Breeze; and we shall see what was to happen to them during this threadbare era.

Out of key with the times was the erection of hunting stables south of the town, a project begun the year before. It was beyond Tashama Farms, and its entrance was on Cato Lane. Hunting had been introduced in 1926 by a Philadelphian who brought a small pack of harriers to Nantucket. The stables built during the winter of 1929 -30 were sponsored largely by Gustavius Town Kirby, of the Nantucket Yacht Club. The building was an open quadrangle and contained thirty-two box stalls. Stables and grounds represented an outlay of $35,000, a considerable sum at the outset of the Depression. A clubhouse and grooms' houses were proposed. Hunting was hardly appropriate to the island and has played a meager role here. Horseback riding enjoyed slightly greater participation. It tied in with events at the Agricultural Society's fairs, which institution had but a few more years of survival.

What saved the Commonwealth of Massachusetts, by appealing to such tourism as existed during the summer of 1930, was the Tercentenary of the old Bay Colony, onto which Nantucket latched for its share of the gains. It called its participation Old Home Week, which began on Saturday, 19 July. Featured on this day was the gathering of the Sons and Daughters of Nantucket for

133 *Perspective rendering of the proposed hunting stables off Cato Lane, 1930.*

lunch at Surfside. Some eighty members of the organization, then in its forty-sixth year, met on the south shore at 1:00 o'clock for a "clam bake." A fire was going, and the clams were steamed, as were the "hot dogs," served on rolls, which completed the collation. It was followed by an "hour or two of sociability" at the Weeweeder Inn. The American Legion Post Band was there and played; and Charles T. Hall, head of the society, presided. Representative Arthur W. Jones read a telegram from Gov. Frank A. Allen. Isabel Coffin recited several of Mary Starbuck's poems, and other speakers were David J. Maloney and William F. Macy, the latter being president of the Nantucket Historical Association, which, like the Sons and Daughters, was founded in 1894.

On Sunday evening there was a mass meeting at the Congregational Church on Centre Street. The band marched through the streets playing stirring music, ending with its final numbers on the lawn of Old North Vestry. James H. Garnett, wearing a Puritan costume, stood at the portal rolling his drum in the manner of calling people

to meeting in the olden days. The program opened with the doxology and then everybody joined in the hymn "Coronation." The organ and choir led in the musical numbers. Frederick W. Cook presented the governor's greetings, and the Hon. Breckinridge Long delivered an historical oration. Hymns sung afterward included "Faith of Our Fathers" and "America the Beautiful." The Rev. Evarts W. Pond pronounced the benediction, and the program closed with the vocalizing of the "Star-Spangled Banner."

Edgar F. Wyer, portraying the town crier, made announcements for the Tercentenary Committee through the streets of Nantucket.

On Monday and Tuesday evenings at 8:30, Prof. Albert Bushnell Hart of Harvard showed a documentary film called "Three Centuries of Massachusetts" at the Unitarian Church. It was prepared by the University Film Foundation of Cambridge, and a door fee of 50¢ was charged.

An "Historic Parade" was the main event on Tuesday afternoon, which had been declared a half-holiday in the town. Floats represented various facets of Nantucket "from the time of the Indians to the departure of the mosquitoes." The largest representation was of the Red Men, including their float of Chief Nickanoose conveying Nantucket to the white man in 1664, probably meaning the deed from him and Chief Wanackmamack of 1660. The female counterpart of the Red Men, the Degree of Pocahontas, followed with a float of "Indian Customs," of which the primary one exploited was war-whooping. The Daughters of the American Revolution had a vehicle portraying Abiah Folger Franklin, the chapter's namesake, and her son Benjamin. Other floats included Arthur H. Norcross's woodworkers; David Gray's of Liddy Worth's cent school; the Whaling Museum's of a whaleboat with crew; two of the Telephone Company, representing old and new modes of communication; and the Gas and Electric Company's commemorating the installing of gaslights in 1854, with Sam Kelley as the lamplighter. The "Boys of 1867," the three Nantucket survivors of the Grand Army of the Republic—Josiah F. Murphy, James H. Barrett, and James A. Wood—rode in a surrey. The Fire Department paraded with the old pumper "Cataract"; and the Legion Drum and Bugle Corps was led by Drum Major Charlie Thurber. The Nantucket Yacht Club had a tender mounted on a truck filled with young people, and the Boy Scouts furnished a representation of a scout camp. The Mosquito Control Committee, at that time an active island force, furnished several young ladies representing the insectile object of their ire. The Monnohanit Club float contained five girls with field and spy glasses, and the last vehicle contained an "old time orchestra," whose members were bedecked in "unique costumes" and false whiskers. The parade started on Washington Street at 2:30, went up South and North Water streets to Cliff Road, through North Liberty to India, thence to Centre, down to Main, past the reviewing stand to Union, down Union to York, over to Pleasant, up to Main, west to Gardner, up to Liberty, back to Main, down Orange to Consue, to Union by Francis, and ending where it began, on Washington Street.

On Wednesday afternoon at 2:30 were the whaleboat races. From the Island Service Company's wharf the vessels rowed around the stake boat off Coatue Point and returned. In the evening the Nantucket Historical Association presented Chester Scott Howland, of New Bedford, in a motion-picture lecture, "The Story of the Early Whalemen." It was for the benefit of the Whaling Museum Fund.

Thursday was the Nantucket Historical Association's special day. The annual meeting was held at 2:30 in the afternoon, and at 3:00 o'clock followed the dedication of the new Whaling Museum at Broad and South Beach streets. The building originally was the Richard Mitchell & Sons candle factory, built in 1847, later the Hadwen & Barney offices, which the association purchased from Henry P. Schauffler of Brooklyn, New York, in 1929. It was a plain, brick, Greek Revival warehouse with slate roof, whose rectangular doorway was given a new fan enframement in the Federal style. Its exhibits (including the sperm whale's jaw and other items formerly at the Atheneum) were arranged casually, to avoid what the newspaper termed the "museummy" look. The dedicatory ceremony consisted of a reading of a message from the governor and three speeches. They were by Austin Strong, spokesman for the yacht club; Abbott P. Smith, of the Whalemen's Club; and Moses Joy, who told about candlemaking.

A stage performance that was prepared for and considered part of the Tercentenary was presented in the Old North Vestry of the Congregational Church two weeks later. It was described as a pageant in thirteen episodes. The setting was an antique shop in which various pieces came to life and told their stories. Among them were a sampler, cradle, armchair, Paisley shawl, china dog, and a fan. There also were a quilting party, Revolutionary-period tea, a spinner, and several other characters. The lines had been written in verse by Ethel Hawthorne Tewksbury. Included on the program was Litta Grimm, a soloist from the Riverside Church in New York who sang "The Waters of Minnetonka" and "The Morning," accompanied by Alfred Boyce. Peter Hussey, the church quartet, and the organist also furnished music.

134   *The Whaling Museum, Broad Street, originally the Richard Mitchell & Sons candle factory (1847),*
    later Hadwen & Barney candle factory (modern photograph).

The Dreamland Theatre needed no lecturers to comment on its films, as it had installed a Western Electric sound system before the beginning of spring in 1930, enabling the presentation of the latest Hollywood releases.

However, the theatrical spotlight of the summer was directed on the Nantucket Players, holding forth in their second year at the American Legion Hall. Top seats were again $2.00, but the lower admission fee had dropped to $1.00 in token of the changed times. There was a new spirit of earnestness about summer theatre beginning this year. Whereas, heretofore, the play given at

Siasconset in 1928 had been postponed almost a fortnight, and the second play of 1929 performed only on one of its two slated engagements, during the 1930s a full summer schedule was posted and fulfilled regularly. Like everything else during the Depression, legitimate theatre in America was hard hit; and an actor's appearance on the island was no longer a personal concession but a bread-and-butter job.

Robert Ross again was to direct and act in all productions during 1930. The first on 10 and 11 July, was George Kelly's *The Show Off,* which initially had been performed in New York in 1924.

At that time it was proclaimed by Heywood Broun the best comedy written by an American. On Nantucket it was interpreted in the old "town-hall style." The cast of eight included six professionals, with Ross playing the part of Audrey Piper. Also included were Olive Russell, another returnee, and Natalie Wykes, David Keating Maloney, and Richard Maloney.

All were to appear in the Nantucket Players' second production, *Uncle Tom's Cabin,* given on 24 and 25 July. The theatre version of Harriet Beecher Stowe's novel dates from 1852. David Keating Maloney portrayed Uncle Tom, Robert Ross played St. Clare, and Richard Maloney played Shelby. Olive Russell was Ophelia, and Natalie Wykes was Topsy. A newcomer, Gibbs Penrose, played Simon Legree. Stage settings were by William McDonald, a Philadelphia artist. The final scene of the melodrama showed Little Eva on the back of a milk-white dove, in the midst of angels, ascending to heaven.

The third play, written by Nantucket's summertime enthusiast Austin Strong, was entitled *Three Wise Fools,* which had enjoyed a run in New York and London and on the road a few years earlier. Miss Russell, Mr. Ross, and the two Maloneys were in the cast, and they were joined by Burgess Meredith—who had been appearing in the New York production of *Candida*—and Mary Lawrence and Marion Tobey.

The last production of the season was George Bernard Shaw's *Candida,* whose copyright performance was given in 1895, followed by a run in London in 1900 and in New York in 1904. It was presented in Nantucket on 21 and 22 August. Olive Russell played the title role, and Mary Lawrence portrayed Prosey. Burgess Meredith was the poet, Marchbanks, and Robert Ross appeared as Morrell. The two Maloneys also had roles. A portion of the proceeds of this show was contributed to the Nantucket Cottage Hospital.

The yacht club engaged in two gala summer events that included theatricals. The first transpired on 30 and 31 July. It was billed as the "Vaudeville de Luxe," and the admission fee of $3.00 went to the Bulkhead Benefit. Conspicu-

ous in the presentation were Austin Strong and Edgar W. Jenney. As in the "Nantucket Follies" of 1927, Frederick Kitson Cawley again impersonated "The Quaker" and Sarah Bunker Winslow was the "Little Gray Lady." Numbers consisted of Mr. Bilby singing "Roses of Picardy," Mrs. C. H. Walling interpreting a humorous scene at the ticket window of Steamboat Wharf, Pepsi Marshall dancing in ballet costume, and William E. Chamberlain performing card and other tricks. The Squidnet Riveters, a jazz orchestra of six, played under the leadership of Austin Strong. Jay Fawcett rendered several monologues. The Nantucket Players gave a skit called "The Awakening of Spring," and Olive Bird, Henry Bartol, and Theodore Steinway rendered another, called "Bared." Frank and Molly Orvitt performed songs and dances. After a brief intermission, Miss Bird, Mr. Steinway, and Beatrix Buel Smith, Leonie Danford, Henry Clapp Smith, and J. Archer Smith presented a farce called *The Bathroom Door.* Tony Sarg appeared and drew caricatures of persons well known to the audience. Barbara West danced; Mrs. Helen B. Reynolds sang two solos; and several girls came out in a dance sketch called "Sea Ponies." The group that appeared in "Bared" and *The Bathroom Door* gave a mystery called *The Forbidden Shrine.* Charles Stratton sang; and two or three young ladies executed some intricate steps in a number called "Beach Nuts." "The Lancers," composed of five pairs of dancers and four musicians, ran through several antique dances. The final number was "The Quaker" reading an epilogue, with the "Little Gray Lady" in a tableau on a roofwalk. Music was furnished by the Art Taylor orchestra.

The second entertainment at the yacht club was "A BAL TRAVESTI COSTUME CABARET," designated "So This Is Paris." It was held on two evenings, 13 and 14 July, from 10:00 p.Mm. to 2:00 a.m., and admission was $5.00. The ballroom was made to resemble a Parisian boulevard, called the "Rue de Nantucket," where guests sat beneath the awnings of sidewalk cafes and danced in the street. American soldiers on hand recalled the days of World War I. Marie Tiffany, of the Metropolitan Opera Company, sang the

"Marseillaise" and the aria from "Louise." In the duet from *Veronique,* she was joined by baritone Milford Jackson. Other features included a "startling Apache Dance" and a "burlesque guillotining." The Art Taylor orchestra was conducted by Austin Strong. Set pieces were designed and painted by Edgar W. Jenny, with parts (like the costumes worn by performers) imported from Paris. The scenery was left intact for an informal dance that was held on Friday night, 15 July.

The creative counterpart of the interpretive arts in 1930 was highlighted from 11 to 13 August by Nantucket's Sidewalk Art Show on Federal Street at the flank of the Atheneum. Miss Maude Stumm is credited with having originated the idea, and it became an annual affair. Twenty painters were represented, attracting a daily average of 300 spectators. The exhibition closed with an auction conducted by Henry B. Coleman, "which brought together the largest crowd of the show." That year's display of pictures at the Easy Street Gallery extended from 1 August to 1 September. Individual shows during the summer included that of Isabelle Tuttle, from 20 July to 1 August, and Harriet Lord and Lucy M. Stanton, from 4 to 16 August at the Candle House Studio. Frank Swift Chase showed his work at his studio, corner of Washington and Francis streets, from 20 August to 1 September, and Lillian Gertrude Rockwood exhibited at Auld Lang Syne in Siasconset during July and August. Outdoor art classes were held by Frank Swift Chase and Emma H. Van Pelt, each having taught here for ten years; and Flora Woodman, of Boston University, conducted her third annual class for children.

While theatre, art exhibitions, and classes lent an aura of glamour and lavished rewards upon the few, the greater number of Nantucketers furnishing accommodations were left to make out as best they could with the prosaic reality of guest shortage. Inns in Nantucket town listed in the 1930 telephone directory were:

Anchor Inn, 66 Centre St.

The Breakers, Point Rd. (Easton St.)

Broadview Tavern, Lincoln Ave.

Grey Gull, 1 Liberty St.

Nantucket House, 1 N. Water St.

Nesbitt Inn, 21 Broad St.

Ocean House, 29 Broad St.

Plymouth House, S. Water St.

Point Breeze Hotel, Point Rd. (Easton St.)

Roberts House, 2 Pearl St.

Sea Cliff Inn, Cliff Rd.

Quanato Terrace, Quanato Ct.

Springfield Lodge, 27 N. Water St.

Veranda House, 3 Step Ln.

Wonoma Inn, 61 Centre St.

White Elephant, Point Rd. (Easton St.)

Out-of-town establishments were:

Wauwinet House

Beach House, Siasconset

Chanticleer, Siasconset

Dine-a-Mite, Siasconset

Tavern-on-the-Moors, Siasconset

Wander Inn, Siasconset and

White Whale, Siasconset

Advertisements show that at the beginning of summer the name of the Veranda House was changed to Hotel Overlook; and although E. S. MacLaughlin remained the proprietor, it was managed by Mary E. Duggan, who later was to become the owner. MacLaughlin still ran the Ships Inn. The former Worth House, at 26 North Water Street, was under the direction of Mrs. Alvira Gayne. Crest Hall on North Water Street, Cottage Inn on Pearl (India) Street, Old Parliament House on Pine Street, and the Woodbox on Fair Street were in existence, though without telephone service. A newcomer was the Spouter Inn, in the old Christopher Baxter lean-to dwelling (1756) at 114 Orange Street, a combination tearoom, gift shop, and guest house. M. C. Ashley was the proprietor.

Nantucket fell victim to the current Depression rage of thinking small, manifesting itself in miniature golf. An eighteen-hole course was on the bathing-beach road, charging a quarter a game, including the use of clubs and balls.

A bit of unpleasantness arose over transportation to the public bathing beach. Elmer F. Pease, proprietor of one of the bus lines, appeared before the Nantucket selectmen with a complaint against town-beach lessee Leon M. Royal for erecting a stand or plank platform specifically for use of Captain Folger's buses. Royal arose and defended his position by accusing the Pease system of favoritism toward the rival beach, by discharging passengers there under the impression that it was the public beach. The matter then came up concerning the two signs at the junction of Town Beach Road and North Beach Street, one or the other continually being shifted to obscure its companion. The selectmen instructed the superintendent of highways to place both boards in plain view.

The beach was in the news again in September, when a survey showed that, due to the buildup of sand, Royal's bathing establishment was over 300 feet out from the nearest boundary line of the land purchased by the town in 1903. It was suggested that the area be taken under consideration by land-court procedure.

The unemployment situation on the island toward the end of the year was alleviated by a general participation in scalloping.

In 1931 the Nantucket Players shifted from the American Legion Hall to the yacht club theatre. Thomas Barrows was manager, and Austin Strong stuck an unofficial finger in the selection and production pies. There were four offerings during the summer, on Wednesday and Thursday evenings of alternate weeks, and admission remained $2.00 and $1.00. The first, on 8 and 9 July, was the mystery thriller *Cat and the Canary,* written for the stage by John Willard. Its set mechanics of opening panels and hinged bookcases were more ingenious than its plot, which focused on frightening a legitimate heir into insanity. Pascal Cowan was the shy hero, Betty Upthegrove the blond "canary," and Mary Lawrence the cryptic West Indian housekeeper. David and Richard Maloney were back again, and the cast included Helen

Huberth, Nadine Norton, William Mercer, John Shaw, and William Miles.

The second play was Bernard Francis Moore's *Belle the Typewriter Girl,* given on 22 and 23 July. A hit at the Comedy Club during the preceding winter, the melodrama of the nineties is about a miner (played by William Mercer) who returns to his Chicago home with a fortune in diamonds, which he leaves with a banker (David Keating Maloney) and then dies of a heart attack. The banker tries to swindle the miner's wife and beautiful daughter, Belle (Betty Upthegrove). Richard Maloney played the banker's clerk and henchman, John Shaw the hero, and William Miles a character bent on seeing that justice is done. Entr'actes included Mercer singing "After the Ball" (just before his death), the showing of the 1903 movie "The Great Train Robbery" (about a decade late for the setting), and Helen Huberth singing "Frankie and Johnny," as well as engaging in a rope-skipping act.

Captain Applejack was the third production, given on 5 and 6 August. It is an Arabian Nights adventure by Walter Hackett about a young man so bored with his existence that he has advertised to sell his home and go off to seek excitement. He finds it, but without leaving home, when an attractive young lady claiming to be a Russian dancer appears, seeking sanctuary from Bolsheviks who are after priceless jewels supposed to be in her possession. In hiding her, a secret parchment turns up revealing one of the hero's ancestors to have been a pirate. This suggests a dream sequence in which the young man identifies with the old buccaneer. John Shaw and Betty Upthegrove played the leads.

Last in 1931 was George Kelly's comedy *The Torch Bearers,* presented on 19 and 20 August. It is about a group using "little theatre" as a means to culturally elevate the community. The hero (Charles Hyde) returns home to find his living room the scene of a rehearsal in which his wife (Olive Russell) plays the part of a "hard-boiled, cigarette-voiced, hip-swinging" female. The second act is a play within a play, being backstage while a performance is in progress, and the audience is treated to a full score of amateur-theatrical blunders. The wife, who had entertained the thought of becoming an actress, reneges when the husband convinces her of her shortcomings.

At the Siasconset Casino on 17 August, Gibbs Penrose (who had played Simon Legree in *Uncle Tom's Cabin* the previous year) staged *Depressions of 1931,* characterized as "A Broadway Revue with Local Appeal." Penrose's part was omnipresent as he "danced, wrote skits, trained the chorus even to the extent of teaching some of them how to tap-dance, he sang not well but loudly, and he managed and directed the show." Special honors went to pantomimist Peter Joray whose impersonations of Louis XIV and Queen Victoria were pronounced priceless. Joray was not billed. He had performed in a recital series at the Tavern-on-the-Moors the evening before, and his appearance in *Depressions* was a last-minute arrangement. Proceeds benefited the Siasconset Casino Association.

On 13 August Tony Sarg's marionette group, The Barn Stormers, on a New England tour, presented "Dick Whittington and His Cat" at the Sea Cliff Inn entertainment hall. A demonstration on the making, costuming, and stringing of marionettes and a variety show were included.

Early in 1931 the announcement had been made that India House, an inn at 37 Pearl Street, was to be under Skipper management, and it would be open throughout the year. The old Frederick C. Sanford residence, 17 Federal Street, formerly serving as the Hospital Thrift Shop, now offered overnight accommodations, and the thrift shop was conducted at 12 Liberty Street. The telephone directory shows that Franklin E. Smith took guests at 63 Main Street, and L. A. Souza at 4 East Dover Street.

Mrs. Elmer E. Ames "converted her spacious reception room at Maddaket into a Fish Grill where she . . . [served] lobsters, steamed clams, little necks, chowders, clam fritters, sandwiches and lunch. Regular shore dinners pre-arranged. Open from 2 p.m. until 11:30."

There must have been some accusation that the group performing at the yacht club during the summer of 1931 differed from that previously at the American Legion Hall, because the following year it was styled the Nantucket Theatre. It was organized by Betty Upthegrove and William Miles, both newcomers in the 1931 season, the latter to serve as the forthcoming director. Business manager was Eva M. Fry, who had held this position at the Henry Street Theatre in New York, and the treasurer was Ruth Tanner, who had served the Nantucket Players in that capacity for four years. P. Ward Beachley was scenic artist, having had design experience at Stockbridge, Massachusetts; Aarden, Delaware; and at the Roerick Museum and with the Juilliard Opera Company in New York City. Miss Upthegrove and Mr. Miles were to perform; they were joined by J. Sayer Crawley and Mary Ward, who had been with the Civic Repertory Company for five years; Maurice Wells, from the Theatre Guild; and Eleanor Bedford, John Gordon, and George Taylor, Jr., who also had some background on the legitimate stage.

It was announced that Mr. and Mrs. George Fawcett would be "associated with the group." The Fawcetts, it will be recalled, had figured prominently in the entertainments at the Siasconset Casino in 1901 and 1902, and they were leading members of the village's summer-theatre colony. The Fawcett's daughter, Margaret, directed a benefit performance at the legion hall on 16 and 18 May 1932, called *The Whole Town's Talking,* sponsored by the Nantucket Shellfish Association. Although the cast was composed of amateurs, it was said that the production was of top quality.

During the following summer the Nantucket Theatre maintained a downtown office at 56 Main Street where photographs of actors and other publicity were displayed. The season began with Dion Titheradge's *Crooked Billet,* the name of an English inn in which four persons find themselves trapped at the headquarters of an international gang. It was given on the evenings of 6 and 7 July and billed as "the first professional performance . . . [Nantucket] has witnessed,"

THE FIRST PRODUCTION

OF THE

THE NANTUCKET THEATRE

———

"THE CROOKED BILLET"

BY

DION TITHERADGE

(Staged by William Miles)

———

CAST

(in order of their appearance)

SLICK PALZER .... David Keating
SIR WILLIAM EASTON .... Maurice Wells
RODGERS .... Albert Valentine
MRS. WIMPLE .... Mary Ward
ALF, THE POTMAN .... Henry Bulkley
PHILIP EASTON .... George Taylor
JOAN EASTON .... Betty Upthegrove
GUY MERROW .... John Gordon
THE DOCTOR .... J. Sayer Crawley
INSPECTOR HITCHING .... William Miles

———

The action takes place in the parlour of "The Crooked Billet", a small village Inn in England.

    ACT I.   An afternoon in September.
    ACT II.   Ten seconds later.
    ACT III. Immediately afterward.

———

Business Manager .... Eva M. Fry
Treasurer .... Ruth Tanner
Designer and Technical Director .... P. Ward Beachley
Stage Manager .... George Taylor

———

The Nantucket Theatre is indebted to Mr. Louis J. Clark
for the furniture used in this production.

———

NEXT WEEK—Miss Percy Haswell in "Mr. Pim Passes By". Seats now on sale at the Box Office.

135 *Program for* The Crooked Billet, *presented at the Nantucket Yacht Club by the Nantucket Theatre, 6 and 7 July 1932.*

meaning in which all phases of the production were handled by people of that status. At this time Austin Strong was quoted as saying: "The theatre is needed now, as never before, to liven the spirits and steady the morale of our citizens." The mission of livening spirits and steadying morale was becoming a serious business.

Other plays given by the Nantucket Theatre in 1932 were: A. A. Milne's *Mr. Pim Passes By,* featuring Percy Haswell (Mrs. George Fawcett), 13 and 14 July; Rachel Crother's *Let Us Be Gay,* starring Betty Upthegrove, 20 and 21 July; William Cotton's *The Bride the Sun Shines On,* a recent success in New York, 27 and 28 July; Emlyn Williams's *A Murder Has Been Arranged,* with setting of St. James's Theatre, London, 3 and 4 August; Edwin Burke's *This Thing Called Love,* a sprightly comedy about marriage, 10 and 11 August; S. N. Behrman's *The Second Man,* a four-character cast and the author's first success (1927); and Leonard Ide's new play, *Peacock,* with Mr. and Mrs. Fawcett and their daughter Margaret in the cast, 24 and 25 August. It was a trial run, as *Peacock* was to open in New York on 10 October.

The summer of 1932 brought competition for the Nantucket Theatre by the appearance—or reappearance—of the Nantucket Players, asserting their prerogative to perform on the island by characterizing this as their fifth season. The announcement in the press in June stated: "Among the original group who will appear again this season are Jane Eichelberger, who played in *Belinda* a few seasons ago; David Keating, son of Mr. and Mrs. David J. Maloney, . . . Olive Russell, founder of the group and star in many of its shows; Mary Lawrence of 'the Wayside Players' and Robert Ross . . . former director of the 'Players.'" It said that Jimmy Russell had "risen from prop-hand to manager," replacing Tom Barrows. The director was Carl Benton Reid, graduate of Carnegie Technical School of the Theatre, with several years' experience in this field at Detroit and Cleveland and recent appearances on Broadway. Actors new with the Players were Effingham Pinto, who had performed in London and was related to the Nantucket Mitchells, and Leon Whitton and Herbert Rawlinson. Mention of

Pinto's and Keating's island family connections and of the policy to "remain semi-professional and use local people" were aimed at establishing a close rapport with Nantucketers, and the latter served as a retort to the all-professional (closed-rank) character of the rival theatre. The Nantucket Theatre presented its shows on Wednesday and Thursday evenings weekly, whereas the Nantucket Players only gave two plays, running for three consecutive evenings, yet both managed to overlap either on its first or last date with one of the yacht club shows. The Players performed at the old stand on Washington Street, now called the Legion Hall Theatre.

The Nantucket Players' first production in 1932, on 28 through 30 July, was C. K. Monroe's comedy, *At Mrs. Beam's,* whose setting was an English boardinghouse and whose plot involved the landlady (portrayed by Madeline Hollerith) and her eleven boarders. Herbert Rawlinson played the latest arrival, and the hero. The director was a replacement, the original being Wadden Murray from Paramount Studios, who used movie techniques, crowding thirty rehearsals into a fortnight. Herbert Rawlinson, at least, experienced no new burden, as he had played in the films. The second offering was Paul Osborn's farce, *The Vinegar Tree,* given on 15 through 17 August. Olive Russell and Herbert Rawlinson took the leads in this story set in a Long Island house. An extra performance was given on Saturday evening, 20 August.

Three Shakespeare recitals were rendered on the evenings of 19, 22, and 26 July by William F. Jones, Percy Haswell (Mrs. George Fawcett), and John Shaw at the Cyrus Peirce School auditorium. They were accompanied by other readings and musical numbers.

An institution called the Nantucket Neighbors came into existence in 1932 to "build a friendly spirit among all classes of people" during the summer months. It was sponsored by the Nantucket Civic League and consisted chiefly of weekly meetings held at the Old North Vestry, with an hour devoted to a talk or other form of program and another of socializing. The first meeting

136 *The cast of* Cappy Cornus, *with Mr. and Mrs. George Fawcett in the center, on stage at the yacht club theatre, 2 July 1933.*

occurred on Monday evening, 11 July, at which 150 persons registered. Civic League president Louis J. Praeger presided and introduced the Rev. Herbert A. Jap, pastor of the Union Congregational Church in Boston and leader of the Boston Friendship Tours (of a social nature), who spoke on "Why I Like Nantucket." James A. Wood, now one of Nantucket's two surviving soldiers of the Civil War, said a few words, expressing the hope that all wars belonged to the past. Writer Edwina Stanton Babcock read a poem dedicated to him, "Grandfather Wood," from her published collection called *Nantucket Windows.* The second Nantucket Neighbors meeting, on 18 July, featured Edgar W. Jenney, artist and illustrator, and Mrs. Frederick Ackerman, formerly of the Columbia faculty and president of the New York Decorators Club, whose subject, "Let's Visit Nantucket," had to do with the island's historic architecture. The Civic League also promoted dances and parties for an "Intercollegiate" group. Notices of events were posted on a bulletin board at the corner of Main and Orange streets.

Professional wrestling put in its first appearance on the island in 1932. The American Legion Post of Nantucket built a ring in the center of the race track at the fairgrounds and arranged four sections of chairs. Leon Burbank of Boston was referee. The bouts occurred on the evening of 2 July. The first was between Manuel Souza of Nantucket and Young Cassidy of New Bedford. The local boy won on a count of points. Four other matches that evening included one between Don George, former world's champion, and "Cowboy" Jack Wagner of Providence. The former champ won but Wagner got the applause for the cleaner fight. The American Legion sponsored further wrestling bouts the next year, headlining "Man Mountain" Dean, the masked "Yellow Peril," and John "Gorilla" Spellman. The second evening, 14 August 1933, witnessed the first "lady" wrestlers on Nantucket, Mary Robertson and Nell Whitney. They were written up in detail in the newspaper.

The Nantucket Players did not return in 1933, and all of the summer's performances were given at the yacht club theatre. The first was an independent affair, a Sunday-evening benefit for the hospital on 2 July. It was Fred Ballard's *Cappy Cornus,* adapted by George Fawcett, who played the part of Eggleston ("Egg") Stern, with Mrs. Fawcett in the role of Carrie Stern, his wife. The other nine members of the cast were nonprofessionals. The plot revolves around the daughter, Florence Stern, and how she was able to attend college, despite the family's strained circumstances and her father's reluctance to work, through her boyfriend's getting his father to offer Egg a job as night watchman at the bank.

The Nantucket Theatre carried on that year, though with only six instead of eight selections, as in 1932. Maurice Wells continued as director, and Mesdames Upthegrove and Fay were back to run the business end. Tickets ranged from $2.20 (with tax) down to 40¢. The season opened with *The Late Christopher Bean,* translated by Sidney Howard from René Fauchois's *Prenez Garder à la Peinture,* starring Helen Mencken, on 19 and 20 July. The second production, originally announced as *Another Language,* was Edgar Wallace's murder mystery *Criminal at Large,* Maurice Wells playing the chief inspector at Scotland Yard, on 26 and 27 July. It was followed on 2 and 3 August by George Haight and Allan Scott's *Goodbye Again,* a comedy about a lecturer who encounters a former lover at the Statler Hotel in Cleveland. The fourth play was Benn Wolf Levy's *Springtime for Henry,* featuring Rose Hobard and Florida Freibus, on 9 and 10 August. Next came the humorous love story, John Van Druten's *There's Always Juliet,* with Violet Heming and Roger Pryor, 16 and 17 August. The last was *By Your Leave,* a new comedy by Gladys Hurlburt and Emma Wells (wife of the Nantucket The-atre's director), which was given with its original Broadway cast on 23 and 24 August.

After fifteen years of Prohibition, the Massachusetts legislature voted in the spring of 1933 to permit the sale and consumption of beer, and a number of dealers on Nantucket applied to the selectmen for licenses. A crowd gathered at the wharf to witness the arrival of the first shipment on 11 April. Among vehicles driving off the boat was a little truck carrying three small cases. The disappointment was somewhat alleviated on the following day when a more ample supply arrived. Legalizing the sale of beer was prelude to the complete repeal of the Eighteenth Amendment toward the end of the year.

A source of some considerable excitement in 1933 was the arrival of Franklin Delano Roosevelt, the fourth incumbent head of state to visit Nantucket. During Roosevelt's New England vacation cruise aboard *Amberjack II,* with a naval escort and press boats, the President was scheduled to arrive here from Edgartown late on Sunday afternoon, 18 June, but heavy seas prevented the trip. Somewhat less heavy waters precluded a planned trip around the tip of the Cape on Monday; and the boat, with the President at the helm, was turned toward Nantucket. The destroyers had to remain outside, but a Coast Guard cutter and the press boats accompanied the *Amberjack II* into the harbor, where anchors were dropped at 11:15 a.m. Roosevelt did not leave the craft. A party headed by William Holland, chairman of the selectmen, and the Democratic town committee set out in the fishing sloop *Beatrice B* to extend welcome. It was intercepted by a Secret Service agent on a patrol boat, and after questioning was allowed to approach within calling distance to deliver its message. In response to the invitation of coming ashore, the President proffered his regrets, saying he did not intend "to set foot on dry land for two weeks." While the elder Roosevelt took his afternoon nap, son James came ashore and was driven around to see the island's high spots and visit the Whaling Museum. The *Amberjack II* did not leave until the following morning, and the newspaper observed that President Roosevelt was the first of his exalted rank to "ever spend the night here." Ten days after the President's visit, the reception committee's conveyance, the *Beatrice B,* burned and sank.

The trying month of this year was March. First the governor and then President Roosevelt ordered the closing of banks. The Nantucket Institution for Savings foreclosed on three island hotels: the Broadview Tavern, Sea Cliff Inn, and Point Breeze, leading to their auction on 24 March.

The Broadview Tavern had been listed among hostelries since 1927, when it was operated by R. S. Deering, and the following year that function was assumed by Fred H. Folger of the Sea Cliff Inn. It may have been the location of the tavern—one of the most desirable on the Cliff with

137 *Perspective sketch of the proposed Broadview Hotel, on the Cliff at Lincoln Avenue, 1930.*

a view of the harbor and Sound—that prompted him, in 1930, to form a corporation called the Folger Hotel Company with himself as president. It presented a grandiose scheme for a new four-storied building on the site to contain 150 rooms with baths, a dining room seating 300 persons, and a spacious ballroom. Such a project was inappropriate for the times; the old tavern building was not replaced. It is the flat-topped house standing southeast of the Lincoln Park circle at the end of Lincoln Avenue. The land had passed from builder Charles H. Robinson to Alonson Cary in 1882, and from the latter or his heirs to Charles A. Snow in 1909, Snow taking out a mortgage for $7,500 on the Nantucket Institution for Savings in 1914. The bank itself bid in the property for $5,000 at the auction in 1933. The Institution for Savings sold the Broadview

to Grafton S. Kennedy II in 1940, and it ceased being a public inn.

The Sea Cliff Inn also was burdened by a heavy mortgage, for which Clifford Folger and William D. Carpenter had contracted with the Nantucket Institution for Savings in 1907. The bank reposessed assumed the property at the 24 March auction for $5,000. On 21 February it was sold to John O. Wilson, Inc., of Bourne, Massachusetts; and on the same day the latter took out a mortgage with the institution for $75,000. The inn on Cliff Road continued to operate a few more years before running into another unfortunate situation.

The Point Breeze Hotel on Easton Street had been acquired by Edward B. Hayes from Bracey Curtis in April of 1920, and at the same time

The New Wauwinet House—from the architect's sketch.

138 *Rendering by Alfred F. Shurrocks, architect, for the new Wauwinet House at the Haulover, 1934.*

Hayes took a mortgage with the Nantucket Institution for Savings for $30,000 at 6% per annum. Mrs. Hayes, widowed, was running the hostelry when the building burned in 1925 (see chapter seven). The bank acquired the building at the 1933 auction for $5,000.

Auctioning hotels due to breach of conditions on mortgages continued into 1934. Frank Worth, who had purchased the Ocean House from William D. and Lawrence A. Carpenter in 1921, took out a $5,000 mortgage with the Nantucket Institution for Savings in the fall of 1927. In the spring of 1934 the bank foreclosed, and the Ocean House was put up for auction on 9 May. The bank bought it. The hotel opened early in June under the management of Merwin J. Bulkley, who had been connected with the Waldorf-Astoria and Vanderbilt hotels in New York City, and was associate manager of the New Alba Hotel in Palm Beach. Bulkley had been proprietor of the Beach House at Siasconset since 1920.

Another Nantucket caravanserai was sold at auction on 31 August 1934, the Quanato Terrace, on Quanato Court off Orange Street. John B. Staples had bought it from Jessie A. Coffin and others in 1909, and Mrs. Staples had mortgaged it in 1922. It was purchased from the estate of Mrs. Mary E. Staples by Mr. and Mrs. Edward Mills of Morristown, New Jersey, who assumed the mortgage. Furniture and household effects were auctioned separately.

Opening under the most auspicious conditions in May of 1934 was the new Wauwinet House at the Haulover. The small story-and-a-half cottage of 1876 had grown until the latest additions made it a three-storied building that could accommodate sixty guests. It contained a new craftsman-style living room and dining room, a new kitchen, and a new casino with a dance floor and stage. The renovation/enlargement was designed by Alfred F. Shurrocks, who had been in charge of the work at the Jethro Coffin house five years earlier. During excavation for the

Wauwinet House, laborers came upon a skull and other bones of a human skeleton, and speculation averred that they were of Wonoma, "the gentle daughter of [Chief] Wauwinet."

Springfield Lodge, at the corner of North Water and Easton streets (or Brant Point Road), advertised that it was the eleventh season of its being under the same management. Florence H. Breithut purchased it from Edwin S. Tirrell in September of 1926.

Mrs. Elizabeth Temple Ludwig was making every effort to keep the White Elephant on its legs, using its waterfront location to advantage and catering to those who arrived in yachts. She provided Russian balalaika-orchestra music for cocktails and dining. Across Brant Point Road was the Riding Light Tea House, offering "meals by day, week or à la carte."

The diversions of the summer of 1934 were provided mainly by the efforts of the third season of the Nantucket Theatre, performing at the yacht club. Among familiar faces back on the island was that of Betty Upthegrove, who had become affianced to W. Warren Kirkbride of New York City, where the wedding was to take place after the summer season. Percy Haswell and Rose Hubert, Maurice Wells and William Miles reappeared, and also P. Ward Beachley, the set designer. The Nantucket Theatre presented two performances of a play a week, beginning 19 and 20 July with Clare Kummer's comedy *Her Master's Voice*, which had enjoyed a thirty-week run at the Plymouth Theatre in New York during the previous winter; Elizabeth McFadden's recent melodrama success, *Double Door*, supposedly concerned with the Wendell family of New York, 26 and 27 July; Rachel Crothers's comedy, *When Ladies Meet*, about what happens when a woman tells a wife she loves her husband, 2 and 3 August; Patricia Collinge (a summer resident of 'Sconset) in *Dulcy*, 9 and 10 August; Kenon Jewett's *Short Circuit*, with Harold Vermilyea and Doris Dalton, 16 and 17 August; Rose Hobart starring in Keith Winter's *The Shining Hour*, 23 and 24 August; and

139 *Living room of the new Wauwinet House, 1934.*

Oscar Wilde's *The Importance of Being Earnest,* with the Misses Hobart and Haswell, 30 and 31 August. The second play, *Double Door,* was to open on Broadway in November, and in the cast was Thomas Barrows, former manager of the Nantucket Players during their first season at the yacht club (1931).

The Nantucket "Cattle Show" held on 15–16 August 1934 was mainly a horse and dog exhibition. There were five trotting- and three running-horse races each day, the latter with "lady" jockeys. The horse show on 16 August was under the management of Betty Lanier. The Sportsmen's Club dog show was on both days, for sporting dogs on the first and others on the second. Also scheduled were music, vaudeville acts, and "plenty of Fakirs." Admission was 50¢ during the day and 85¢ evenings. Parking was free. As often had been the case during the 1920s, weather conditions were unfavorable. Rain caused the vaudeville acts to be canceled, and few hucksters were present. The newspaper noted afterward: "The management is endeavoring to keep interest in the annual fair alive from year to year, but like all country fairs, that at Nantucket does not prove an attraction to the present generation that it did in years gone by." Thus ended the seventy-ninth—and last—of the Nantucket fairs. The Agricultural Society sold the fairgrounds in 1949.

Inspired by the hospital fete of 1929, the Nantucket Civic League fabricated an exposition on Old North Wharf from 2:00 to 6:00 o'clock on Tuesday afternoon, 28 August 1934. For the benefit of the Nantucket Neighbors, it was known as the Neighbors' Water Front Festival. There were no sideshows, but boathouses were open for inspection, and there was a sequence of entertainments. It began with the "Strolling Players," the King family of Polpis, accompanied by Herbert Brownell, Nantucket's blind accordionist. Included were the members of Camp Nickanoose (a boys' camp) performing a sailor's hornpipe and "Indian Adagio" dances. Brownell again accompanied some adult sailors' songs. Pupils of the Duncan School of Dance (Siasconset) performed on the old landing at the end of the wharf. And the concluding number was a "Nantucket Tea

Party," with guests arriving in an old box wagon. Catboat and pony rides were available, and there were children's games, a raffle and an auction, and prizes for historic costumes. Cigarettes, refreshments, and fancy articles were sold.

As has been seen repeatedly, it was an old Nantucket custom for widows of deceased landlords to assume responsibilities at public houses. At the beginning of the 1935 season, "MRS. MERWIN J. BULKLEY . . . [announced] the opening . . . of [the] BEACH HOUSE," which would maintain "the same standard of courtesy and service and the same traditional hospitality, as under the late MERWIN J. BULKLEY." He had died in December of the preceding year.

An innovation that year was the Summer School of Interior Design. It was conducted by Lucy D. Taylor in the Capt. Paul West house, 5 Liberty Street. Homemakers and professional workers were offered classes in color; elementary decoration, with architectural details; outdoor sketching; and dyeing and weaving. Instructors included Dean Ross, Mrs. Seidmore, and Prof. A. Morin of the College of Home Economics, Cornell University; Frederick Huston, architect and educator; Melville Melendy, director of the Willard Cottage Weavers; and Edgar W. Jenney, Nantucket artist, designer of yacht club festivities, and speaker before the Nantucket Neighbors three years earlier.

With Betty Upthegrove cast in the role of a wife in real life, the Nantucket Players had lost their organizer; and a new dramatic group was at the yacht club in 1935, calling itself the Island Theatre. The director was Robert Ross, who had been with the Nantucket Players at the American Legion Hall. Except for Ross Hobart, the performers were not past frequenters of the Nantucket stage.

As in recent years (excepting the last play in 1934), the selection was of recent offerings. There were seven plays in 1935: Wilbur Steele and Norma Mitchell's *Post Road,* about kidnapping along the Connecticut stretch of the Boston turnpike, 16 and 17 July; Benjamin McKaye's *On Stage,* a play whose reality is elusive, 22 and 23

140 *The Frederick C. Sanford house, Federal at Broad Street.*

July; also McKaye's *The Curtain Rises,* 29 and 30 July; Edward Chodorov's *Kind Lady,* adapted from a short story by Hugh Walpole, 5 and 6 August; Mark Reed's *Petticoat Fever,* about a lonely radio operator in Labrador who plays host to an attractive couple thrust upon his precinct by a plane wreck, 12 and 13 August; Sidney Howard's *Ned McCobb's Daughter,* about a restaurant in Maine, 19 and 20 August; and on 25 and 27 August, Noel Coward's *Private Lives,* in which the author and Gertrude Lawrence had played in New York.

Miss Maude Stumm, credited with having originated sidewalk art shows in Nantucket, died in March of 1935. The first two annual events had been held by the side of the Atheneum. Skipping 1932, in August of 1933 the show moved up to the corner of Federal and Broad streets, at the fence by the Frederick C. Sanford house. In 1934,

an exhibition of crafts replaced that of paintings. It was held inside the old residence and included weavings, hooked rugs, furniture, and pottery. In 1935, the Hospital Thrift Shop, which had moved from 12 Liberty Street to the corner of Federal and Pearl (India) streets in 1934, took up headquarters in the Sanford house. The art show from 15–17 August 1935 once more was held outside, and it contained more than 200 pictures. Special features were the work of Miss Stumm, and a poet's corner, in which Nantucket writers of verses were invited to contribute their "favorite compositions," mounted, hopefully to be sold.

Evidently to compensate for the defunct cattle show and fair, a dog show was held in Wallace Field, alongside the yacht club, on the afternoon of 14 August. It was sanctioned by the American Kennel Club, and a silver cup went to the best-in-

141 *Bennett Hall, at the First Congregational Church, Centre Street (modern photograph).*

show. Door proceeds went to the hospital fund.

In 1935, after a lapse of six years, the hospital festival combined a Main Street fete and a waterfront carnival on Old North Wharf. It was held on Wednesday, 7 August, starting with lunch at the yacht club for 75¢. The "carnival" nearby got under way at 1:00 o'clock. Old North Wharf was bedecked with hundreds of brightly colored balloons and presented a midway atmosphere with barkers promoting fortunetellers, games of chance, pony rides, and refreshments. The usual stretch of Main Street was open from 2:00 to 6:00 p.m. As before, it was a setting for figures in period costumes. A tea party was in the yard of the

Henry Coffin house. The Charles G. Coffin house, across the street, had pillow and bag tables in front and a cent school in the side yard, and inside was a Nantucket antiques and heirlooms exhibition gotten up and arranged by Mrs. Emerson (Isabelle) Tuttle which remained open until Saturday. The Coffin School on Winter Street displayed the products of its domestic-science and woodworking courses. A section of Main Street was devoted to a sidewalk art show; and 89, 99, 100, and 102 were open for public inspection. Proceeds amounted to $13,577.86.

In 1936, Lieut. Parker W. Gray inaugurated Mayflower Airlines with new tri-motored Stinson planes that carried ten passengers and were equipped with two-way radios. The system offered daily round-trip service between Nantucket and Edgartown, New Bedford, Hyannis, Provincetown, and Boston. Fares were becoming lower for air travel, and by 1938 one could fly via Mayflower from Nantucket to Boston for $7.50.

In the spring of 1936 the Rev. Fred D. Bennett, minister of the First Congregational Church, promoted the idea of using the recreational rooms of the Point Breeze Hotel as a meeting place for Girl Scouts, where they could engage in such sports as basketball and volleyball. It brought a return of life to the premises, which had been closed for several years, and was prelude to its new role in accommodating summer guests. At the beginning of June the plant was purchased by Gordon M. Folger, formerly connected with the Sea Cliff Inn. No sale price was given in the deed, but a mortgage was taken out on the same day with the Nantucket Institution for Savings for $17,500. The newspaper pointed out that inasmuch as the hotel had been founded forty-five years earlier by Charles Folger, who had the same family name as the new owner, it should be called The Folger House. The purchaser went one step further, calling it the Gordon Folger Hotel, after his father. Today it is known as the Folger Hotel.

Also during the early part of 1936, the Nantucket Institution for Savings sold the Sea Cliff Inn with a mortgage covenant of $75,000, and the Ocean House with a mortgage of $48,000, to John O. Wilson, Inc., of Bourne, Massachusetts. On 25 April the Wilson company transferred both properties, for the same amounts plus current taxes, to Nantucket Hotels, Inc. The chief investors in the latter enterprise were Robert A. Ide of Buck Falls, Pennsylvania; Constance Ekstrand of Staatsburg, New York; and Henry S. Duncan of New York City. Under the new regime, the Ocean House was opened on 28 May, and the Sea Cliff Inn on 23 June. The manager of both was David F. Tuttle, whose experience had ranged from Westchester County, the Catskills, and New Jersey to Sebring, Florida. D. C. McLeod was associate manager. Howard Chisholm continued as driver for the Sea Cliff, which had been his occupation for the past thirty years. The Sea Cliff Inn had its own orchestra, with Guido Antonelli leader and violinist; C. James Murphy at the piano, Donald W. Haywood on clarinet and flute, and Luis Doten on percussion. It played for dancing during cocktails from 4:00 to 6:00 p.m. daily, and Thursday and Saturday evenings from 8:30 to 11:00.

The Island Theatre launched its second season on Nantucket under the management of Peg Wangler, who strove to make evenings at the yacht club brilliant social and artistic affairs. Luther Greene was director, Richard Maloney business manager, and Harry Davis designed and built settings that got rave notices. The eight plays produced were: Lawrence Riley's *Personal Appearance,* 6 and 7 July; George Bernard Shaw's *Arms and the Man,* 13 and 14 July; Lynn Riggs's *Russet Mantle,* 20 and 21 July; Benn W. Levy's *Springtime for Henry,* 27 and 28 July; Gladys Hurlburt's *Lovers' Meeting,* 3 and 4 August; Lawrence Percy's *Beyond the Terrace,* 10 and 11 August; Frederick Jackson's *The Bishop Misbehaves,* 17 and 18 August; and Sidney Howard's *They Knew What They Wanted,* 25 and 26 August. The last won a Pulitzer Prize in 1924–25. The great *coup* of the summer was getting Dorothy Gish to play the leading role in *Russet Mantle,* which, of course, proved a sellout. Publicity brought out the childhood friendship between the Gish sisters and Gladys Smith, who was to take the name of Mary Pickford in the movies. Alexander Dean, who directed the New York production, undertook that play. *Springtime for Henry* had been given by the Nantucket Theatre in 1933. Among the 1936 presentations were two being tried out here for fall openings in New York City. The first was *Lovers' Meeting,* which had been adapted from a Harry Haller novel. Its adapter, Gladys Hurlburt, had collaborated in writing *By Your Leave* with Emma Wells, wife of the director of its 1933 run at Nantucket. The other to go from the island to Broadway was the mystical play *Beyond the Terrace.*

The theme of the yacht club ball in 1936 was the Arabian Nights. It was held on Thursday evening, 27 August. The ballroom was bedecked with hundreds of balloons suspended from the ceiling, and one corner was filled with pillows for the "sheik" and his harem (the judges), with a Turkish man in the moon swinging leisurely above the stage. Donald Gifford produced the decorations. "Rajahs, sheiks, ladies of the harem, and slaves were everywhere, garbed in beach towels, coats, cheese cloth, spangles, rope, and, now and then, chiffon. Real elaborate Turkish costumes were at a premium, as was seen at the time of the grand march, when the judges found it almost easy to make their decision." Phil Williams conducted the march, which transpired at 11:30 to strains of "The Road to Mandalay." First prize went to Mr. and Mrs. Jules Thebaud, whose costumes represented "Rajah Not" and "Not-he but Nice," and were universally proclaimed the handsomest. The prize for the best girl's costume was won by Mrs. Alexander Hagner, dressed all in white and with a crimson velvet sultan's cap atop her blond hair. C. H. Polly, as a "Representative of the Foreign Legion," took the prize for the best men's costume. The group award went to the "Sultan and His Hectic Harem," led by Neal O'Hara. Meyer Davis conducted the orchestra, which had added three extra musicians for the event, and all were garbed in bright costumes.

The Rev. Fred D. Bennett's mission of securing a place where young people could socialize and frolic, as in the old Point Breeze Hotel early in 1936, bore fruit as the year progressed. By the end of August, plans were formulated by the First Congregational Church for erecting a recreation hall adjoining its building. Construction was begun in September and was almost finished in seven weeks. John Ring contracted for the masonry, Huram Macy for the carpentry, Ralph Bartlett for the plumbing, and Robert Blair for the wiring. The building was somewhat submerged into the hillside so as not to detract from the church proper, and it housed a large (37 x 107-foot) hall, with a stage at the west end and raised tiers for seats at the east, or front entrance. The hall could be used as a gymnasium, being provided with transparent backboards for basketball hoops to allow spectators a view of the throws. A kitchen was appended at the west. When dedicated on 16 December it was called the Parish House, but by April of the following year it had become Bennett Hall. In the fall of 1938 the Rev. Fred D. Bennett transferred to a post in Boston.

The Cliff Bathing Beach was the subject of a good deal of controversy during the first half of 1937. Leon M. Royal, who had leased it in 1924 at $3,300 per annum for fifteen years, due to the Depression and the practice people had assumed of wearing their beach clothes from home, asked that the fee be reduced twenty percent, in consequence of which it was set at $2,640 in 1933. The same year the proprietor had built and opened what he called the Club Royale, an inn serving clam chowder, soups, salads, sandwiches, desserts, and beer and ale on draught from 11:00 a.m. to midnight. It also employed several girls as singers. In 1934 the question came up whether a "night club" should be maintained and operated, and a liquor license permitted (Nantucket had no entertainer-license requirements at that time), at a public beach. The selectmen detailed Sgt. L. F. Mooney of the police force to ask for the surrender of the permit. The matter then was tried on 10 July before Judge Fitz-Randolph, who declared it a technical violation. In the spring of 1936 Leon M. Royal offered the town $100 for all the bathing beach park it owned. At the beginning of summer he "flatly refused to pay one cent of rent [on Cliff Beach]. The reason given was that the land of the bathing beach was not owned by the Town but belonged to Franklin E. Smith."

Upon investigation it was found that Smith was indeed the owner. The developer of Tom Nevers Head had purchased a number of pieces of property throughout the island, most of them taken up for back taxes. Smith offered to sell the town Cliff Beach for $6,000, with a legal fee for himself of $500.

At the beginning of April 1937 the selectmen posted a notice concerning the "rental, for the term of one year, of Cliff Beach (so-called) bath houses and equipment." Bids were to be in by 15 April. Before the latter date, a counter announcement was inserted in the *Inquirer and Mirror* by Franklin E. Smith. It read: "All persons . . . are hereby notified that I own said land and that the Board of Selectmen has no right to rent it." However, on 6 May Paul F. Klingelfuss signed a lease for the use of the beach buildings for five years, with an option on another five, for $3,500 per annum. Klingelfuss had been with the White Elephant on Nantucket and the Mid-Ocean Club, Bermuda. Some agreement must have been made between the town and Smith. During the last week in May the Massachusetts senate passed a bathing-beach bill (over the governor's veto), and on 3 June Franklin E. Smith sold the waterfront property to Nantucket. Royal's buildings were purchased, and on 15 June Klingelfuss opened the former Cliff Beach under the new name of The Jetties. A few days, or rather evenings, later, the former club, now also called The Jetties, opened with Buddy Hotin and the Jettians playing nightly from 6:30 for dinner and supper dancing. The former proprietor opened Royal Manor, a guest house on Centre Street.

The yacht club's theatre season of 1937 was a mixed endeavor, consisting of dancing, music, readings, and a lecture for the first half, and a series of one-act plays during August. The first presentation was on the evenings of 5 and 6 July and consisted of Addison Fowler and Florenz Tamara, "international dance duo," accompanied by pianist Charles Ruetchi. The dancers performed an East Indian modern number, a Versailles gavotte, Viennese waltz, a contemporary fantasy to Nacio Brown's "Night and Day," Ravel's "Bolero," and several Spanish dances. Miss

Tamara executed a solo to "Valse Triste," and a number inspired by a bullfight, "La Corrida," in appropriate costumes. Mr. Ruetchi played several pieces from Mozart, Chopin, Lecuona, and Liszt. The program was followed by social dancing. The second event was John Mulholland entertaining with "Adventures in Magic" on 13 July. Joan and Betty Rayner, the Strolling Troubadors, gave two evenings of ballads and "folk-lure" on 19 and 20 July. Cornelia Otis Skinner appeared in such sketches as "The Wives of Henry VIII" and "The Loves of Charles II" on 26 and 27 July. On 22 August Robert de Bruce talked on astrology, singling out the Duke and Duchess of Windsor, Hitler, and Mussolini for special analyses. He was available for personal readings by appointment at the White Elephant for a week afterward.

For the second month the yacht club was committed to the Playmakers Company of Chapel Hill, North Carolina, directed by Harry Davis. Three one-act plays were given on 9 and 10 August, consisting of Beverly Hamer's *Funeral Flowers for the Bride,* Loretta Carol Bailey's *Job's Kinfolks,* and Gertrude Coffin's *Magnolia's Man.* On 16 and 17 August the group performed Lulu Vollmer's *Sun-up.* For 23 and 24 August the announcement merely stated that there were to be "three comedies."

A balloon released by the R. H. Macy department store in New York City in December of 1929 was found by Rudolph Matland while he was hunting rabbits near Gibbs Pond on 15 February 1930. The coincidence becomes striking when one recalls that Rowland Hussey Macy, founder of the metropolitan emporium, was born on Nantucket in 1822. Macy's had presented an annual Thanksgiving Day Parade in New York since 1924. The parades were designed by Tony Sarg and featured huge balloons in a variety of shapes ranging from fairytale and storybook characters to popular mythical and other figures having to do with the Thanksgiving and Christmas holidays. Sarg, who was always ready for a prank, conceived the idea of bringing one of the latest full-size parade creations to Nantucket at the height of the summer season in 1937. It was a gigantic being, which was to be presented as the fabled

142 *Tony Sarg's sea monster at South Beach, 19 August 1937.*

sea monster. The editor of the *Inquirer and Mirror* was consulted, and it was arranged that a respected Nantucket fisherman first would glimpse and report on the monster; then he and a companion would discover its footprints in the sand at Madaket beach. The first story was reported on 7 August and the second the following week, with photographs. On Wednesday, 18 August, the monster in all its rubber majesty was plainly in view across the harbor on Coatue. By this time, off-island newspaper and newsreel media had been alerted to the phenomenon, and the fact of its being a hoax had leaked out. On Thursday the sea monster was brought across to Mrs. Henry Lang's land at South Beach, where the children (and others) could enjoy it at close range. Sarg himself was on hand and had his picture taken with about eighty youngsters at and in the mouth of the inflated being, which, despite its 20-foot forked tongue and 4-foot fangs, was more comical than terrifying. R. H. Macy had asked that its name not be mentioned, that whatever publicity

was accrued might go to Nantucket; but the matter went awry along with the secrecy that was to have preceded the manifestation. The "sea monster" appeared in the forthcoming parade in its originally intended role as St. George's dragon.

The wind-up of the season, with its anxieties and activities concentrated on the shore of the harbor, was the Civic League's second waterfront carnival on 25 August. An estimated 1,400 persons enjoyed the games, refreshments, and entertainments.

In September of 1937 the Nobadeer "airport" was purchased by Alexander Hagner of Washington, D. C., a summer resident of Nantucket and owner of his own plane. In November, Hagner offered to give the field to the town, so that W. P. A. funds might be utilized to improve it properly. Many Nantucketers felt that although the island needed a landing field, it was not desirable to have an airport, and disapproved of the location at Nobadeer because planes would be passing directly over the town. David Raub, who had been running a charter air service for several years, wrote in favor of the project; and while the matter was in limbo, he kept his planes at the Fairhaven airport (New Bedford). In the summer of 1938 Raub's flying service was again in operation. The Nobadeer property was made over to Nantucket in June of 1941, and Raub was appointed airfield manager by the selectmen.

While presenting a full season of entertainments in 1938, the yacht club departed even further from legitimate theatre than it had during the previous year. Its offerings included Peter Joray (at the 'Sconset Casino in 1931) in "Royalties of the Past," in which he impersonated not only Louis XIV and Queen Victoria but Frederick the Great of Prussia, Catherine the Great of Russia, Napoleon III, and others, on 11 July; the Yale Puppeteers gave an "up-to-the-minute, smart, sophisticated entertainment" on 16 July; Victor Coty showed his natural-color motion pictures of sports and activities on 1 and 2 August; Dr. Harlan Tarbell demonstrated magic and his "eyeless vision" on 8 August; the University Gilbert and Sullivan Company presented the operettas *H. M. S. Pinafore* and *Trial by Jury* on 15 August, and *The Mikado* next evening; and Cecilia Loftus impersonated Gertrude Lawrence, Fannie Brice, Noel Coward, Ethel Barrymore, Beatrice Lillie, Lynn Fontanne, Sarah Bernhardt, and others on 22 and 23 August.

The theatre colony of Siasconset took up the torch of giving plays at the casino this year with a bill of eight during July and August. The theatre was called the Nantucket Playhouse, and its directors were Morgan Farley, William Beers, and Bertram Yarborough. Farley, Lawrence Fletcher, Ivan Triesault, Blanche Yurka, Kay Strozzi, and Violet Heming were feature performers. Shows were given on Thursday, Friday, and Monday evenings. The sequence was Gerald Savoy's *George and Margaret*, 7, 8, and 10 July; S. N. Behrman's *Biography*, 15, 16, and 18 July; G. B. Shaw's *Candida*, 29 and 30 July and 1 August; Porter Emerson Brown's *The Bad Man*, 4, 5, and 7 August; Mark Reed's *Yes, My Darling Daughter*, 11, 12, and 14 August; Rachel Cruther's *Susan and God*, 18, 19, and 21 August; and A. W. Pinero's

Enchanted Cottage, 25, 26, and 28 August. Blanche Yurka, who had starred in *Yes, My Darling Daughter*, gave a special matinee at Robert O'Connor's studio in Siasconset, portraying "Great Scenes from Great Plays," on 13 August at 4:00 o'clock.

During July and August, on Tuesday, Thursday and Sunday afternoons, the 2:45 steamer from Nantucket connected with the Colonial Line's S. S. *Meteor* in New Bedford, and after an overnight trip reached New York the next morning. The return connection was made in New York at Pier 11 at the foot of Liberty Street on Monday, Wednesday, and Friday evenings at 6:00 o'clock. Fare was $5.00, with staterooms ranging from $1.50 to $5.00. Automobiles could be transported for $5.00, except on Sundays, when the cost was $7.50. The service remained the same in 1939; and in 1940 fare for passengers was reduced to $4.00, or $7.50 round trip.

The twenty-year-old Lodge on Tom Nevers Head began burning around 4:30 on Friday morning, 26 August 1938. The place lately had become the rendezvous for "parties," and it was showing the effects of depredations. There was little doubt about the blaze being set intentionally. Fire engines from town arrived too late to save the building itself, which was totally destroyed, but the firemen kept the flames from spreading to adjoining structures. The press account recalled that the Lodge was an integral part of the "Tom Nevers boom," which "bubble burst," and although the Lodge had been "conducted as a restaurant and for one or two seasons it seemed to prosper," at last it had "gone up in smoke."

Although the abandonment of the Lodge on the south shore was somewhat indicative of the hotel situation on the island as a whole, still, a number of hostelries continued in business. David F. Tuttle, who had been appointed general manager of the Sea Cliff Inn and Ocean House in 1936, two years later was operating the Breakers on Brant Point. The Eltinge brothers (Ernest W. and Raymond D.) were running the Sea Cliff, with A. C. McLeod remaining as associate manager and head clerk. Edward P. Moloney, former

S.S. "METEOR" is a steel-hulled. 325 foot, twin screw vessel.

NEW YORK

by *Direct* Steamship

FARE

$5

Staterooms
$1.50 to $5.

**AVOID
TRAFFIC**

TAKE YOUR CAR
TO NEW YORK
BY SHIP!
Autos $5 weekdays.
Fridays. Sundays,
Holidays, $7.50

For tickets, reservations, free booklet, see PAGE, Tel 306.

The S. S. "Meteor" leaves New York Wharf, New Bedford (Next to N. B. M. V. & N. Steamboat Co. Wharf), Tuesdays, Thursdays, Sundays at 7:30 P. M. (DST).

- From Nantucket take the 2:45 P.M. (DST) boat.
- From Marthas Vineyard take the 4:45 P.M. (DST) boat.
- From Hyannis take the 4:50 P.M. (DST) Bus which connects with the ship at New Bedford.

Returning the S. S. "Meteor" leaves Pier 11 North River, N. Y. C. (Foot of Liberty St. near Hudson Tube, Cortlandt St. Subway) on Mondays, Wednesdays and Fridays at 6 P. M. (DST).

GO COLONIAL LINE

THE "PUBLIC BE PLEASED" ROUTE

143 *Advertisement for steamboat service to New York City, via New Bedford, by the Colonial Line, 1938.*

steward at the Prince George Hotel in New York City and lessee of the Fritz-Carlton (not Ritz-Carlton) in Boston, was in charge of the Ocean House; and Frank Worth, the former owner, was back as resident manager. These were three of eight Nantucket hostelries discussed in an article in the periodical *Hotel and Restaurant News* in 1938. The others were the Gordon Folger Hotel, Ships Inn, White Elephant, Wauwinet House, and the Old 'Sconset Inn. The last was at the east corner of Ocean and Magnolia avenues on Sunset Heights, Siasconset, and its proprietors were Mr. and Mrs. Clement H. Reynolds.

David F. Tuttle called a conference, held 10 September, of Nantucket officials and hotel proprietors to discuss the future of Nantucket as a summer resort. The group included the selectmen, members of the finance and publicity committees, Mrs. Bulkley of the Beach House, the Reynoldses of the Old 'Sconset Inn, Mrs. Ludwig of the White Elephant, the Eltinge brothers of the Sea Cliff Inn, E. S. McLaughlin of the Ships Inn, and Carl Stig of the Grey Gull. They were treated to a chicken dinner at the Breakers. William Hull, chairman of the publicity committee, introduced the speaker of the evening, James Wales of the Wales Advertising Company of New York City. The substance of Wales's recommendations was that for better business Nantucket needed to encourage long-term guests rather than short trippers. He suggested that with proper advertising visitors to the New York World's Fair in 1939 could be induced to come to Nantucket. The right media, he felt, were the big newspapers like the *New York Times*, the *Herald-Tribune*, the *Boston Transcript*, and the *Christian Science Monitor*. George Lattimore, publisher of the *Lake Placid News* as well as being connected with the Wales company, suggested the issuing of attractive posters for display at travel agencies; and he advocated lengthening the season by holding golf and tennis tournaments after Labor Day. At someone's query as to how much money would be needed for such a program, a sum of between $5,000 and $10,000 was suggested. It was pointed out that a state law allowed no more than $3,000 be spent for such a purpose, of

which $500 should be for an information bureau. Mr. Hills, secretary of the publicity committee, stated that $500 was not enough to keep the information office open every hour of the day. He mentioned having had 18,700 booklets printed, publicizing Nantucket, of which there were about 300 left. Lists of hotels were included, but they did not give rates. One drawback in mailing out this literature was that the clerk of the information bureau had no typewriter, though sometimes rented one. Another point brought out was that the New York, New Haven and Hartford Railroad had taken movies of Nantucket, which were to be shown throughout the Midwest and Central states.

The conference at the Breakers prompted Representative Robert S. Backus to petition the Massachusetts legislature for authority to let the town meeting appropriate $6,500 for advertising the recreational attractions of the island. The senate amended the bill, requiring $3,500 of the amount to come from sources other than the town treasury. The finance committee recommended setting aside $2,500 for advertising and $750 for the information bureau, and at the town meeting held at the Dreamland Theatre on 21 February those amounts were approved. Nantucket was illustrated in the New Haven Railroad travel folder that came out in the summer of 1939, which did not extract one cent from the town purse.

Nantucket made a good initial effort in the summer of 1939 by putting on an unusually spectacular Fourth of July celebration. It was an "old fashioned" affair, with George Haddon as "chairman extraordinary, master-of-ceremonies, general handy-man, dispenser of good cheer and a complete one-man show in himself." The festivities began with a bonfire on the Madaket Road at twelve o'clock on the eve. A tremendous pyre, intensified with buckets of gasoline and accompanied by nearby rockets, blazed dramatically in the clear, moonlit night. Athletic events were held next morning in front of the post office. Races and a blueberry-pie-eating contest were for youngsters. A rolling-pin throw was for ladies, the target of their skill being a dummy.

144 *Scenes from the Fourth of July parade in 1939. The Ships Inn box wagon; Arthur Parker as the New Bedford "Whaleman's Statue," for Stevens' Sporting Goods Store; and the group from Young's Bicycle Shop.*

Margaret Fawcett Wilson hit it three out of four throws, but Maud Haddon accomplished as many hits in three tries and won. Also included were a fat-man's and over-forty races, and a fisherman-versus-landlubber tug-of-war. A doll-carriage parade concluded the exercises.

The "Big Parade" was in the afternoon. It formed on Washington Street and went up Main past the reviewing stand before turning on Centre Street. The Legion's Drum and Bugle Corps led, and its float had Charlie Brown peering from behind a machine gun. Among the two-dozen participants, the more interesting were the Wannacomet Water Company's vehicle professing to be a reproduction of Nantucket's former railroad engine; the Nantucket Nursery School's float with a group of tots inside a wire pen; the Island Service Company's entry, consisting of an old fish shanty mounted on a truck, with skiff, barrels, and nets, and a fisherman (Dick Barnett) mending the nets, which was considered the best bit of local color in the parade. The Ships Inn had a horse-drawn boxcart, driven by its porter, Tom Mulkern, with passengers in old costumes. The North Church resorted to a Hansel and Gretel fantasy. Eleanor Manter had a rose garden on wheels. The example that won the prize was from Stevens' Sporting Goods Store, representing the "Whaleman's Statue" in New Bedford, with Arthur Parker, gilded, and poised with harpoon in a whaleboat prow in front of a stele.

Nantucket's foremost entertainment medium of the 1930s—live stage shows—reached its zenith during the last summer of the decade. Three theatres were on the island, and they opened on 6, 22, and 24 July. From the last week in July to about the end of August there was at least one offering every night, except Sundays, and mostly a choice of two, a few of three.

The most ample program was at the Siasconset Casino. Bertram Yarborough again was director, but there was a change in title from the Nantucket Playhouse of the previous year to the old name of the early 1930s, the Nantucket Players. The season consisted of Sutton Vane's *Outward Bound*, 6, 7, and 9 July; Moss Hart and George S.

Kaufman's *You Can't Take It with You*, 14, 15, and 17 July; Noel Coward's *Tonight at 8:30*, made up of three short plays, *Hands Across the Seas*, *Fumed Oak*, and *Ways and Means*, 20, 21, and 23 July; Arnold Ridley's *The Ghost Train*, 27, 28, and 30 July; Ian Hay's *Bachelor Born*, 3, 4, and 6 August; Paul Osborn's *Oliver, Oliver*, 11, 12, and 14 August; Samson Raphaelson's *Accent on Youth*, 17, 18, and 20 August; and Thornton Wilder's *Our Town*, 24, 25, and 27 August.

As it had during the preceding two years, the yacht club theatre in 1939 resorted to a variety of programs, only one of which was a play. Its first presentation on 24 July was Clyde Eddy's "The River Thames from Source to Mouth," a color film with commentary. Helen Howe gave character sketches in a program called "These People" on 31 July and 1 August. The Yale Puppeteers appeared with "It's a Small World" on 14 and 15 August. Three evenings of Gilbert and Sullivan operettas included *The Pirates of Penzance* and *Trial by Jury* on 21 August, *The Gondoliers* on 22 August, and *Iolanthe* on 23 August. The first program was a repeat of one the previous season. The Fawcett Players presented Shakespeare's *The Taming of the Shrew* on 28 and 29 August. It had been given on the island by the same group in March and was the Samuel French abridged version. Robert Wilson played Petruchio, and his wife, Margaret Fawcett Wilson, was Katharina.

George Fawcett died 6 June 1939, and to perpetuate his memory his daughter and son-in-law, the Robert Wilsons, formed the Fawcett Players, which provided the third theatre that summer. Their repertory was short plays about the island that originally were scheduled to be given at the yacht club on the last evening of July and first of August. With the founding of the Fawcett Players a boat shed at the end of Commercial Wharf was leased, and it was furnished with a stage, proper lighting, and folding chairs, becoming the Commercial Wharf Theatre and the Players' headquarters. Robert Wilson, originally an architect by profession, did much of the work, and he designed and built the settings. Wilson also wrote the first four plays, known collectively as *In Old*

Nantucket, consisting of *As It Was in the Beginning, Keziah Coffin,* the enterprising businesswoman smuggler during the American Revolution; *The Newbegin Distaff,* about the three strange Newbegin sisters of the early nineteenth century; and *1890,* a comedy having to do with the replacement of whale oil for lighting. Later, Wilson added *The Great Russell,* a fictionalized account of Lillian Russell's visit to Nantucket. Margaret Fawcett Wilson directed the plays, was in charge of costumes, and she and her husband played in them. Two plays were given each evening at 9:00 o'clock, Monday through Saturday, and the admission charge was 85¢. The season began on 22 July and continued through August, except for the last Monday and Tuesday evenings, when the Fawcett Players appeared at the yacht club.

The annual Nantucket Yacht Club costume ball took place on the evening of 17 August with 200 members and guests in attendance. Isaac Hills was master of ceremonies, dressed like town crier Billy Clark, and Lester Lanin's orchestra furnished the music. There was no special theme. Prizes for the best costumes went to Mrs. R. C. Brownlee as "The Brown Maid of Hawaii" and Jules Thebaud as a gardener. Second prizes were awarded to Mr. and Mrs. Morton of Siasconset as "A Little Bit of Old Nantucket." Third prizes were given to Bunny Schlottzhauer as "The Nantucket Rainbow Fleet" and Bill Rowland as "Ferdinand the Bull." Six men on a tandem, "the Sullivan Sextette," were given the group prize.

Like the earlier thespians of the same name, the Nantucket Players quit Siasconset and came to town. It was announced in the fall of 1939 that they would appear at the yacht club during the summer of 1940. Bertram Yarborough remained director; he was now similarly ensconced at the Grand Rapids Civic Theatre in Michigan throughout the winter months. Originally announced as opening with *Roland,* a play written by Yarborough and Morgan Farley, instead the Nantucket Players launched the 1940 season by repeating one first given here in 1932, *The Vinegar Tree,* on 7, 8, and 9 July. It was followed by Florence Johns and Wilton Lackaye II's *America Very Early,* 14, 15, and 16 July. Others in sequence were: Ayn

Rand's *Night of January 16th,* 21, 22, and 23 July; Clifford Goldsmith's *What a Life,* 28, 29, and 30 July; the old-timer, Mrs. Henry Wood's *East Lynne,* 4, 5, and 6 August; Victor Wolfson's *Excursion,* 11, 12, and 13 August; S. N. Behrman's *End of Summer,* 18, 19, and 20 August; and Eugene O'Neill's *Ah, Wilderness,* 25, 26, and 27 August.

The owner of the boat shed on Commercial Wharf complained that the theatre people made too much noise, and he refused to rent it for another season. The Fawcett Players secured a new home in 1940. It was the old Benjamin Gardner Store (ca. 1849) on Straight Wharf, which recently had been used as a storehouse for plumbing equipment, a tinsmith shop, and a livery stable. Offered the building for $5,000, the Players raised a portion of that sum and took out a mortgage for the balance. Robert Wilson remodeled the building, tearing out part of the second floor and building the stage. It originally had room for 110 seats, but a new balcony, later installed, provided seating for 75 more. Other subsequent changes included wood over the concrete floor and a false ceiling, the latter so that rain on the roof would not drown out the players' lines. Christened the Straight Wharf Theatre, it opened on the evening of 20 July with *Keziah,* Robert Wilson's *Keziah Coffin* lengthened into a three-act play. *1890* was retained from the previous season, and there was a new show about the Nantucket astronomer, *Maria Mitchell,* written by Margaret Fawcett. Also new, a drama about present-day sabotage and spies on the island, *Night Watch,* was included in the season's repertory.

Having their own headquarters at the Straight Wharf Theatre, the Fawcett Players undertook to extend the drama season around the calendar. On Thanksgiving and the two following evenings they played Austin Strong's *Three Wise Fools,* with a dance after the final show. On 26, 27, and 28 December they gave a dramatic version of Charles Dickens's *A Christmas Carol.* In January and February of 1941 they put on *Ten Nights in a Bar Room,* and in May, *Believe Me, Xantippe,* with Mary Walker, principal of the Nantucket High School, in the leading role. Margaret Fawcett Wilson conducted a children's

145 *The Straight Wharf Theatre, ca. 1940.*

acting class, and in March and April her mother, Percy Haswell, delivered a series of readings from Shakespeare. The great problem was trying to get the theatre warm enough for the comfort of performers and audience, and because it was not satisfactorily solved, a winter program was not again attempted until the end of the decade.

At the beginning of summer, 27 June 1941, the English film "Thumbs-Up" was shown at Bennett Hall, its proceeds (75¢ admission) to go to British War Relief. This cause was of great concern to the island. The annual old-house tours for the benefit of the hospital fund were called off this year as the owners were sufficiently occupied "giving unstintingly of their efforts in behalf of the British War Relief and the Red Cross." The former furnished the theme and purpose of the yacht club ball held on 25 July.

Patriotism was more in evidence than usual at the July Fourth celebration in 1941. Main Street shops were decked in red-white-and-blue bunting. The usual features were repeated. In the street parade the Fawcett Players had a wagon representing *Little Women,* one of their forthcoming plays. The conclusion and highlight of the day's events was a marine parade during the evening. It was conceived by Samuel A. Boyer and sponsored by the steamboat company. South Wharf and the yacht club were blazing with lights, and the Breakers, White Elephant, and a number of cottages on Brant Point were aglow. The steamer *Nantucket* was decorated with strings of electric bulbs, outlining the upper deck and reaching to the top of the smokestack. A band played on the forward deck, and invited guests were aboard, amply furnished with refreshments. The *Nan-*

tucket left Steamboat Wharf shortly after 8:00 o'clock, proceeded around the point and through the jetties, where it met the other boats that were to be in the parade. It led them back toward town. No two in the floating procession were alike. The judges awarded the top prize to Stanley Whelden's boat carrying a representation of the Brant Point lighthouse. Second prize went to Arthur McCleave's lobster boat *Squam*, which displayed a map of Nantucket Island outlined by electric lights. Third prize was awarded to the sloop *Argonaut,* built, owned, and skippered by Charles Sayle, with lights creating a huge red cross and singers providing music. The parade was followed by an aquaplaning demonstration, the motor boat and board-rider spotlighted by the searchlights of the *Nantucket* and *New Bedford.* Also illuminated were fountain displays thrown up by the cruiser *Ark,* ending with the hoisting of "Old Glory" on the forward staff and the band playing the "Star-Spangled Banner." Group singing continued until midnight.

Governor Saltonstall had appointed Selective Service Board No. 172 on Nantucket in the fall of 1940, and the first registration for the draft occurred on 16 October. The backwash filling the void left by the departure of young men for service was the brackish gloom of pending disaster emanating from the Nazi-fascist maelstrom consuming Europe. But the momentum of alleviating the depression doldrums propelled a double-theatre program through one more summer.

Josephene Bender joined Bertram Yarborough as co-managing director of the Nantucket Players at the yacht club. The eight plays of the 1941 season were: Lynne Starling's *Meet the Wife,* 6, 7, and 8 July; Jean Ferguson Block's *Penny Wise,* 13, 14, and 15 July; Patrick Hamilton's *Gaslight,* 20, 21, and 22 July; Lawrence Riley's *Personal Appearance,* 27, 28, and 29 July; J. B. Priestley's *Dangerous Corner,* 3, 4, and 5 August; Moss Hart and George S. Kaufman's *George Washington Slept Here,* 10, 11, and 12 August; Anna Cora Mowatt's *Fashion,* 17, 18, and 19 August; and Francis Swann's *Out of the Frying Pan,* 24, 25, and 26 August.

The Fawcett Players appeared at the Straight Wharf Theatre on Saturday evening, 12 July, with the play they had presented at the beginning of 1941, William W. Pratt's *Ten Nights in a Bar Room.* The weekly schedule ensued, with *In Old Nantucket* (*The Newbegin Distaff* and *Night Watch*) on Monday and Tuesday, *Maria Mitchell* on Wednesday and Thursday, and the Pratt production on Friday and Saturday nights. In mid-August, *Little Women* was added to the repertory. It was given on Wednesday and Thursday, and the Nantucket subjects were limited to one night each on Monday and Tuesday.

Summer art activities kept abreast of theatre during the late 1930s and early 1940s. Frank Swift Chase continued teaching classes in landscape painting and showing his own work. His studio in 1941 was on Commercial Wharf. George Parker also offered art classes at Barnsite Studio, lower Main Street. Exhibitions of Nantucket artists recurred during August at the Easy Street Gallery, and in 1941 the Sidewalk Art Show was presented on 18, 20, and 21 August, the second day (a Tuesday) skipped because of inclement weather.

During recent years the *Inquirer and Mirror* had run a summer column on "The Hotels," mostly giving the names and addresses of current guests. Those caravanserais meriting inclusion in 1941 were the Sea Cliff Inn, the Gordon Folger, White Elephant, the Breakers, Ships Inn, and 5 Fair Street, which had been owned by Jessie T. Bennett since 1928.

Other guest houses advertising this year included the Anchor Inn, 66 Centre Street; the Grey Gull, 1 Liberty Street; the Nantucket House (formerly Mrs. Anna Mooers' and Mrs. Calvert Handy's), 1 North Water Street, owned and run by Dr. and Mrs. C. Kenneth Veo since 1939; the Wauwinet House, at the Haulover; and the Chanticleer, at Siasconset. Also, the Joshua Coffin House, Centre Street at the north corner of Gay, let three-room apartments. Other places remained open in silence.

The denouement of the decade of depression occurred late in 1941. On 7 December the Japanese bombed Pearl Harbor. The following day the United States declared war on Japan, and two

146 *A scene from* Keziah, *performed by the Fawcett Players, 1940.*

days later it made the same declaration against the two European confederates, Germany and Italy. On Nantucket the Public Safety Committee took up headquarters in the second story of the Sanford house on 9 December. Shortly thereafter, radio messages were received that enemy planes were approaching the Atlantic coast. Schools were dismissed, and people were advised on what to do in the emergency. It was a false alarm. Air-raid wardens were appointed, one to each fifteen houses in a section. Civil Defense instructed the islanders in detail how best to preserve themselves in case of attack. The newspaper published helpful information, like clearing out inflammable materials from garrets, keeping buckets of water and sand to extinguish incendiary bombs, and keeping passages clear. The selectmen designated David Raub special police officer at the airport. They called an emergency meeting of the citizens at the Dreamland Theatre on 29 December for authorization to spend a sum not exceeding $10,000 to purchase equipment and supplies for public safety. The full amount was sanctioned within ten minutes. Nantucket had never acted on an expenditure measure so quickly.

EPILOGUE

THE ECONOMIC SLOWDOWN occasioned by the Wall Street disaster in 1929 was a mild affliction compared to the aftermath of Pearl Harbor a dozen years later. Nantucket was in sound working condition at the time of the former: It came after a prosperous season, and the island was not really aware of what the effects would be. The nation had no choice but to take it and its consequences passively: It was an interval affair that would heal itself in time. But plunging into a world war was a different matter: The United States had been attacked and had itself become an aggressor. It had not fully recovered from the Depression, and there was an undercurrent of suspicion that a plunge into the new ordeal was a technique for promoting the interests of industrialists—at the people's expense. There were lingering memories of sea skirmishes during the 1914–18 war with Germany, and Nantucketers already were in a frenzy gathering bundles for Britain and processing Red Cross paraphernalia. Vivid in their minds was the picture of what happened on 7 December 1941 to that other island in the Pacific Ocean. Warnings had not been heeded when disaster struck, and the same thing could befall Nantucket. The Cape Cod satellite had no means of defense; and apparently there was little or no consideration of the fact that the magnet in the Pacific for the Pearl Harbor attack was its tremendous stockpile of war equipment, of which Nantucket had none. Its citizens saw only that its own warriors were sent abroad by the draft, that this channeling of manpower robbed the island of its patrons from America as well, that with the rationing of gasoline, certain foods, and wearing apparel, supplies were short, and things in general looked pretty bad.

The *Inquirer and Mirror* kept the war consciousness alive by inserting two new weekly columns, "Red Cross Notes" and "Men in Service." It also published longer articles and pictures of the local boys in uniform, telling where they were in training, or perhaps in action. Occasionally there were casualties to report. Early in February 1942 Daniel J. Murphy, aged fifteen, whose father was an officer stationed in the Pacific, gave to the Winter Club an eye-witness account of the Japanese attack on Pearl Harbor. A month later the island received news of the loss of one of its summertime favorites, Tony Sarg, who died in New York on 7 March. Sixty-year-old Sarg had entertained Nantucketers with his marionettes, personal appearances at the yacht club, participation in the fetes, his art work and caricatures, antics such as the sea-monster hoax; and he had a shop at the Choo-Choo near the head of Steamboat Wharf.

Nantucket adjusted to its home-front existence. A safety order issued on 26 April called for a dimout on the streets that became a full blackout at times. On 24 May two boatloads of survivors from a vessel torpedoed off Bermuda were picked up and landed at Nantucket. Citizens were asked to contribute bedding and other comforts. The Red Cross took charge of forty-two men, thirteen of them Chinese, who were sheltered at Bennett Hall. In June, due to the rubber shortage, the Office of Defense Transportation ordered the cessation of sightseeing bus tours. Charter bus ser-

147 *The restored Jared Coffin House (1845), formerly the Ocean House, Broad Street (modern photograph).*

vice was limited to essential trips. Horse-and-buggy tours were permitted. Because business looked so unpromising, Paul Klingelfuss asked to be released from his contract at the bathing beach, and it was granted by the selectmen. Leslie Martin, who had worked for the steamboat company for a number of years, took over the management of the beach for the season at $250.

Boat service began with two trips a day to the Cape up to 20 June, when it was increased to three, with water routes to Boston and New York.

But on 9 July the government appropriated the *Naushon*, and on 4 August it conscripted the *New Bedford*. In the fall of 1943, a Nantucket boy serving in England found the *Naushon* being utilized as a hospital ship on the Thames. The *New Bedford* became a freighter on our coast. The *Martha's Vineyard*, which had been lying at New Bedford out of service, was reinstated on the island run. Trips were cut; boats were painted a battleship gray. Crest Hall, which as the Springfield House had served as navy barracks during World War I, became headquarters for Military Police Unit 709 for eight months after army contingents moved in on 25 and 26 August. With the Coast Guard occupying Brant Point, Madaket, Coskata, and Sankaty, uniforms became a common sight on the streets of the town; and one was likely to run into mock skirmishes along many of the farther-away beaches. Toward the end of October, Nantucket leased its airfield to the government, which contracted with the Bianchi Company for its development. It was taken over officially by the Navy in August of 1943 for a training field. Toward the end of 1942 Nantucket erected an "Honor Roll" bronze plaque containing the names of those currently serving in the armed forces in the side yard of the Sanford house, which structure was to be replaced by the present Town Building in 1964, the honor roll remaining.

The local newspaper did not report effects of the war on the island such as the sight of stacks of sandbags in the streets, the observation tower erected next to the old mill that was manned around-the-clock, the arrival of the refugees, or the explosions from mock battles that were audible in town.

The 13 June 1942 edition of the *Inquirer and Mirror*, partially sponsored by businessmen, was then the largest ever printed, consisting of 11,600 copies of eight pages. It was a mail-away meant to attract visitors to the island. It contained numerous pictures, featuring street scenes and old buildings and prominent citizens at historic spots. At this time the Nantucket Golf Course, Sankaty Head Golf Course, and Old 'Sconset Links were in operation for the summer. The yacht club was to open in two days; but its facilities were limited, having no lunch or cocktail service, no orchestra or other form of entertainment, its old bar serving as a meeting room. The tennis courts were available. Guest houses announcing themselves in readiness for visitors were the same as in 1941 with the single addition of Haddon Hall, 56 Centre Street, Mrs. George Haddon, proprietress. The Siasconset Casino offered movies during the summer, beginning with "The Man Who Came to Dinner," on 2 July. At the Straight Wharf Theatre the Fawcett Players started their fourth season with *Rip Van Winkle,* on 11 July. During the summer they were to add two titles to their historic series. They were Margaret Fawcett's *The China Trade*, about a friendship between a Chinese mandarin and a Nantucket whaling captain; and Robert Wilson's *The Man from Salem*, concerning the first John Gardner and the half-share men's revolt. There were no performances on Monday nights, which were given over to "military balls." At the end of July, Leroy H. True built a band-stand on the grounds of the Sanford house, and concerts were furnished by the school band. The Easy Street Gallery was open during August, and the Sidewalk Art Show was held from the 17th to the 19th. A carnival was at the Siasconset Casino on the evening of 18 August. A few dances were held at the yacht club during the summer with music furnished by Gus Bentley's orchestra from the Wauwinet House. Boats were reported as arriving with fewer passengers than a person has fingers, perhaps a single automobile, and several crates and parcels. It was a slow summer.

Because of war restrictions, Nantucket's foremost hostelry, the Sea Cliff Inn, remained closed during 1942 and 1943. In the latter year, the Nesbitt Inn, Broad Street, was taken over by the Coast Guard for offices and an infirmary, remaining until May of 1944. With Crest Hall occupied by the military police at the time the Coast Guard absorbed the Nesbitt Inn, two hotels on Nantucket were officially closed to guests for most of the duration of the war.

The conditions imposed by the national catastrophe remained through 1945. Germany surrendered on 7 May and Japan on 2 September. The United States, of course, was at war until the latter date, which was post-season on the island's calendar. The return to a civilian routine and appearance was the main endeavor for 1946. The Massachusetts Steamship Company took over the New Bedford, Martha's Vineyard and Nantucket Steamboat Company's equipment and premises on 1 March. The *Nantucket*, once more painted sea-gull white, rounded Brant Point on 6 April. The line was to change hands again two years later, when it was acquired by the New Bedford, Woods Hole, Martha's Vineyard and Nantucket

Steamship Authority, the present owner—New Bedford no longer being either in the name or itinerary. Old Progress Hall (1904), on South Water Street, lately a servicemen's club, reopened in June as the Marine Appliance and Lumber Company center. On 20 June the Navy turned the Nobadeer airfield back to the town, and it was named the Nantucket Memorial Airport in honor of the eleven islanders who had died in service. Also on 20 June Northeast Airlines initiated regular flights between the island and Boston and New York. The return to normal transportation facilities by sea and air reestablished the full peacetime approach to Nantucket.

Harriet S. Ross, who had purchased the New Springfield House (1883) and adjoining Dining Room House (1902) from Edwin S. Tirrell in 1920, and had conducted them as Crest Hall for over a quarter of a century (and now vacated by the military police), sold the property on 18 April 1946 to Harbour House, Inc. The name of the concern reflected that to be given to the hotel. The rear of the lot was cleared and landscaped and the lower east side, on Beach Street, became the new front. Lawrence W. and Marjorie K. Miller bought the Harbour House in 1950, and Miller brought it with him when he and his son Lawrence K. joined Walter Beinecke, Jr., in forming Sherburne Associates in 1964. Subsequently, the "u" was dropped from the name of the hotel. In 1977, stair towers were built on both fronts of the New Springfield pavilion, the clapboards were replaced by rustic shingles, and the Dining Room House became the entrance to the establishment.

Sherburne Associates would also play a role in the fate of Nantucket's greatest hotel, the Sea Cliff Inn. The management after the war was encumbered by a large mortgage, which was more than a third of the purchase price when the New Sea Cliff Inn of Nantucket sold the hostelry to Sherburne Associates for $80,000 early in 1965. The Sea Cliff Inn was conducted for seven more summers, then it was razed in 1972. The upper land, on Cliff Road, was offered as building lots. In six years' time, one house was erected, and nine tennis courts were installed immediately below the cliff.

The Nantucket Institution for Savings repossessed the Ocean House, and at the end of 1944 sold it to Eben Hutchinson. A few months later Hutchinson sold it to Nantucket Ocean House, Inc. This concern ran it for ten years, and in May of 1955 it was acquired by Margaret Wilson Manchester. The hotel became the rendezvous for scores of boisterous young people. On 6 October 1961, Margaret Manchester conveyed the property to the Nantucket Historical Trust, a corporation consisting of Walter Beinecke, Jr., Henry B. Coleman, and George W. Jones. The new owners set out to remove the excrescences and restore the building, hiring H. Errol Coffin, formerly of Coffin and Coffin, New York, to handle the architectural work. The interiors were decorated professionally, and the parlors furnished with antiques. The result was Nantucket's most elegant hostelry, rechristened the Jared Coffin House, from the name of the original builder. After 114 years—the entire life of the building's occupancy—the old name of the venerable Ocean House was dropped and given a new appellation. The annex, on the southwest corner of Centre and Gay streets, and the building to the east of the hotel were razed, the former site made into a vest-pocket park and the latter replaced by a new building set far back from Broad Street. The Nantucket Historical Trust sold the Jared Coffin House for $545,000 to Philip W. Read on 28 October 1976.

The White Elephant Hotel, Easton Street, had been a guest house since before World War I. It was purchased in 1919 by Mrs. Charles H. Walling, who sold it in 1945 to Mrs. Elizabeth Temple Ludwig, its manager for the past twenty years. When she sold it to Mr. and Mrs. Paul F. Klingelfuss at the beginning of May 1951, the White Elephant was the second-largest hotel on the island, containing ninety guest rooms and nine cottages. Paul Klingelfuss, after relinquishing management of the bathing beach, had been in charge of the Harbor House. He sold the White Elephant in June of 1962 to Walter Beinecke, Jr. The old structure had been demolished and replaced by a complex designed by H. Errol Coffin. The name was retained, and the property has undergone subsequent renovations.

148 *The Kenneth Taylor Galleries, originally the Thomas Macy Warehouse (1846), now the Nantucket Historical Association's Museum of Nantucket History, Straight Wharf (modern photograph).*

The Breakers, a few lots to the east of the White Elephant, was acquired by Wendell Miller during World War II, and in the fall of 1966 it was sold to Sherburne Associates. This building, also, was replaced by another pavilion of the same name, becoming an annex of the White Elephant.

The old Point Breeze Hotel of 1891, the Gordon Folger from 1936 onward, was sold to Mr. and Mrs. Robert B. Bowman for $250,000 in 1972. It still operates as the Folger Hotel and is the largest hostelry in Nantucket Town to retain its pre-World War II configuration.

The Woodbox, the mid-eighteenth-century George Bunker house on Fair Street at the south corner of Hiller's Lane, and attached building, conducted as an inn by Maude E. Stovell since the 1920s, was sold to the Woodbox, Inc., in 1950. Afterward it was run by the proprietress, Mrs. Marie W. F. Tutein, and now by her son Dexter Tutein.

The Overlook (Veranda House before 1930), retains both designation and visual characteristics antedating World War II. Purchased by Frederick M. Gardner in 1922, it was acquired in 1944 by Mary E. Duggan and sold in 1946 to Mr. and Mrs. Thomas J. Devine, who managed it themselves. In 1951 they purchased the adjoining dwelling from Helen Cash to serve as an annex and their own residence. The appearance of the inn on Step Lane has changed little since Nathan Chapman was the proprietor in the 1880s.

Another inn whose image has remained much as it was in the middle of the nineteenth century is the Roberts House, at the corner of Centre and India streets. After the death of Mary E. Roberts, the last of John Roberts's daughters, the building passed in 1960 to Ellen T. Winter and Lucille Sanguinetti, who renamed it the Bayberry Inn. Three years later it was acquired by Mr. and Mrs. Lester C. Ayers. On 22 April 1975 Mr. and Mrs. Michael O'Reilly purchased it and restored the name to Roberts House. A Chinese restaurant, the China Clipper, was conducted in the adjacent old Quaker meeting-house pavilion in 1975–76. It now houses the Meeting House Shops and includes the Off-Centre Cafe. The

Manor House, formerly Royal Manor, is now part of the Roberts House complex.

The Ships Inn, the old three-storied Capt. Obed Starbuck home (1831) on Fair Street, the adjoining Defriez house (on the south side) and the modern annex to the north (between Mooers and Mott lanes, now the Barnacle Inn) were sold by Helen M. Barnes (formerly Helen M. MacLaughlin) to Mr. and Mrs. Harold W. Lindley in 1956. The Ships Inn was resold to Timothy A. Clark in 1964, then to Rogers W. Cabot four years later, to Howard M. Jelleme, Inc., at the end of 1971, and to Mark and Ellie Gottwald in 1991. The Ships Inn has been maintained without appreciable change since midway between the two world wars.

Mr. and Mrs. Harold W. Lindley bought the former Bay View House, on Orange Street at the corner of Gorham's Court, in 1952. It was run as an inn called the Four Chimneys. After the Lindleys left the Ships Inn in 1964, they removed to the Four Chimneys and made it their private residence. Later operated as a hostelry by Betty York, Four Chimneys Inn has been owned by Bernadette Mannix since June 1990.

The Nesbitt House on Broad Street, built in the late 1870s, functioned under this label after it and the adjacent house to the east were purchased by John D. and Mary B. Nesbitt in 1895 and 1896. Lizzie Burgess acquired the Nesbitt House in 1914. She and her husband, George W. Burgess, presided over it as the Nesbitt Inn. It was transferred to the second generation bearing their name in 1966. And it is still in the family, currently owned by Charles and Dolly (Burgess) Noblit.

The building to the west, Harriet M. Hooper's The Gables at the turn of the century, was being operated by George W. Burgess, Jr., when he sold it to Arthur Krause in 1971. The basement today functions as a restaurant called The Brotherhood of Thieves.

On Centre Street, old Central House, later known as Swain's Boardinghouse, at the north corner of Lily Street, remains a guest house, called Holiday Inn since the close of World War II. It now is conducted by Mrs. James K. Moriarty.

The Archelaus Hammond house (1806), at 66 Centre Street, Marie Louise Miller's Anchor Inn of the 1920s, still goes by that name, formerly under the direction of Rogers W. Cabot and now Charles and Ann Balas.

Anna Ward's Wonoma Inn of 1923 at 61 Centre Street became Vivian Holliday's Martin's Guest House, and is now the Martin House Inn owned by Channing and Cecilia Moore.

The old silk-factory building at the top of Gay Street, known from the 1870s over the next half-century as the Waverly House, the Summit, the Waverly House (again), and the Summit Inn, took a few guests under the proprietress, Mrs. Claire G. Worek. It is now called the Sherburne Inn.

Albert Easton's boardinghouse of the 1880s, 17 North Water Street, which was Mrs. H. S. Ross's Colonial Inn before World War I, today, under her grandson Cyril Ross, Jr., once more has assumed the name Easton House.

Franklin Worth's boardinghouse of the 1880s, at 26 North Water Street, run by Mrs. Calvert Handy during the 1910s, now operates as the Carlisle House Inn.

The former boardinghouse of Mrs. G. G. Fish, later that of Mrs. Calvert Handy, was moved in the 1930s from the corner of Broad and North Water streets to the east side of the block. With a new front pavilion on South Beach Street, for several decades it served as Robert White's antiques shop, and is still an antiques shop owned by Hudson Holland, Jr. In the 1960s the adjoining house, 1 North Water Street (formerly owned by Mrs. Mooers, Mrs. Handy, and Dr. and Mrs. Veo), was demolished, and on the site was built the Nantucket Historical Association's Peter Foulger Museum, opened in 1971.

India House, 37 India Street, survives as an inn owned by Charles Kesser.

Number 7 Union Street, a boardinghouse owned by Cromwell Barnard in 1864, Mrs. Avis M. Enas during the 1870s and 1880s, and more recently the guest house of Mrs. Ida L. Ayers, has become the Union Street Inn.

Out of town, the hotel with the longest unbroken history is the Wauwinet House, operating since 1876. Although frequently added to and completely renovated in 1934, it retained its natural setting and charm. James A. Backus operated it from the mid-1890s and became the owner soon after the turn of the century. It was taken over by Wauwinet House, Inc., in 1962; but the Backuses regained the controlling interest and sold it to the Robert B. Bowmans (of the Folger Hotel) in 1978. Mr. and Mrs. Stephen Karp bought the Wauwinet House in 1988 and had it extensively renovated and redecorated, now calling it simply The Wauwinet.

In Siasconset, the Beach House, acquired by Mrs. Miriam Barbara Bulkley in 1935, was sold to Siasconset Beach House, Inc., early in 1947. The inn continued to run for ten summers. It was torn down in 1957, and its materials were used for constructing cottages for the new Moby Dick Inn. Private summer houses were built on the land.

Nearby Old 'Sconset Inn was enlarged when its proprietor Clement H. Reynolds purchased adjoining Swiss Cottage, on Cottage Street, from Mrs. Bulkley's estate in 1949. The property was taken over by the Bass River Savings Bank of Yarmouth in 1961. Robert N. Wiley acquired it in 1963 and continued to run it. The complex around the building was the Moby Dick Inn, which name had been adopted from the old restaurant, below the bank, that burned in the early 1960s. Today it operates as the Summer House Restaurant and Cottages.

The Chanticleer on New Street in Siasconset continues under the chef-owner Jean-Charles Berruet. Like the Old 'Sconset Inn or Summer House Restaurant, it is surrounded by a miniature village of summer cottages, now privately owned.

The Robert Wilsons were off-island in 1943 engaged in war work, and the Straight Wharf Theatre was rented to the Repertory Players. The Wilsons returned in 1946. Margaret Fawcett's *Macy's Bright Star* and other modern plays were added to their presentations, which continued through 1950. Then the theatre was rented to various professional groups each summer until Mrs.

Wilson sold the building to Sherburne Associates, in 1966, with the proviso that it be leased to the Theatre Workshop for maintenance costs over a ten-year period and that a Nantucket play be given annually. At the expiration of the lease it was to be let to a different group, but it burned down on 19 April 1975, thus obliterating a landmark that had been a major contributor to the island's culture. The Theatre Workshop transferred its productions to Bennett Hall.

In 1985 Richard Cary formed the Actors Theatre of Nantucket. It performed seven seasons at the Folger Hotel and then moved to the Methodist Church.

The function of the Easy Street Gallery, as a place where artists on the island could exhibit their works, passed back to the Candle House on Washington Street at Commercial Wharf in 1944. The Waterfront Artists Group held a show there during July and August.

A bigger institution was in the making. In 1940 seventeen gentlemen banded together as the Nantucket Foundation. The leaders were Kenneth Taylor, Austin Strong, and Everett U. Crosby. In the summer of 1944 the Nantucket Foundation purchased the Thomas Macy brick warehouse built in 1846, next west of the Straight Wharf Theatre. The building lost two-thirds of its roof in the hurricane during September, but it was repaired, and the interior was renovated to be opened as an art gallery at the beginning of July 1945. It was called the Kenneth Taylor Galleries after the founder who had died at fifty-two in June of 1941. Everett U. Crosby was chairman and spokesman until the appointment of the first director, William C. Stevens.

The initial exhibition at the Kenneth Taylor Galleries honored Nantucket artists of the past in an assemblage of paintings by Eastman Johnson; his friend John A. MacDougall, who retired to the island in 1916; Henry S. Eddy; and Edgar W. Jenney. Subsequent shows were of the work of current artists, including Mrs. Kenneth Taylor, Mr. and Mrs. H. Emerson Tuttle, Mr. and Mrs. Peter Kerr, Mrs. H. G. Chatfield, Mrs. Charles E. Congdon, Mrs. Ansley Sawyer, Harriet Lord, Ruth Sutton, Mimi Goelet, and several young "modernistic" painters, called the "45 Group," led by Max Schallinger. Generally, fine arts were displayed on the first floor and crafts upstairs, and there might be walls devoted to old maps, prints, and ship paintings, or to Tony Sarg's designs. There were weekly talks on art. Prizes were awarded, only instead of the usual numerical rating for oil paintings the first year the four best were all given honorable mention. One was bestowed upon Elizabeth Saltonstall, who also was recipient of the best in the black-and-white class. On 27 August Everett U. Crosby scheduled a meeting for the purpose of organizing what was to become the Artists Association of Nantucket. It was to use the Kenneth Taylor Galleries for exhibition. Then in 1984 the Nantucket Foundation dissolved and, in the interest of historic preservation, transferred ownership of the Thomas Macy Warehouse to the Nantucket Historical Association. The building henceforth was devoted to familiarizing visitors with island history. The Artists Association of Nantucket currently rents the Little Gallery next door.

The first commercial art gallery of the post-war period was George Vigoroux's Lobster Pot on South Wharf, opened in 1959. Five years later it moved to Easy Street across from the former gallery begun by Mrs. Lang. The Lobster Pot survived until 1972, by which time a number of other such establishments had come into existence.

The brave new world of Nantucket following World War II was one in which there were to be made many serious and concentrated efforts to keep the town and its monuments as intact as possible, but they were in conflict with the natural order of change that was accelerating around the globe. The foremost agent was recognized as being the Nantucket Historical Association, which had already acquired several historic monuments and was operating them as permanent museums. It had aquired the old windmill on Popsquatchett Hills, and the Friends schoolhouse/meetinghouse (1838) on Fair Street during the 1890s. To the latter it had added a fireproof addition to serve as its headquarters in 1904. In the late 1920s it acquired and converted the Jethro Coffin House on Sunset Hill into a house museum, and the Richard Mitchell & Sons/Hadwen & Barney candle factory (1847) at 11 Broad Street into the Whaling Museum. Mid-twentieth-century acquisitions began in 1948 with the old log jail (1805) on Vestal Street. It was followed by a number of old residences: the Richard L. Coleman House (1801), 4 Mill Street, opened as "The 1800 House" in 1952; the William Hadwen House (ca. 1845), 96 Main Street, in 1963; and the house built by Thomas Macy (after 1723) and given to his son Nathaniel (in 1745), at 12 Liberty Street, in 1972. The Nantucket Historical Association also received Greater Light, formerly the studio and summer home of the Misses Gertrude and Hanna Monaghan on Howard Street, remodeled in the 1930s from a barn in which they incorporated elements from old European and American buildings. It has been available for inspection on a limited schedule since 1973. Most recently, the handsome Federal Thomas Macy house at 99 Main Street was bequeathed to the NHA, which uses it for receptions and housing distinguished guests. Though not belonging to the historical association but similarly serving as a museum since 1902 is the Hezekiah Swain House (1790), later the William Mitchell residence and birthplace of his daughter Maria in 1818. Located at 1 Vestal Street, it is the nucleus of the Maria Mitchell Association complex, which includes a library and observatory.

In 1955 a two-year endeavor to establish a law creating an "Old and Historic Nantucket District" bore fruit with commonwealth approval. The "District" encompassed most of Nantucket Town and the ancient part of Siasconset Village. The jurisdiction of the Historic District Commission was extended over the entire island in 1971.

In 1965 Sherburne Associates began redevelopment of the harbor, involving Straight, South, and Commercial wharves. Some of the older buildings were retained, whereas an elaborate yacht marina with modern conveniences replaced the former whaling-ship piers. New structures mostly were in keeping with traditional waterfront architecture, but pilings with blue plastic caps (to discourage gulls) were used decoratively, and a large parking lot filled the area between Straight Wharf and Salem Street, and from the water to Candle Street. The varied use of materials—asphalt, brick, and old paving stones from New Bedford—and its planting including the preservation of pre-existing trees render the parking lot perhaps the most acceptable specimen of its kind in the world. In December 1986, all Sherburne Associates properties were acquired by First Winthrop Corporation.

Inevitably, change would come to Nantucket in ways perhaps ordained when the Nantucket Railroad made its final run and the Automobile Exclusion Act was repealed in 1918. Some changes, especially those brought by the proliferation of motor vehicles in the summer season, have not been entirely welcome. Efforts continue to relieve the impact of the automobile on the narrow streets and lanes of Nantucket Town, and the overhead clutter of utility wires is gradually being laid underground.

Although the small grocery stores and specialty markets — like Ashley's and Charlie's — have disappeared from Main Street and given way to the mainland convenience of well-stocked supermarkets, the homely, intimate exchange between summer resident and purveyor survives in the fresh farm produce and island-grown flowers that are still seasonal features in Nantucket Town and Siasconset, albeit on trucks, not wagons.

The innocent seasonal activities of yesteryear have been succeeded by perhaps more seriously organized occasions that attract visitors and entertain residents. Events like the Christmas Stroll keep lodging establishments, restaurants, and shops open long past the time they had closed in years gone by . . . and see them open earlier so people can enjoy the Daffodil Festival that welcomes springtime on Nantucket.

A happy alternative to the development that might have consumed much of the open land on the island is in the conservation efforts of recent years: of the 32,000-acre land mass of Nantucket, more than a third is in the hands of organizations committed to preserving the land in its natural state.

RECORDED HERE is the nostalgic enchantment of a Nantucket that pulled itself out of desperate times after the demise of the whale fishery and sustained itself up to the modern era and a future that would be uncertain and sometimes foreboding.

The earlier Nantucketers introduced in these pages—the frugal boardinghouse keepers and ambitious hoteliers, the entrepreneurs and entertainers, the shopkeepers and restaurateurs, the actors and artists—all have their successors in today's breed of Nantucketer offering a time-honored brand of gracious hospitality, providing a cherished aftertaste of the great banquet that flourished during the simpler times remembered in this chronicle.

Perhaps nowhere on earth can be found a spot as affectionately embraced and nurtured. Protected by its remoteness, isolated betimes by fog, held in happy memory of all who discover its potent magic. . . . Nantucket, a Holiday Island for all time.

SOURCES

Quoted matter in this work was transcribed from primary sources on Nantucket. Copies of the fully annotated manuscript are deposited at the Nantucket Atheneum and with the Nantucket Historical Association in the Edouard A. Stackpole Library in the Research Center at the Peter Foulger Museum. The manuscript is available for on-premises research upon application to those institutions, both of which possess microfilmed copies of the Nantucket newspapers quoted.

BOOKS AND MONOGRAPHS

Margaret Fawcett Barnes. *'Sconset Heyday.* Nantucket, 1969.

J. Hector St. John de Crèvecoeur. *Letters from an American Farmer.* London, 1782. Reprint, New York, 1957.

Everett U. Crosby, ed. *Nantucket in Print.* Nantucket, 1946.

Thomas J. Devine. *Veranda House and the Overlook Hotel.* Brochure. Nantucket, n.d.

The First Residence and Business Directory of Nantucket, Edgartown, Cottage City, Vineyard Haven, Tisbury, West Tisbury, and Chilmark. South Braintree, 1897.

Henry Chandlee Forman. *Early Nantucket and Its Whale Houses.* New York, 1966.

Will Gardner. *The Coffin Saga.* Cambridge, Massachusetts, 1940.

Edward K. Godfrey. *The Island of Nantucket.* New York, 1882.

Mary Wheeler Heller. *A Casino Album, 1899–1974.* Nantucket, 1974

R.B. Hussey. *The Evolution of Siasconset.* Nantucket, 1912.

Clay Lancaster. *Two Sketches of Lower Main Street Nantucket Before and After the Great Fire of 1846.* Monograph. Nantucket, 1975.
  The Far-out Island Railroad: Nantucket's Old Summer Narrow-gauge. Nantucket, 1972.

Lothrop's Nantucket Blue Book and Directory. Boston, 1927.

Nantucket Telephone Directory, 1927, 1929.

*The Residence and Business Directory of Nantucket . . . .*Boston, 1909, 1914, 1919.

Alexander Starbuck. *The History of Nantucket County, Island and Town.* Boston, 1927.

Harry B. Turner. *Nantucket Argument Settlers.* Nantucket, 1960.
The Story of the Island Steamers. Nantucket, 1916.

George F. Worth. "Island Reminiscences." Unpublished manuscript, 1841.

Henry S. Wyer. *Sea-Girt Nantucket.* 2d edn., Nantucket, 1906.

NEWSPAPERS

Nantucket Inquirer, 1821–1865

Inquirer and Mirror, 1865–1941

Nantucket Journal, 1879–1899

PERIODICALS AND JOURNALS

42nd Annual Report of the Board of Railroad Commissioners. Boston, 1911.

Harper's New Monthly Magazine.

Historic Nantucket. Bulletin of the Nantucket Historical Association.

NANTUCKET TOWN AND COUNTY RECORDS

Nantucket County Books of Plans

Nantucket County Deed Books

Nantucket County Probate Books

Nantucket County Court Proceedings

Proprietors' Books of Plans

INDEX

Mowry, Charles H., 101
Murry, J. F. (restaurant), 25–26
Myrick, Andrew M., 65, 67, 133
Myrick, W. Clark, 104
Myrick, W. H. (boardinghouse), 57, 104
Myrick's Grove, 57

Nantucket Agricultural Society, 25, 116–17,
174–75, 182, 191, 206
Nantucket and Cape Cod Steamboat Company,
23, 68–69
Nantucket Athletic Club, 137, 148, 167, 169
Nantucket Brass Band, 25
Nantucket Central Railroad, 116, 129, 137–41,
144–46, 155–56, 158–59
Nantucket Company, The, 133
Nantucket Cottage Hospital, 168, 179, 187, 195
Nantucket Historical Association, 123–24, 192,
193, 229, 230
Nantucket Historical Trust, 226
Nantucket Hotel, 91, 93–94, 112, 136, 191
Nantucket House, 182, 196, 220
Nantucket Memorial Airport, 226
Nantucket Neighbors, 200–1, 206
Nantucket Players, 185–86, 194–95, 197–98,
200, 201, 206, 218
Nantucket Playhouse, 213, 217
Nantucket Railroad Company, 70–73, 80–83,
115–16
Nantucket Roller Skating Rink, 86
Nantucket Sea Shore Enterprise, 63
Nantucket Spa, 186
Nantucket Steamboat Company, 17–19, 22–23
Nantucket Theatre, 198, 200, 202, 205–6
Nantucket Yacht Club, 137, 167, 169, 184–85,
195–96, 197–98, 201–2, 205, 210, 211, 213,
217, 218, 220, 225
Narwhal Guest House, 177, 183, 186
Nautican Realty Company, 179, 180 (fig. 127)
Nauticon (land development), 65
Nauticon Saloon, 21, 33
Nesbitt (Inn), Mr. and Mrs. John D., 105–6,
130, 143, 153, 182, 186, 196, 225, 228
Nevins Mansion, 142
New Bedford, Martha's Vineyard and Nantucket
Steamboat Company, 23, 224, 225
New Bedford, Woods Hole, Martha's Vineyard
and Nantucket Steamship Authority, 225–26
Nicholson, John B., 13, 33
Nickerson, Judah (boardinghouse), 95
Nickerson, Thomas G. (boardinghouse), 55, 95
Nicoletos Brothers, 178, 181

North Quaker Meeting House, 10
Northrup, A. Judd, 66
Norton, John M., 71

Ocean House, 19, 21–22, 25, 31, 34, 43, 45, 91,
101, 130, 135, 143, 144, 149, 153, 174, 183, 196
209, 213, 226
Ocean Park, 184
Ocean View Cafe, 133
Ocean View House, 45–48, 80–81, 91, 101, 130,
143, 153, 163, 191
O'Conor, Charles, 77
Old Colony Restaurant, 86
Old Garden Gate, 170
Old Nantucket Candy Kitchen, 135
Old Parliament House, 174 (fig. 123), 174, 196
Old 'Sconset Inn, 215
Old Virginia, The (tearoom), 171
Olympian Cottage, 150
orchestras, see bands and orchestras
Orr (Cottage), Mrs. Imogene F., 109, 130, 143
Orr, Isabella A., 65, 76
Our Island Home, 104, 111–12
Overlook, The, 196, 228

Paddack, George, 79
Paddack, Henry, 79, 90, 133
Paddack, Rachel (inn), 6
Palmer (House), Mrs. Mary E., 143, 153
Pantheon Hall, 27
Parker, John A. (boardinghouse), 10, 16
Parker, Mrs. Pearl (boardinghouse), 183, 186
Parker, Mrs. R. F. (boardinghouse), 13, 19, 21,
33
Patterson, F. L., 111
Patterson, James, 76, 88, 91, 115
Peter Foulger Museum, 229
Peter Rabbit Candy Shop, 177
Paterson and Newhall, 172
Pettee, Mrs. Charlotte W., 100, 102, 105, 132
Phillips (House), H. R., 153
Pinkham, Mrs. A. (boardinghouse), 13
Pioneer Inn, 153
Pitman (House), T. C., 107, 130, 143, 153, 183
Plymouth House, 196
Point Breeze Hotel, 101–2, 103–4, 134–35, 137,
143, 153, 174, 178–79, 183, 191, 196, 202,
203–4, 209, 228
Prentice, Margaret, 167–68
Progress Hall, 133, 141, 226
Providence House, 55
Purdue, Helen (shop), 172